Lotus SmartSuite® Millennium Edition For Dummies

SO-AHF-944

Sheet

SmartSuite Millennium Edition Shortcuts

SmartIcon	Keyboard equivalent	Function
	Ctrl+N	Create a new file (except in Approach)
	Ctrl+O	Open an existing file
	Ctrl+S	Save the current file
	Ctrl+P	Print the current file
	Ctrl+?	Print Preview
	Ctrl+X	Cut selection and store on Windows Clipboard
	Ctrl+C	Copy selection and store on Windows Clipboard
	Ctrl+V	Paste Clipboard contents into current file
	Ctrl+Z	Undo last action
B	Ctrl+B	Make selected text bold
I	Ctrl+I	Make selected text italic
U	Ctrl+U	Make selected text underlined
	Alt+Enter	Move between InfoBox and selection

Word Pro Shortcuts

SmartIcon	Keyboard equivalent	Function
	Ctrl+F2	Check spelling
	Text⇨Text Properties	Open Text Properties InfoBox
	Right-click, Page Properties	Open Page Properties InfoBox
		Cycle attribute options
		Cycle alignment options
	Ctrl+L	Left-align text
	Ctrl+E	Center text
	Ctrl +R	Right-align text
	Ctrl+J	Justify text
	View⇨Show/Hide⇨Ruler	Show/Hide ruler
	Text⇨Named Styles⇨Reset to Style	Reset to style
	Text⇨Named Styles⇨Create	Create a style

...For Dummies: #1 Computer Book Series for Beginners

Lotus SmartSuite® Millennium Edition For Dummies®

Cheat Sheet

1-2-3 Millennium Edition Shortcuts

SmartIcon	Function
	Open Sheet Properties InfoBox
	Open Range Properties InfoBox
	Copy range's format to other ranges
	Size columns to widest entry
	Sum values above or to left
	Create a worksheet
	Create a chart
	Create a text box
	Create an ellipse
	Create an arrow
	Go to a range or graphic object

Freelance Graphics Shortcuts

SmartIcon	Function
	Run screen show
	Create a chart
	Create a text block
	Create or edit a speaker note
New Page	Create a new page
	Show InfoBox
	Zoom to show whole page
	Zoom in to selected area
	Duplicate page
	Group objects
	Ungroup objects

Approach Shortcuts

SmartIcon	Function
	Go to first record
	Go to previous record
	Go to next record
	Go to last record
	Sort field in ascending order
	Sort field in descending order
	Delete current record
	Duplicate current record
	Insert today's date
	Insert current time
	Insert value from previous record

Organizer Shortcuts

SmartIcon	Function
	Return to previous page
	Open Show Through dialog box
	Create a new entry in the Calendar section
	Create a new entry in the To Do section
	Create a new entry in the Address section
	Create a new entry in the Calls section
	Create a new entry in the Planner section
	Create a new entry in the Notepad section
	Create a new entry in the Anniversary section
	Find text

IDG BOOKS WORLDWIDE

...For Dummies: #1 Computer Book Series for Beginners

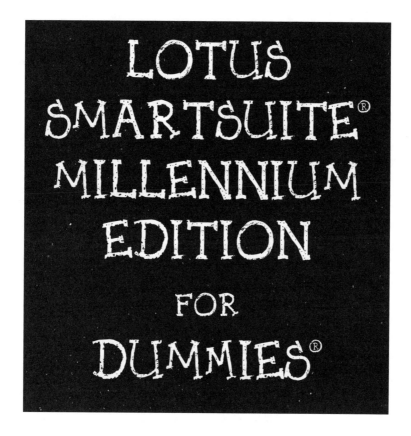

LOTUS SMARTSUITE® MILLENNIUM EDITION FOR DUMMIES®

by Michael Meadhra and Jan Weingarten

IDG Books Worldwide, Inc.
An International Data Group Company

Foster City, CA ♦ Chicago, IL ♦ Indianapolis, IN ♦ New York, NY

Lotus SmartSuite® Millennium Edition For Dummies®

Published by
IDG Books Worldwide, Inc.
An International Data Group Company
919 E. Hillsdale Blvd.
Suite 400
Foster City, CA 94404
www.idgbooks.com (IDG Books Worldwide Web site)
www.dummies.com (Dummies Press Web site)

Library of Congress Catalog Card No.: 98-85675

ISBN: 0-7645-0353-7

Printed in the United States of America

10 9 8 7 6 5 4 3 2 1

1O/QZ/QX/ZY/IN

Distributed in the United States by IDG Books Worldwide, Inc.

Distributed by Macmillan Canada for Canada; by Transworld Publishers Limited in the United Kingdom; by IDG Norge Books for Norway; by IDG Sweden Books for Sweden; by Woodslane Pty. Ltd. for Australia; by Woodslane (NZ) Ltd. for New Zealand; by Addison Wesley Longman Singapore Pte Ltd. for Singapore, Malaysia, Thailand, Indonesia and Korea; by Norma Comunicaciones S.A. for Colombia; by Intersoft for South Africa; by International Thomson Publishing for Germany, Austria and Switzerland; by Toppan Company Ltd. for Japan; by Distribuidora Cuspide for Argentina; by Livraria Cultura for Brazil; by Ediciencia S.A. for Ecuador; by Ediciones ZETA S.C.R. Ltda. for Peru; by WS Computer Publishing Corporation, Inc., for the Philippines; by Unalis Corporation for Taiwan; by Contemporanea de Ediciones for Venezuela; by Computer Book & Magazine Store for Puerto Rico; by Express Computer Distributors for the Caribbean and West Indies. Authorized Sales Agent: Anthony Rudkin Associates for the Middle East and North Africa.

For general information on IDG Books Worldwide's books in the U.S., please call our Consumer Customer Service department at 800-762-2974. For reseller information, including discounts and premium sales, please call our Reseller Customer Service department at 800-434-3422.

For information on where to purchase IDG Books Worldwide's books outside the U.S., please contact our International Sales department at 650-655-3200 or fax 650-655-3297.

For information on foreign language translations, please contact our Foreign & Subsidiary Rights department at 650-655-3021 or fax 650-655-3281.

For sales inquiries and special prices for bulk quantities, please contact our Sales department at 650-655-3200 or write to the address above.

For information on using IDG Books Worldwide's books in the classroom or for ordering examination copies, please contact our Educational Sales department at 800-434-2086 or fax 317-596-5499.

For press review copies, author interviews, or other publicity information, please contact our Public Relations department at 650-655-3000 or fax 650-655-3299.

For authorization to photocopy items for corporate, personal, or educational use, please contact Copyright Clearance Center, 222 Rosewood Drive, Danvers, MA 01923, or fax 978-750-4470.

About the Authors

Michael Meadhra is an author and consultant who writes about Windows and a variety of Windows programs. After several years of experience in the corporate world, he began writing monthly software journals, and now he writes books such as this one. To date, he has co-authored or contributed to more than two dozen titles on topics such as DOS, Windows, Lotus Freelance Graphics, the Internet, and Quicken.

Jan Weingarten is a software trainer and consultant in the Pacific Northwest. She has written or co-authored more than 20 books, including titles on SmartSuite, Windows, 1-2-3, Paradox, Excel, Microsoft Office, WordPerfect, and CorelDRAW!.

Authors' Acknowledgments

Publishing a book is a true team effort. Once again, I have been privileged to work with the team at IDG Books Worldwide, Inc. Ryan Rader, the project editor for this book; Mike Kelly, the acquisitions editor; and their cohorts at Dummies Press, have made the experience of revising this book for the current edition a truly pleasurable experience. And that's a remarkable feat in a business where deadline pressures and the uncertainties of beta software all too often conspire to create tensions between the author and the publisher.

The copy editors, Tina Sims and Ryan Rader (yeah, Ryan did double duty as project editor and copy editor), did a great job of making sure my prose possessed the proper grammar and style, and the layout artists, Kathie Schutte and Janet Seib, did their thing to make the book look good.

My friend, Steve Rindsberg, deserves thanks for contributing his talents as technical reviewer. His many suggestions significantly improved this book.

Thanks also to my agent, David Fugate of Waterside Productions, for his help in getting the contract for this book.

I want to extend a special thanks to Adam Frary of Lotus Development Corp. for his assistance in resolving technical questions about the software.

Thanks also to John Weingarten, Wallace Wang, and Deborah Christy for their contributions to previous editions of this book.

ABOUT IDG BOOKS WORLDWIDE

Welcome to the world of IDG Books Worldwide.

IDG Books Worldwide, Inc., is a subsidiary of International Data Group, the world's largest publisher of computer-related information and the leading global provider of information services on information technology. IDG was founded more than 25 years ago and now employs more than 8,500 people worldwide. IDG publishes more than 275 computer publications in over 75 countries (see listing below). More than 90 million people read one or more IDG publications each month.

Launched in 1990, IDG Books Worldwide is today the #1 publisher of best-selling computer books in the United States. We are proud to have received eight awards from the Computer Press Association in recognition of editorial excellence and three from *Computer Currents'* First Annual Readers' Choice Awards. Our best-selling *...For Dummies*® series has more than 50 million copies in print with translations in 38 languages. IDG Books Worldwide, through a joint venture with IDG's Hi-Tech Beijing, became the first U.S. publisher to publish a computer book in the People's Republic of China. In record time, IDG Books Worldwide has become the first choice for millions of readers around the world who want to learn how to better manage their businesses.

Our mission is simple: Every one of our books is designed to bring extra value and skill-building instructions to the reader. Our books are written by experts who understand and care about our readers. The knowledge base of our editorial staff comes from years of experience in publishing, education, and journalism — experience we use to produce books for the '90s. In short, we care about books, so we attract the best people. We devote special attention to details such as audience, interior design, use of icons, and illustrations. And because we use an efficient process of authoring, editing, and desktop publishing our books electronically, we can spend more time ensuring superior content and spend less time on the technicalities of making books.

You can count on our commitment to deliver high-quality books at competitive prices on topics you want to read about. At IDG Books Worldwide, we continue in the IDG tradition of delivering quality for more than 25 years. You'll find no better book on a subject than one from IDG Books Worldwide.

John Kilcullen
CEO
IDG Books Worldwide, Inc.

Steven Berkowitz
President and Publisher
IDG Books Worldwide, Inc.

Eighth Annual Computer Press Awards ≥1992

Ninth Annual Computer Press Awards ≥1993

Tenth Annual Computer Press Awards ≥1994

Eleventh Annual Computer Press Awards ≥1995

Publisher's Acknowledgments

We're proud of this book; please register your comments through our IDG Books Worldwide Online Registration Form located at http://my2cents.dummies.com.

Some of the people who helped bring this book to market include the following:

Acquisitions, Editorial, and Media Development

Project Editor: Ryan Rader

Acquisitions Manager: Michael Kelly

Copy Editor: Tina Sims

Technical Editor: Steve Rindsberg

Editorial Manager: Elaine Brush

Editorial Assistant: Paul E. Kuzmic

Production

Associate Project Coordinator: Tom Missler

Layout and Graphics: Lou Boudreau, Angela F. Hunckler, Todd Klemme, Jane E. Martin, Heather Pearson, Brent Savage, Janet Seib, M. Anne Sipahimalani, Kate Snell

Proofreaders: Christine Berman, Kelli Botta, Michelle Croninger, Nancy Price, Robert Springer, Janet M. Withers

Indexer: Sherry Massey

Special Help

Ted Cains; Leah P. Cameron; Rowena Rappaport; Stacey Riebsomer

General and Administrative

IDG Books Worldwide, Inc.: John Kilcullen, CEO; Steven Berkowitz, President and Publisher

IDG Books Technology Publishing: Brenda McLaughlin, Senior Vice President and Group Publisher

Dummies Technology Press and Dummies Editorial: Diane Graves Steele, Vice President and Associate Publisher; Mary Bednarek, Director of Acquisitions and Product Development; Kristin A. Cocks, Editorial Director

Dummies Trade Press: Kathleen A. Welton, Vice President and Publisher; Kevin Thornton, Acquisitions Manager

IDG Books Production for Dummies Press: Michael R. Britton, Vice President of Production; Beth Jenkins Roberts, Production Director; Cindy L. Phipps, Manager of Project Coordination, Production Proofreading, and Indexing; Kathie S. Schutte, Supervisor of Page Layout; Shelley Lea, Supervisor of Graphics and Design; Debbie J. Gates, Production Systems Specialist; Robert Springer, Supervisor of Proofreading; Debbie Stailey, Special Projects Coordinator; Tony Augsburger, Supervisor of Reprints and Bluelines

Dummies Packaging and Book Design: Robin Seaman, Creative Director; Jocelyn Kelaita, Product Packaging Coordinator; Kavish + Kavish, Cover Design

◆

The publisher would like to give special thanks to Patrick J. McGovern, without whom this book would not have been possible.

◆

Contents at a Glance

Cartoons at a Glance

By Rich Tennant

"It's a ten step word processing program. It comes with a spell-checker, grammar-checker, cliche-checker, whine-checker, passive/aggressive-checker, politically correct-checker, kissy-fit-checker, pretentious pontificating-checker, boring anecdote-checker and a Freudian reference-checker."

page 53

"IT HAPPENED AROUND THE TIME WE SUBSCRIBED TO AN ON-LINE SERVICE."

page 343

"Of course graphics are important to your project, Eddy, but I think it would've been better to scan a picture of your worm collection."

page 253

"I think the cursor's not moving, Mr. Dunt, because you've got your hand on the chalk board eraser and not the mouse."

page 187

"IT'S CHAOS – BUT IT'S CHAOS THAT WORKS."

page 285

"NIFTY CHART, FRANK, BUT NOT ENTIRELY NECESSARY."

page 135

WHAT'S THE DIGITAL BATHROOM SCALE DOING IN MY LAPTOP CASE?

...PROMPT...?

page 9

"YES, WE STILL HAVE A FEW BUGS IN THE WORD PROCESSING SOFTWARE. BY THE WAY, HERE'S A MEMO FROM MARKETING."

page 381

Fax: 978-546-7747 • E-mail: the5wave@tiac.net

Table of Contents

Introduction

．．．

Welcome to *Lotus SmartSuite Millennium Edition For Dummies*. Just the fact that you're holding this book in your hands proves — at least to us — that you're no dummy. You're just someone who wants to get the essential information about how to use all those terrific features that you know must be lurking somewhere in the Lotus SmartSuite package.

So, what the heck is SmartSuite, anyway? Glad you asked. We start with what Lotus SmartSuite is not. SmartSuite has nothing to do with fancy first-class hotel rooms — although you get plenty of room to "spread out" with this package. SmartSuite is actually an integrated set of first-class computer programs (a *suite* in computerese) that can make your day-to-day work at the computer a whole lot easier. In fact, by using the SmartSuite programs individually or in combination, you can perform just about any computing task you can possibly imagine — if, of course, you take the time to find out a bit about how SmartSuite operates. Well, you're in luck. Showing you what SmartSuite can do — and how you can best use its interconnected programs — is exactly what we're here for.

About This Book

This book is a reference. You don't need to read it front-to-back or cover-to-cover. Instead, think of a topic that piques your interest. Look it up in the index, turn to that page, and just start reading. Generally, each topic has its own section, and no section assumes that you've read anything else in the book. (If you need some background knowledge, or you want more information, you can use the references sprinkled throughout to guide you to the pertinent topic.)

This book can help you perform any of the following feats:

- Use Lotus Word Pro to create beautiful word-processing documents, such as letters, memos, reports, and even — dare we say it? — the great American novel, without breaking a sweat.

- Put together Lotus 1-2-3 spreadsheets to juggle numbers and perform death-defying calculations. You can even persuade your boss that you actually *know what you're talking about.*

✔ Keep track of vast amounts of data by using SmartSuite's Approach database program. Yes, thanks to Lotus, database management is finally approachable.

✔ Conquer your paralyzing fear of public speaking by using Lotus Freelance Graphics to create professional presentations. The next time you need to make a presentation, you'll get "Ooohs!" and "Aaaahhhhs" rather than yawns.

✔ Organize your life by using (what else?) Lotus Organizer. What's Organizer? (Funny you should ask. . . .) It's much like a computerized version of one of those pocket day planners — on steroids. If you can't get organized by using this program, you just can't get organized.

✔ Create even more complex documents than any one of these programs can handle by itself. (But don't worry. The documents themselves may be complex, but the steps to create them aren't.)

How This Book Is Organized

This book is arranged so that you can easily find the information you're looking for. The first step on your quest to knowledge is to head toward the appropriate part of the book. To help you in that goal, here is a handy description of the book's eight main parts:

Part I: A Suite Deal

This part of the book looks at SmartSuite as a whole. Here's where you can find out how to use SmartCenter, for example, to launch the SmartSuite programs, open documents, and access other features; how to work with SmartIcons and save your work; how to use SmartCenter with the Internet; how to get help if you're stuck; and how to figure out exactly which SmartSuite program to use — and when. If you haven't played around with SmartSuite at all yet, we strongly suggest that you read through this part of the book before jumping ahead to another section that catches your fancy.

Part II: Take a Letter, Word Processor

The average computer user spends more time using a word-processing program than performing any other computer-related activity. This part shows you all the skills you need to put Word Pro's wordsmithing capabilities to work. By using Word Pro as outlined in this part, you can create, edit, format, and print documents — pieces of paper with words on 'em — in less time than you used to take to change a typewriter ribbon. You'll never need to dust off that old typewriter again. (You *do* remember typewriters, don't you . . . ?)

Part III: Spreadsheets As Easy As, Well — 1-2-3!

If working with numbers is your middle name (hmmm, that's a really weird middle name), 1-2-3's your game. If you think that pocket calculators are cool, wait till you get a load of what 1-2-3 can do for you. Spreadsheet programs are generally credited with starting the personal computer revolution. After reading this part of the book, you'll know why. We show you how to create and format worksheets for any purpose you can imagine, use formulas to automatically calculate results, and turn those results into charts and graphs to make the results understandable even to those folks whose eyes routinely glaze over at the sight of too many numbers.

Part IV: Caution — Database Approaching

If you need to manage piles of data; create forms, reports, and queries; and deal with other strange-sounding stuff about which you're currently clueless (if you have a life, that is), Approach should be your SmartSuite tool of choice. This part of the book covers all the database basics that you need to create anything from a simple name and address list to an integrated accounting system. Okay, so you need to know about accounting to create an integrated accounting system, but we still show you the basic steps you need to get rolling.

Part V: Freelance's Presentation Power

Whether you're pitching next year's budget to your corporation's board of directors or making a proposal to the local homeowners' association, presentations can be scary. If giving presentations makes you sweat, turn to this part of the book before you even *start* thinking about your next presentation. Freelance Graphics makes preparing and organizing all your presentation materials as easy as . . . well, *easy!* (Trust us.) This part shows you how to put together all the bits and pieces you need for a top-notch presentation, including title pages, charts, bulleted lists, text — you name it. You even find information on how to put together an on-screen electronic presentation. Gee, maybe you won't even need to show up at all.

Part VI: Organize Your Life

This is the part of the book to turn to if you want to computerize all the entries you *should* have made in your pocket day planner. These chapters tell you how to keep track of appointments, names and addresses, anniversary dates, and notes. You still need to enter the data yourself, but by using Organizer, at least you can *find* that data when you really need it.

Part VII: Spinning a Web

The Internet and the Web are all the rage these days. This part of the book shows you how to move from being an observer to being a participant in the Web publishing realm. This part is where you find information about how to use the Web publishing features of the various SmartSuite programs to transform documents, spreadsheets, and presentations into Web publications. You also get plenty of insight into FastSite — the new member of the SmartSuite family that makes fast work of building a Web site by assembling documents and converting them to Web pages.

Part VIII: The Part of Tens

You want the top ten shortcuts for the SmartSuite programs, ten best tips, ten of this, and ten of that? Here they are. If you can't find the answer to your SmartSuite questions or dilemmas elsewhere in the book, check out this part. You may get lucky.

A Word about Teamwork and Passing Notes

SmartSuite includes some powerful features to facilitate team computing. The component programs all incorporate specific features to help you share your work with others and collaborate on projects. In particular, the SmartSuite programs are designed to integrate with Notes, the popular Lotus groupware program. However, these are relatively advanced features that involve using networks of computers more than using the SmartSuite programs themselves. As such, these features are beyond the scope of this book. When you're comfortable with SmartSuite, we encourage you to check with your network administrator to find out more about how you can reach out across the network to extend the capabilities of SmartSuite.

Foolish Assumptions

We don't make too many assumptions about our readers. We do, however, assume several things:

- ✔ You have a computer.
- ✔ You use Windows 95 or Windows 98.
- ✔ You have SmartSuite loaded onto your computer. (If not, stick that SmartSuite CD into the drive and follow the on-screen instructions to get SmartSuite installed — posthaste!)

We don't assume that computers are your life — or even that you like computers, for that matter. We figure that you just want to find the answers to your questions so that you can use SmartSuite to get your work done with the least amount of fuss and bother. If any of the following items apply to you, we wrote this book for you:

- ✔ You're scared to death of computers and want gentle guidance through the SmartSuite minefield.
- ✔ You know a bit about computers in general but haven't a clue about SmartSuite and don't want to remain clueless.
- ✔ You hate computers and want nothing to do with them, but your boss is forcing you to learn this stupid program.

Read More ...For Dummies Books

Because this book covers all the SmartSuite programs in a limited number of pages, we can't cover every aspect of every program. We also don't cover a great deal about what you may need to know about computer basics and Windows.

Don't despair. You can find a ...*For Dummies* book for every occasion. If you want to know more about the basics of computer operations, for example, check out *PCs For Dummies,* 6th Edition, or *Windows 98 For Dummies.* For specific terms that you don't recognize, try the *Illustrated Computer Dictionary For Dummies,* 3rd Edition. If you want more detail about some of the individual programs in SmartSuite, look for *Lotus 1-2-3 Millennium Edition For Dummies* and *Approach 97 For Dummies.*

Conventions Used in the Book

If you believe the old saw, consistency is the hobgoblin of small minds. Okay, we admit to having small minds when it comes to making things easy for you so that you have no trouble figuring out what the heck we mean when we tell you something about SmartSuite. So we adopted some conventions for this book.

You may notice that whenever we tell you to choose menu commands or click buttons to perform some task, the names of these commands usually contain underlined letters. These underlined letters are called the *hot keys* for those commands. You can either use the mouse to click menu commands directly off the menu bar or opened menus, or you can use these hot keys instead. If we tell you to choose Edit⇨Undo, for example, you can either click the name of the Edit menu, as it appears on the menu bar, and then click the Undo command after the Edit menu opens — or you can press the Alt key and hold it down as you press the E key and then press the U key, all on your keyboard. (Pressing keys together like this is called using *key combinations*. Oh, and whenever you see that little arrow between a couple of menu commands, as in Edit⇨Undo in this example, it always means that you first open the menu named before the arrow and then choose from that open menu the command named after the arrow. Got it? No? Well, hang in there; we cover this more later, too. And if you don't know what we mean when we tell you to *click* a command, well . . .)

If we tell you to *click* the mouse (or click a command or even to *single-click* something), that means to press and rapidly release the left mouse button. *Double-click* means to press and release the left mouse button *twice* in rapid succession. *Right-click* means to press and release the right mouse button.

If we want you to type something specific, such as on a page in a document, in a text box of a dialog box, or in a cell of a spreadsheet, that something appears in **boldface** type, just like the following:

Type **this text** in the Filename text box.

(Oh, and if we *really* want to be tricky, we put the words that you type in regular text if the rest of the surrounding text is bold, as is the case in numbered list paragraphs that tell you specific actions to take.)

If we want to show you something that appears on-screen — particularly text that appears in list boxes — we put that text in a special typeface (like this). Just remember, that whenever you see that kind of type, you're seeing something here on the page that you should also be seeing on-screen.

When we mention a dialog box, a menu command, or an option by name, we use initial caps (capitalizing the first letter of each word) to make the name stand out from the rest of the sentence. That means that the capitalization of the text you see in this book and the text you see on your computer screen may not match — particularly in the case of options in dialog boxes. But this convention changes the phrase "Check the Turn to entry after Create/Edit check box" into "Check the Turn To Entry After Create/Edit check box," which helps you avoid having to reread sentences to figure out what we're trying to say.

Text that appears in *italic* type indicates a new term (which we try to explain in the surrounding text) or something we think is important enough to emphasize. Italics are also used for book titles, words in foreign languages (no, not computerese), and so on.

If you see several paragraphs of text with a gray background surrounded by a box stuck smack-dab in the middle of a page of regular text, you've encountered a *sidebar*. Sidebars provide useful, or at least interesting, information that you can often safely skip. The following is an example of a sidebar:

Sidebars are cool!

You don't have to read any of the sidebars to get all the essential information that you need to use SmartSuite. On the other hand, you'll usually find the sidebar information interesting and enjoyable. Well, at least we enjoyed writing them.

Icons Used in This Book

The following *icons* (little circled pictures clueing you in to special portions of the text) are strategically placed in the margins to point out stuff that you may — or may not — want to read right away.

This icon alerts you to nerdy technical discussions that you may want to skip (or read — for the nerd in each of us).

Any shortcuts or new insights on a topic are marked with this icon.

Figures and features

SmartSuite has many options and customizable features. We have tried to write instructions and descriptions and capture screens for figures using the default settings for each SmartSuite program. However, the programs may look slightly different on your screen, depending on the settings you are using and your computer system.

 This icon provides a friendly reminder to do something.

 This icon provides a friendly reminder *not* to do something.

 This icon indicates a feature that two or more SmartSuite programs share or a way to use the various SmartSuite programs together.

 This icon indicates a link to the Internet or a feature that enables you to use the Internet.

 This icon indicates a bit of supplemental information, explanation, or something to watch out for.

Where to Go from Here

Before diving into the text, scour the Table of Contents to find the topic you want to know more about — and *then* jump right in. If you don't find what you seek in the Table of Contents, check the index. Remember that this book is a reference, not necessarily a cover-to-cover read. (If you're having a *really* good time reading it, however, we certainly won't mind if you devour every word.)

Ready to get going with SmartSuite? Well, what are you waiting for? Go to it!

Part I
A Suite Deal

In this part . . .

SmartSuite Millennium Edition is more than just a group of independent computer programs. SmartSuite is actually a tightly integrated suite of programs (Smart*Suite*, get it?) with a ton of features that are the same in each of its programs. This part looks at SmartSuite as a whole entity — how to launch and switch among the programs and how to use its common features. So don't be a SmartSuite dummy — read this part and become a SmartSuite . . . er, *smarty*.

Chapter 1

Boot Camp for SmartSuite

• •

In This Chapter

▶ Introducing the SmartSuite family members

▶ Learning about the SmartSuite family's common commands

▶ Getting caught up in SmartSuite's Internet capabilities

• •

A suite is more than just a collection of popular programs in the same box. Although all the component programs in SmartSuite Millennium Edition are powerful, stand-alone applications designed to fulfill specific computing needs, each program is also designed to work with all the other programs in the suite. SmartSuite enables you to easily share information among its component programs. You can develop a table in 1-2-3, for example, add that table to a letter you write in Word Pro, and then merge names and addresses into the letter from an Approach database.

All the SmartSuite programs share a strong family resemblance. They look alike (or at least as much alike as a word processor and a spreadsheet or other program can look). But the family resemblance goes beyond appearances — the various SmartSuite programs work alike, too. Common actions are exactly the same in all the SmartSuite programs. That makes discovering how to use all the SmartSuite programs easier for you. After you figure out how how to open a file in one SmartSuite program, you know how to open a file in all the other SmartSuite programs.

This chapter shows you how to do all sorts of things in 1-2-3, Word Pro, Approach, Freelance, and Organizer, even though the individual programs aren't covered until later. Amazing — *but true!*

How Suite It Is: The SmartSuite Family

Now that you know what a suite is, you need to meet the members of the SmartSuite family. Each family member has its own specialty and a distinctive character that makes that program the tool of choice for particular tasks. But remember that each SmartSuite program is also designed to complement all the other SmartSuite programs.

Word Pro is the SmartSuite word processor. You use this program to dash off a quick memo, write a letter to Aunt Gertrude, prepare a report, or write a manuscript. Word Pro is likely to be your most-used SmartSuite program.

Lotus 1-2-3 is SmartSuite's resident number-crunching expert. You can use 1-2-3's columns and rows of numbers and formulas to prepare a budget or a price list, compare the cost of buying or leasing your next car, or calculate how much retirement income you are going to need. But 1-2-3 does more than numbers — the program also creates charts, graphs, and more to help you make sense of your calculations.

If you need to make a presentation, SmartSuite's *Freelance Graphics* can help you make your best impression. Freelance can help you organize your thoughts and turn your ideas into colorful visuals to support your presentation. Freelance may not make the knot in your stomach go away, but the knot may loosen a bit after you know that you're well-prepared, thanks to this program.

Approach is the name of SmartSuite's database program. The idea of working with a computer database may seem intimidating, but this database is very, well, approachable. A database is, after all, just a place to keep lists. Approach can handle everything from simple mailing lists to inventory systems.

Organizer helps you clean up the clutter of a busy life by providing a place for you to keep track of all your appointments, telephone calls, to do lists, and addresses. Best of all, you already know how to use the program. Organizer looks just like the pocket calendar systems that are so popular — except that Organizer taps the power of your computer to do things that no paper calendar can do.

FastSite is the newest member of the SmartSuite family. It's designed to help you easily publish documents on a Web site. FastSite works equally well on Internet Web sites or on corporate intranet Web sites. So you can publish your documents for the whole wide world to see, or share them with your team or coworkers.

SmartCenter provides a convenient master control for all the SmartSuite programs and documents. With SmartCenter running, no SmartSuite program is more than a couple of mouse clicks away. SmartCenter also provides you with quick access to Internet sites, addresses, e-mail, and online Help for SmartSuite programs.

ScreenCam is a nifty little utility that lets you record screen activity and, if you have a sound card and microphone installed, a narration in your own voice. It's great for creating training demos that simultaneously show and tell someone how to do something on the computer. Of course, like your VCR, you're more likely to use ScreenCam to play back recordings that someone else makes than to create your own "movies." You don't need special training for simple playback of ScreenCam movie files created by someone else, so we won't cover ScreenCam in this book.

It's All in the Family

As already described, all the SmartSuite programs share some of the same features — after you know how to use a common feature in one program, you know how to use that same feature in all the SmartSuite programs. This interchangeability is all part of that family resemblance we've been talking about.

The following sections briefly describe just a few of the many features shared by all (or most of) the SmartSuite programs. We introduce many more of these common features in later chapters. We mark each of these common features with the Linking icon (described in the Introduction to this book) — so get into the habit of looking for the ubiquitous little critter.

Get smart — icons, that is

All the SmartSuite programs (except ScreenCam) include a variety of icon palettes, called *SmartIcons,* that put access to many common features a mere click away. So what exactly is a SmartIcon? A SmartIcon is simply a button that displays a little picture (called, naturally enough, an icon). Clicking a SmartIcon causes the program to perform some common task, such as saving your document. You can also perform the same action by choosing the equivalent command from a menu — the SmartIcon is just faster and more convenient to use.

Sets of SmartIcons designed for performing related tasks are grouped together into palettes. In most SmartSuite programs, you usually find palettes of SmartIcons positioned just below the menu bar. You can, however, drag SmartIcon palettes to any on-screen position that is convenient for you. SmartIcon palettes can cling to the sides of the SmartSuite program window or even float on top of your document, as shown in Figure 1-1.

That different SmartIcons exist for each different SmartSuite program only makes sense. After all, each program performs different functions. Those nice folks at Lotus, however — always trying to make your life easier — tried their best to make as many of the SmartIcons as possible appear and work exactly the same from program to program. Figure 1-2 shows typical SmartIcon palettes.

SmartIcon palette   Floating SmartIcon palette   Another SmartIcon palette

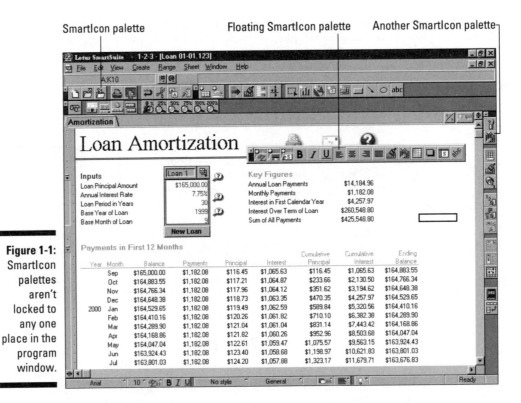

Figure 1-1:
SmartIcon
palettes
aren't
locked to
any one
place in the
program
window.

Approach

1-2-3

Word Pro

Figure 1-2:
Typical
SmartIcon
palettes.
Notice how
many of the
icons are
the same
for each
program.

As you work with SmartIcons, keep the following points in mind:

✔ You don't need to remember what each SmartIcon does (although you're likely to start remembering them as you use them regularly). Whenever you position the mouse pointer on a SmartIcon for a couple of seconds, a bubble appears describing the icon.

✔ To use any of the SmartIcons, just point to one and click the left mouse button. If you know how to use the SmartIcons in one program, you know how to use them in all the programs.

   As you read through the chapters of this book, you see the most useful SmartIcons for each program pointed out and described.

✔ Although you can use most features in SmartSuite without a mouse, you must use your mouse to access SmartIcons. (Fortunately, alternatives are available for most SmartIcon functions. You could, for example, choose File⇨Save from the menu bar or press Ctrl+S instead of clicking the Save SmartIcon.)

Checking your status (bar)

Each of the SmartSuite programs (except Organizer and ScreenCam) features a status bar at the bottom of the screen. As you discover in each of the book's SmartSuite program sections, the status bar provides valuable information; you can also click various portions of the status bar to display a list of options, which enables you to make changes to your document and window more easily than you can by choosing commands from a menu.

You can choose which paragraph style to use, for example, by clicking the portion of the status bar displaying the paragraph symbol and style name, as shown in the Word Pro status bar in Figure 1-3.

Figure 1-3:
The Word
Pro status
bar displays
a list of
paragraph
styles.

Keep the following points in mind about status bars:

✔ Although the status bars in each program are a bit different from one another, each status bar generally offers you the most efficient way to change styles and formats, fonts (typefaces), and type sizes.

✔ Get used to looking at the status bar for useful information about your current document or environment. You can usually ascertain such information as the current style, font, type size, and page number.

✔ You find tips for using the status bars in the different programs in each of the program sections of the book, but all the status bars work pretty much the same.

✔ You can completely avoid status bars if you have some sort of status bar allergy. You miss out on some good information, but anything you can do with the status bar you can also do with menus and dialog boxes. Give status bars a try, however, because they save you a lot of time.

Keeping tabs on dialog boxes

Many of the dialog boxes in the SmartSuite programs are tabbed dialog boxes, such as the one shown in Figure 1-4. These dialog boxes have a row of labels across the top that look similar to the tabs in a three-ring binder or a box of index cards. The tabs enabled Lotus to squeeze more information or options into these dialog boxes than would normally fit, and the tabs enable you to work with several related groups of settings without opening multiple dialog boxes.

Figure 1-4:
Click a tab
to access
another
page of
options.

Each tab represents a separate page of options. You just click a tab to bring that page of options to the front where you can work with them. Then you can select another tab and adjust the settings on that page and so on. You can jump back and forth among the tabs as much as you want. After you're through working in the dialog box, just click the OK button to apply the settings and close the dialog box. You can also close the dialog box by clicking the Close button (the button with the X, located in the upper-right corner of the dialog box).

InfoBox — the super dialog box

The major SmartSuite programs (1-2-3, Word Pro, Approach, and Freelance) all use a special kind of dialog box for formatting text and such. Called an *InfoBox,* this handy little feature pulls all sorts of formatting options together.

An InfoBox, such as the one shown in Figure 1-5, is essentially a tabbed dialog box that displays the properties of a selected object but has several more unusual features. Unlike with normal dialog boxes, any settings that you change in the InfoBox take effect immediately. You don't need to click OK to close the dialog box and apply the settings. You can also leave the InfoBox open and select another object (a block of text, a picture, or what-ever), and the InfoBox displays the settings for the newly selected object, which replace those of the previously selected object. The InfoBox also features a drop-down list at the top to enable you to choose between different levels of formatting — for example, between Text formatting and Page Layout formatting.

Use Fast Format to make quick work of copying styles

Suppose that you format a row of numbers just so in 1-2-3. You select a different font and color for the numbers and add a shaded background to make the numbers stand out from the surrounding information. Now you need to add the same formatting to another area of your spreadsheet. Instead of tediously noting the formatting settings and then manually

Figure 1-5:
The InfoBox
handles
formatting
chores.

duplicating the same settings elsewhere, you can use the Fast Format feature to copy formatting with a sweep of your mouse. This feature is available in Word Pro, 1-2-3, Approach, and Freelance.

Simply select a spreadsheet cell or range that's formatted the way you want. Then choose the Fast Format command. (In 1-2-3, for example, the command is Range⇨Fast Format. In other programs, the command appears on other menus or SmartIcon buttons, but it always operates in a similar fashion.) The pointer changes to a paint brush, as shown in Figure 1-6. All you need to do is drag the pointer across another range of numbers to apply the formatting from your sample to the new area. Pretty slick, huh?

After you finish "painting" with the Fast Format brush, choose the command again to turn Fast Format off and return to normal operations.

Cut, Copy, and Paste

All the SmartSuite programs enable you to select some text (or numbers or graphics) in one place, cut the selected text from your document and store it temporarily, and then move to another place in your document and paste that text back in at the new location. If you don't want to remove the text from the first location, you can copy it instead of cutting, and then you can paste a copy of the text in the new location. The process is simple. First you cut (or copy); then you paste. Voilà! You moved or copied whatever items you were trying to move or copy.

This cut/copy/paste thing works within all the SmartSuite programs (and nearly all other Windows programs as well), and you use exactly the same commands. You find the commands on the Edit menu, and they're called (I'll bet you'll never guess) Cut, Copy, and Paste. It doesn't make any difference whether you're cutting and pasting text in a Word Pro document, numbers in a 1-2-3 worksheet, graphics in a Freelance presentation, or data in an Approach database — the commands are all the same. We explain this whole process in more detail in Chapter 4, where you can see how it works in Word Pro. Just remember that it works in all the other programs, too.

You're not confined to cutting, copying, and pasting within one document. You can cut or copy stuff from one document and paste it into another document. You don't even have to be using the same program when you cut and paste. For example, you can copy a table or a chart out of a 1-2-3 worksheet and paste it into a Word Pro document. In fact, when you copy stuff that you created with one program and paste it into a document that you created with another program, you have some special options for how you want to edit and update the copied material. This goes by the fancy name of *Object Linking and Embedding,* or *OLE* for short. You can learn more about OLE by reading *Windows 98 For Dummies,* by Andy Rathbone (published by IDG Books Worldwide, Inc.).

Paintbrush pointer

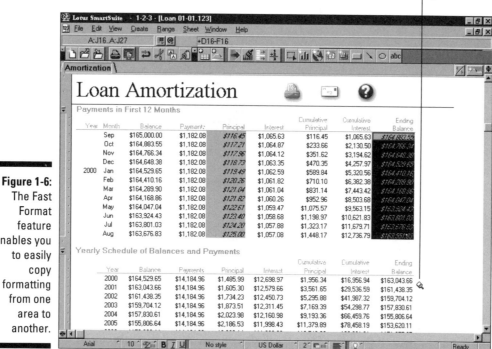

Figure 1-6:
The Fast
Format
feature
enables you
to easily
copy
formatting
from one
area to
another.

Impress your mom — spell it right

If you've used most any modern word processing program recently, the fact
that SmartSuite enables you to check the spelling in your documents
probably comes as no great surprise. You would, in fact, be more surprised
if SmartSuite didn't have this capability. Okay, so what's the big deal?

The big deal is that all the SmartSuite programs (except poor little Organizer,
which has no spell-checker) share the same spell-checking dictionary. After
you tell one SmartSuite program that how you spell your name really is
correct, you don't need to tell any of the other programs the same thing.
They already know. Trust us when we tell you that this feature is really cool.
You start the spell-checking process in all the programs exactly the same
way — by choosing Edit⇨Check Spelling. The Spell Check dialog boxes that
appear vary somewhat depending on which program you're using. The Spell
Check dialog box in Approach, for example, offers different options than the
one for 1-2-3 does, as you can see in Figure 1-7.

Spell Check dialog box for Approach

Figure 1-7:
The Spell
Check
dialog
boxes vary
slightly but
perform the
same basic
operation.

Check Spelling dialog box for 1-2-3

In some cases, you need to specify what portion of the document to check. After you've specified, the Spell Checker searches for possibly misspelled words. If the Spell Checker finds an unfamiliar word, the dialog box displays the word, along with suggested replacements.

As you use the Spell Checker feature in the various SmartSuite programs, keep the following points in mind:

✔ If the word that the Spell Checker flags is spelled just the way you want, you can click the Skip button to ignore this one occurrence or you can click Skip All to ignore all occurrences of this spelling in the document.

✔ If the word is one you think that you intend to use again in the future — and you're sure that the word's spelled correctly — you can click the Add To Dictionary button so that the Spell Checker doesn't bother you if it encounters that word again.

✔ If the Spell Checker offers some suggested alternatives, you can click the correct alternative and then click the Replace button to replace this occurrence with the alternative, or you can click Replace All to replace any occurrence of this word in the document with the alternative.

As important as spell-checking is to your documents, using a spell-checker is no substitute for proofreading. The Spell Checker doesn't stop at a correctly spelled word that just isn't the right word for the context. The feature is not that smart. Suppose that you type *to* or *two*, but you really meant to type *too*. The Spell Checker can't catch that error. Word Pro includes a grammar-checker that works similarly to the spell-checker and can catch some context errors, but nothing can replace a careful proofread by a real person. (Thank goodness something is left for us to do.)

Master your tasks with SmartMaster templates

SmartMasters are another common feature of all the major SmartSuite programs (Word Pro, 1-2-3, Approach, and Freelance). Basically, SmartMasters are templates. You probably know what templates are — patterns that enable you to easily make copies of something so that you don't have to start from scratch each time. But SmartMasters can be, well, *smart*. The folks at Lotus understand that you aren't likely to want to create an exact duplicate of the file they chose as a template. So the SmartMasters are smart enough to actually help you customize the document, worksheet, presentation, or whatever it is you create with the SmartMaster. For example, many SmartMasters include features such as Click Here blocks — spaces where you can enter your own text into the document based on the SmartMaster.

As you might expect, the SmartMasters in the different SmartSuite programs differ in the details of what you can do with them and exactly how you do it. That makes sense because the differences among SmartMasters resemble the differences among a word processor, a spreadsheet, a database, and a presentation program. The common thread in all the programs is that, when you are creating a new file or document, you have the option of basing that new file or document on a SmartMaster. SmartMasters are available for most of the common tasks that you want to perform in the SmartSuite programs. If you need to write a letter in Word Pro, you can find a SmartMaster for it; if you need to create a loan amortization schedule in 1-2-3, you can find a SmartMaster for it; if you need to create a sales contact database in Approach, you can find a SmartMaster for that, too.

Save your stuff

No matter which SmartSuite program you use, you need to save the stuff you're working on in a file on your hard drive. And no matter which program you use, you save files in exactly the same way. Simply choose File⇨Save As to open the Save As dialog box, as shown in Figure 1-8. You can select the disk drive and folder to which you want to save the file and give your file a name. Depending on which program you're using, you can also select different options, such as saving a portion of the document or using different file formats for compatibility with other programs. After you name the file and select any appropriate options, click the dialog box's Save button to record the information on your disk.

Figure 1-8:
You can name your file in the Save As dialog box — in this case, the one used in Word Pro.

 After you save a file the first time, subsequent saves are even easier. If you're working on a file, you can choose File⇨Save (or click the Save The Current File SmartIcon, or press Ctrl+S) to update the file with your latest changes without bothering with the Save As dialog box or entering the name of the file each time.

 If you want to reuse or edit a file you saved, choose File⇨Open (or click the Open An Existing File SmartIcon) to open a dialog box very similar to the Save As dialog box. Just as you did when you saved the file, you can select the drive and folder and then select the file from the large list box. Then click the Open button to open the file. This operation works the same in all the SmartSuite programs.

A quick trip to the printer

 Another operation that's essentially the same in all the SmartSuite programs is printing. Regardless of which program you're using, you start the printing process by choosing File⇨Print. This command opens the Print dialog box, which enables you to choose the printer you want to use (assuming you installed more than one printer) and to specify what portion of the current document to print. The details of this dialog box vary slightly depending on which program you're using. After you adjust the settings as needed, click OK to start printing.

Click the Properties button in the Print dialog box to open a standard Windows dialog box in which you can adjust your printer settings.

Before you print, check the document's page layout to make sure that margins and such are set correctly. In Word Pro, press Alt+Enter to open the InfoBox and then select Page Layout from the drop-down list in the InfoBox title bar to access the margin settings. In the other programs, choose File➪Page Setup (or a similar command) to open a dialog box containing settings appropriate to that program's output.

Go team!

All the SmartSuite programs include features that make the often-complicated task of collaborating on projects with other members of a team or workgroup easier. The Team Computing features, as they are called, include some or all of the following, depending on which program you're using:

- **TeamMail** enables you to send an e-mail message to a colleague and include all or part of the document you're working on.

- **TeamReview** enables you to send a document, spreadsheet, or presentation to other team members for review and comments. You control who gets what editing privileges and can review their comments and suggestions.

- **TeamConsolidate** helps you evaluate review comments by combining multiple documents into one.

- **TeamShow** enables you to show a presentation to several team members simultaneously over a network.

- **TeamSecurity** makes handling file-sharing controls for Approach and Word Pro files easier on a network.

These Team Computing features are cool stuff — provided that you and the other members of your team have access to the SmartSuite programs, network connections, and e-mail systems required to make them work.

We're not going to delve into SmartSuite's Team Computing features in this book, however, because many readers probably aren't able to take advantage of them. Those who can use the Team Computing features surely also have access to system administrators and a corporate computing services staff to help in using these features. If you're one of those lucky ones, make sure that you check out the Team Computing capabilities in SmartSuite.

Installing extra stuff

If you have a friend or coworker who also uses SmartSuite, you may notice that your friend's copy of SmartSuite includes some features that you don't have. Perhaps your friend has more SmartMasters, clip art, or fonts available, or perhaps you are missing an add-on feature, such as IBM ViaVoice, which adds voice recognition and dictation capabilities to Word Pro.

Don't worry. You haven't been shortchanged. SmartSuite is a very large set of programs, and few people use all the bells and whistles. So the standard SmartSuite installation doesn't include all the optional stuff. If you want some of those extra features, you can add them by simply re-running the SmartSuite installation. It's a rather long and drawn-out process, but all you really have to do is start the setup program and follow the on-screen instructions. (To start the setup program, place the SmartSuite CD in your CD-ROM drive and then use Windows Explorer to display the contents of the CD and double-click Setup.exe.) When you get to the point in the installation where you can choose between the minimal, default, or custom installation, choose custom. After you choose custom, the installation program presents a series of dialog boxes where you can pick and choose, in excruciating detail, which SmartSuite components you want to install. At the end of the normal installation routine, you have the option of installing the add-on components such as ViaVoice.

Caught Up in the Net

The Internet is in the process of revolutionizing the way many of us work.

All the SmartSuite programs are Internet-aware to one extent or another. This awareness starts with the simple (but unusual) capability of each program to open files from and save files to remote computers that are connected to the Internet. All the SmartSuite programs except Organizer and ScreenCam can also use the Internet's File Transfer Protocol (FTP) to save files to an FTP site — and can do so directly from within the program. You don't need to save the file on your local hard disk and then use a separate utility to transfer the file across the Internet to the FTP server.

You can use the File⇨Save As command to open the Save As dialog box, and then just click the Internet button to open the Save to Internet dialog box, where you can enter all the information your SmartSuite program needs in order to locate the other computer on the Internet. Then just click the Save button to save your file.

Word Pro, 1-2-3, and Freelance Graphics can all save their respective documents as HTML files (the standard file format for World Wide Web pages) that can be posted on a server on the Internet or a corporate intranet and viewed by anyone with a standard Web browser such as Netscape Navigator or Internet Explorer. And that's not all! The SmartSuite programs have access to a special printing option that enables you to print documents and reports in a format that you can publish on the Web — complete with all the formatting you expect to see in the output from your regular printer. We tell you more about creating Web documents in Chapters 22 and 23. And don't forget that after you create Web documents, FastSite is there to help you publish them on the Web site of your choice.

SmartSuite's Internet connections aren't confined to the output of the SmartSuite programs either. SmartCenter has its own links to the Internet that give you instant access to Web sites for news, reference, technical support, and more. You can find out more about SmartCenter in Chapter 2.

Chapter 2

Taking Control: Working with SmartCenter

In This Chapter

▶ Getting to know SmartCenter

▶ Exploring drawers and folders

▶ Having it your way — Customizing SmartCenter

▶ Utilizing SuiteStart's SmartSuite program icons in your taskbar

*Y*ou can think of *SmartCenter* as the glue that holds all the SmartSuite programs together. It's not — but you're welcome to think of it that way. SmartCenter is really a group of buttons that make starting and switching among your SmartSuite programs unbelievably easy. SmartCenter is your central command center for SmartSuite — and more.

What Is SmartCenter?

SmartCenter is a little like the Windows 95 and Windows 98 taskbar — a button bar that always lurks at the edge of your computer screen to help you launch and switch among programs. But SmartCenter is more than just a convenient way to start SmartSuite programs. SmartCenter also provides easy access to document files, Internet sites, an address book, and much more. In other words, SmartCenter helps you organize your computer desktop so that everything is kept neatly in its place.

SmartCenter normally resides in a strip situated across the top of the computer screen. And SmartCenter jealously guards its turf. Even if you maximize a program window, SmartCenter stays visible — and available — right at the top of your screen. Other program windows never cover up SmartCenter (unless, of course, you configure SmartCenter to act otherwise).

If you installed SmartSuite on your computer by using the standard installation procedure and you didn't change the setup, SmartCenter automatically swings into action right after you start Windows. After Windows starts, you see the Welcome to Lotus SmartSuite logo. Then the row of buttons that make up SmartCenter appears on-screen, as shown in Figure 2-1. If all the buttons don't fit on your computer screen, a couple of arrows appear at the right end of the SmartCenter bar. Just click the right-arrow button to slide more SmartCenter buttons into view. Click the left-arrow button to bring the other buttons back into view.

Figure 2-1: SmartCenter Main Menu button   Use these buttons to slide more drawer buttons into view
This row of
buttons is
the Lotus
SmartCenter.

SmartCenter simulates a filing cabinet with drawers and folders. Each SmartCenter button corresponds to a filing cabinet drawer. (Lotus even *calls* the buttons *drawers*.) Click a drawer button, and the "drawer" itself slides open, revealing — you guessed it! — *folders*. (See Figure 2-2.)

SmartCenter menu button

Open drawer

Open folder

Figure 2-2:
Like those
of a real
filing
cabinet, a
SmartCenter
drawer
contains
folders that,
in turn,
contain
useful
items.

Program icon

Other folders

Folders can contain a variety of items depending on the kind of drawer in which the folder is located. The Lotus Applications folder, shown open in Figure 2-2, for example, contains shortcut icons for all the SmartSuite programs. Other folders in the drawer contain shortcut icons for the documents you create using your SmartSuite programs. The folders in other drawers offer things like address-book entries, access to reference materials, links to Internet sites, and so on.

Opening Drawers and Folders

You can start your SmartSuite program just as you start other Windows programs — click the Start button in the taskbar, point to Programs, point to Lotus SmartSuite in the cascading menu that appears, and finally, select (or click) the SmartSuite program you want to start from yet another cascading menu. Yeck! Surely SmartSuite offers an easier way to get started. (Fortunately, it does.)

If SmartCenter is visible on-screen, any SmartSuite program is just a few clicks away (and you don't need to concern yourself about menus that seem to slip from your grasp and close unexpectedly). To start a program, just click the SmartSuite drawer button in the SmartCenter to open its drawer, click the Lotus Applications folder tab, and then double-click the icon for the program you want to start. Before you realize what's happening — or shortly thereafter — that program appears on-screen. To close the SmartCenter drawer, click the drawer's Close button (the button on the open drawer front with the X on it) or simply click the drawer front again.

Here are a few points to keep in mind as you work with SmartCenter:

✔ SmartCenter is always visible, no matter which Windows program you're running. Even if you're using a Windows program that isn't one of the SmartSuite programs, SmartCenter stays with you like a guardian angel.

✔ If you want to get rid of SmartCenter, click the SmartCenter Main Menu button (the black button at the left end of SmartCenter with Lotus written on it), and choose Exit SmartCenter. SmartCenter goes away, and the other program windows get a bit bigger to use the space previously occupied by SmartCenter.

✔ If SmartCenter isn't running and you want to use it, click the Start button in the taskbar, point to Programs, point to Lotus SmartSuite, and then select (click) Lotus SmartCenter.

> ✔ If SmartCenter starts automatically when you start Windows (as it normally does) and you don't want it to start automatically, you need to edit your Windows Start menu to remove SmartCenter from the Programs⇨ Startup folder. You can find instructions for editing the Start menu in *Windows 98 For Dummies,* by Andy Rathbone (IDG Books Worldwide, Inc.). Or you can persuade your friendly neighborhood Windows weenie to do it for you.

SmartSuite programs and documents

The first of the default SmartCenter drawers is the one you're likely to use the most. The SmartSuite drawer, as it's aptly named, provides quick access to your SmartSuite programs and documents. In addition to the Lotus Applications folder you've already seen in action, this drawer contains folders for templates and for documents (files) that you create in each of the major SmartSuite programs. The SmartSuite drawer even contains a folder set up for Notes Databases for those of you using Lotus Notes to share information among members of your workgroup. The following list details some things you can do with SmartCenter drawers:

> ✔ You can add to a SmartCenter drawer shortcut icons that enable you to open non-SmartSuite programs and documents. SmartCenter makes it easy to add shortcuts to a folder in a SmartCenter drawer. All you need to do is click a shortcut, hold down the mouse button as you drag the shortcut from your Windows desktop or from an Explorer window, and drop the icon on an empty space in an open SmartCenter folder.
>
> ✔ You can drag a file icon from a Windows Explorer window and drop that icon onto a program icon in the Lotus Applications folder. SmartCenter starts the program and tries to load the file you dropped.

> ✔ You can easily get rid of any folder you don't need. Just right-click the folder and choose Delete Folder from the pop-up menu that appears. Confirm the action by clicking Yes in the dialog box that appears, and — poof! — the folder is gone.

If you are not experienced in the ways of using shortcut icons and drag-and-drop techniques, you can read up on these subjects in *Windows 98 For Dummies.*

Internet

SmartCenter's Internet drawer enables you to reach out beyond the limits of your own computer and tap into the resources of the Internet, putting some handy information at your fingertips. SmartCenter uses your existing Internet connection and either your existing World Wide Web browser software or its own browser to deliver the information you select in the Internet drawer. For the most part, SmartCenter's Internet drawer just provides a collection of useful Web sites in a convenient and easy-to-use format. On the other hand, some of the folders, such as Headlines, Stock Quotes, Weather, and Web Reference, can display Internet information right in the folder.

Obviously, you need an Internet connection in order for this to work. SmartCenter is designed to work best on a computer that has a full-time Internet connection (usually provided by a local area network that is linked to the Internet), but SmartCenter also works pretty well over a dial-up connection to an Internet service provider. Configuring an Internet connection and Web browser are beyond the scope of this book. Fortunately, once your Internet connection and Web browser are set up to work properly in Windows, SmartCenter requires little or no additional setup to use the same connection.

If your connection to the Internet is via a local area network, your network system administrator should be able to get you set up. (If your network uses a security device called a proxy server, you'll need to enter its address in the Internet Settings dialog box — which you can reach by opening the Folder Properties dialog box, as explained in the upcoming numbered list of steps — and then click the Internet Settings button.) If you use a dial-up Internet connection, try to get a knowledgeable colleague to configure the various settings for you. Otherwise, you probably need to consult with the technical support staff at your Internet service provider, and perhaps read up on the subject in *The Internet For Dummies,* 5th Edition, by John Levine, Carol Baroudi, and Margaret Levine Young (IDG Books Worldwide, Inc.).

If possible, you want your system configured to automatically launch your Web browser and initiate a dial-up network connection when you attempt to open or run a URL (a *Uniform Resource Locator,* or Internet address). Getting this to happen automatically requires just the right settings in Windows — which is why it's probably worth bribing your favorite computer geek with a free lunch to set your computer up for you.

The features of the Internet drawer require a full-featured Internet connection capable of supporting a connection to the World Wide Web. Most direct network connections will work just fine, as will dial-up connections that go by names such as SLIP and PPP. However, a text-only, e-mail Internet connection just won't get the job done. Talk to your network administrator or Internet provider to find out if your Internet connection has what SmartSuite needs; most connections do, but it pays to check. (If you can use a Web browser on your existing Internet connection, SmartSuite should be able to use that connection, too.)

SmartCenter's Internet drawer comes with an assortment of folders that provide you with easy access to Internet resources for news, weather, reference material, and more. The default folders include the following:

- **Headlines.** The Headlines folder connects to Yahoo! — a powerful and popular Internet index and search site — to download the wire service headlines displayed in the folder. Click an underlined headline to retrieve the story from Yahoo! and display it in your Web browser.

- **Stock Quotes.** After you tell SmartCenter what stock ticker symbols you want to track, you can view reasonably current (15-minute delayed) price quotes for those stocks in the Stock Quotes folder.

- **Weather.** Just tell SmartCenter what city you're interested in, and it will display a brief summary of current and forecast conditions in the Weather folder. From there, you can click links to detailed weather maps and other stuff.

- **Web Reference.** This folder is a collection of links to useful reference sites on the World Wide Web. Click an underlined item to connect to that site.

- **Travel Reservations.** Opening this folder takes you to a Web site where you can get information on airline flights, car rentals, cruises, and hotels, and then you can book reservations if you like. You can even get a map of where you're going.

- **Favorites.** Do you have favorite Web sites that you want to revisit? If you saved the locations on the Favorites list in your Web browser, SmartCenter displays the list of Favorite sites in this folder. This is really just a convenient window into the Windows Favorites folder. Double-clicking a folder icon opens an Explorer window showing the contents of that folder; double-clicking a shortcut icon to a Web site opens your Web browser and starts loading that Web page.

The folders in the Internet drawer need to be customized in order to meet your needs and make the best use of your Internet connection. For instance, you need to select what news category you want to see in the Headlines folder, what city you want weather reports for, and what stocks you want to track in the Stock Quotes folder. You can also specify whether you want to update the information in the folders manually or whether you want SmartCenter to handle the updates automatically at preset intervals. To customize a folder's settings, follow these steps:

1. **Right-click the folder tab you want to customize and choose Folder Properties from the pop-up menu that appears (or just double-click the folder tab).**

   This opens the Folder Properties dialog box for that folder. The dialog box contains a Basics tab plus another tab, depending on what kind of folder it is. For instance, the Folder Properties dialog box for a Headlines folder contains a Basics tab and a News tab.

2. Click the Basics tab and adjust the folder's color, label, and icon settings, if desired.

You probably won't need to adjust these settings, but it's easy to do. To change the folder label, simply type the new label text into the Folder Label text box. To change the color of the folder's tab, click the arrow button at the right end of the Color box and select a color by clicking the desired color in the color palette that appears. To change the icon, simply choose a new icon from the Icon drop-down list.

3. Click the News (or Weather, or Stocks) tab and select the options specific to that folder type.

The options available on this tab vary depending on the folder type. For example, on the News tab, you can choose what news category you want to see in the folder. Your choices include the following: Top Stories, World News, Technology, Business, and Sports. (By the way, after you select a news category, the folder label changes to reflect your choice.)

Want to see news from more than one category? No problem. Just create another folder for the additional news category. See the "Adding drawers and folders" section later in this chapter for instructions.

Other folder types have other options appropriate to those folders. You can specify what stocks you want to track in a Stock Quote folder or the city for which you want weather reports in a Weather folder.

4. If you want SmartCenter to update the information in the folder automatically, click the Refresh Every check box and enter an appropriate number in the Minutes text box.

Automatic updates are great if you enjoy the luxury of a full-time Internet connection. However, if you have a dial-up Internet connection, you probably want to leave the automatic refresh option disabled and refresh the folder information manually after establishing an Internet connection.

5. If your Internet connection goes through a proxy server, click the Internet Settings button to open a dialog box where you can enter the proxy settings; then click OK to close the Internet Settings dialog box.

This is an advanced setting. You need to consult your network system administrator to determine whether your network uses a proxy server and get the address of the server.

6. Click OK to close the Folder Properties dialog box and record your settings.

Now your folder is ready to use.

If you have a dial-up Internet connection, you need to establish your Internet connection manually and then update the folders in SmartCenter's Internet drawer. To manually update the information in a folder, right-click the folder tab and choose Refresh from the pop-up menu that appears.

You can print the contents of a SmartCenter drawer folder (such as a folder that is displaying a Web page). To do so, simply right-click the folder tab and then choose Print from the pop-up menu that appears.

Calendar

The Calendar drawer in SmartCenter is at its best when you link it to your Organizer file. Just open the Calendar drawer to view a display of your appointments for the day, as shown in Figure 2-3. Need to see appointments at earlier or later times? Simply click the Morning or Evening arrows, which are located above and below the Time column, respectively, to scroll the calendar display up or down. To view entries for a different date, click the middle of the date number icon. SmartCenter opens a calendar dialog box in which you can click another date to display appointments for that day. If you just want to look at the previous or next day's appointments, click the left or right side of the date number icon. The following list tells you more stuff you can do with the Calendar drawer:

✔ To link the Calendar folder to your Organizer file, right-click the Calendar folder tab and choose Folder Properties from the pop-up menu that appears. This action opens the Folder Properties dialog box. Click the Calendar tab, open the File Type drop-down list box and choose Lotus Organizer file, fill in the filename for your Organizer file in the Name Of Lotus Organizer file text box, and then choose the appropriate section in the Section drop-down list box. Click OK to complete the link.

✔ You can set the Calendar drawer to open automatically to remind you of appointments. The Open Drawer check box is located at the bottom of the Calendar tab in the Folder Properties dialog box. You can even set how much in advance of each appointment you want to be notified.

✔ To add an appointment to the Calendar folder, simply drag the mouse pointer down across the appropriate time span in the Calendar display. For example, to schedule a two-hour meeting starting at 2:00 p.m., simply click at the top of the 2:00 time block and drag down to 4:00. SmartCenter displays a small Create Appointment dialog box in which you can enter a description of the appointment and then click OK to record that appointment in the Calendar. This also records the appointment in your linked Organizer file. To enter more information about an appointment, you need to set up the appointment in Organizer. (See Chapter 19 for more details.)

Morning arrow

Date number icon

Evening arrow

Days to display box

Figure 2-3:
The
Calendar
drawer
keeps track
of your
appointments.

✔ You can display appointments for more than one day by clicking the corresponding columns in the Days to Display box, located in the lower-right corner of the Calendar folder. For example, to see three consecutive days of appointments, click the third column. SmartCenter automatically widens the Calendar drawer to accommodate the additional days.

✔ To make a drawer wider (or narrower), open the drawer and position the mouse pointer anywhere along the right edge of the drawer. After the pointer changes to a double-headed arrow, you can drag right or left to make the drawer wider or narrower. You can also drag the bottom edge of the drawer up or down to change the number of hours displayed.

Addresses and maps

The Addresses drawer is another of SmartCenter's default drawers. After you open the Addresses drawer, you see a display reminiscent of those flip-top phone directories with the alphabet tabs along the side. Click a letter tab to display a list of address entries with last names that start with that letter. Next, click an entry name to display more details on an address card for that listing, as shown in Figure 2-4. The buttons on the address card that appears enable you to start a letter in Word Pro, dial the phone number, dial the fax number, or send an e-mail message.

To add a new name and address to the folder, just click the Add Name entry in the address list or right-click the address list and choose Add Name And Address from the pop-up menu. SmartCenter opens a dialog box in which you can fill in the information for the new entry. Then click OK to record the name and address in the folder. To edit an existing entry, open it and click the Edit button or just double-click the address card to open the same dialog box you used to enter information for the address entry.

Figure 2-4: Each address card entry has room for home information as well as the business information shown here.

SmartCenter can maintain a separate list of addresses but, like the Calendar drawer, it's at its best if you use the feature to access the address section of your Organizer file. To link the Addresses folder to your Organizer file, right-click the Addresses folder tab and choose Folder Properties from the pop-up menu that appears. In the Folder Properties dialog box, click the Name & Address tab, select Lotus Organizer file in the File Type drop-down list box, fill in the filename for your Organizer file in the Name Of Lotus Organizer File text box, and then choose your Address Book section from the Section drop-down list box. Click OK to complete the link.

In addition to the Addresses folder, the Addresses drawer includes a Maps folder. Opening the Maps folder takes you to a Web site where you can enter an address, click a button, and view a map of the vicinity. It's a great way to make sure that you'll be able to find the address of the person or business that you're planning to visit.

Reminders

The SmartCenter Reminders drawer (shown in Figure 2-5) is a convenient place to keep a simple to-do list. By default, the Reminders drawer contains folders for Home and Business reminders. But you can add folders for projects and other special uses if you want. (See the section "Customizing SmartCenter," later in this chapter.)

Unlike the Calendar and Addresses drawers, the Reminders drawer does not have any provision for linking to your Organizer file. You must keep track of which items you list in the Reminders drawer and which items you track in Organizer.

The following list describes some of the things you can do in the Reminders drawer:

- ✔ To add a reminder, select a reminder folder to open that folder, click the empty rectangle, and type in the reminder text.

- ✔ You can mark a reminder as completed by clicking the check box beside the reminder item.

- ✔ To delete any reminder item from the list, right-click the item and choose Delete Reminder from the pop-up menu that appears.

- ✔ To change the order of the reminders on the list, just click a reminder that you want to move and keep holding down the mouse button as you drag the reminder up or down the list, dropping it in a new location in the list.

- ✔ You can delete all the completed reminder items at once by right-clicking the folder tab and choosing Delete Completed Reminders from the pop-up menu that appears.

Figure 2-5:
The Reminders drawer keeps your to-do list handy.

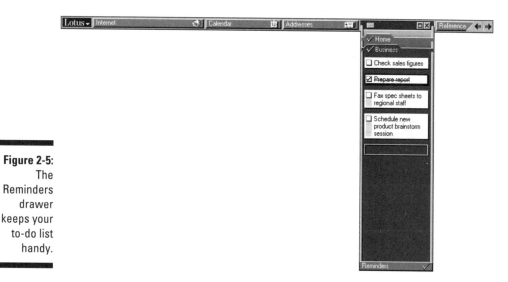

Reference

Did you ever wish that you had a dictionary or thesaurus at your fingertips as you worked on some project? Well, now you do. The SmartCenter Reference drawer contains Dictionary and Thesaurus folders.

To use the dictionary, open the Reference drawer, click the Dictionary folder tab, type a word into the text box, and press Enter. SmartSuite's dictionary responds by displaying the definition, part of speech, and pronunciation guide for the word.

The Thesaurus folder works just like the Dictionary folder except that the display includes only a very brief definition of the word you type, followed by some synonyms for the word.

Business Productivity

The Business Productivity drawer contains an assortment of templates and SmartMasters that Lotus thoughtfully includes with SmartSuite. In this drawer you can find templates for many routine business documents you need to create, all arranged in folders according to functional groups — not which program you use to create them — so you can just double-click an icon for what you want to do. For example, if you choose Amortize A Loan in the Business Management folder, SmartSuite launches 1-2-3 and loads a workbook with a template for doing loan calculations. If you choose Positioning Proposal in the same folder, SmartSuite opens Freelance and starts a presentation based on the proposal SmartMaster.

Suite Help

The Suite Help drawer puts lots of resources that help you use SmartSuite just a mouse click away. The drawer contains folders for Help files, online documentation, and links to Internet Web sites. You see more of the Suite Help drawer in Chapter 3.

Customizing SmartCenter

If SmartCenter isn't set up just the way you want, you can make some modifications so that the feature performs more to your liking. You can, for example, make SmartCenter appear at the bottom of the screen instead of the top. (No, we don't know why you'd want to do that, but you can.) You can change the look of the drawer fronts, add and remove drawers and folders, and add items to folders. The point is that you can have it your way, as the folks at one of those fast-food burger joints used to say.

To start customizing, click the SmartCenter Main Menu button — the first one on the left end of the SmartCenter. To open the SmartCenter Properties dialog box, shown in Figure 2-6, choose SmartCenter Properties from the menu that appears. This dialog box is one of those tabbed ones we talk about in Chapter 1. You find the first set of options on the Basics tab.

Figure 2-6:
Most SmartCenter customization options are contained in the SmartCenter Properties dialog box.

Redecorating SmartCenter

So you want to know what you can — and should — customize? Fair enough. Here's a bit about the Basics tab:

- ✔ You can reduce the amount of screen space SmartCenter requires by clicking the check box next to the Reserve Minimum Space For SmartCenter option. A check mark in this box tells SmartCenter to share its little strip of your computer screen with other programs.

- ✔ If you don't want to see the pop-up Help labels that appear as you rest the mouse pointer on a SmartCenter button for a few seconds, you can hide these labels by removing the check mark from the Display Popup Help option. Just click the check box to deselect this item.

- ✔ You can move SmartCenter to another portion of the screen by choosing the Top Of Screen or Bottom Of Screen option button.

Click the Effects tab in the SmartCenter Properties dialog box to see the next set of options, as shown in Figure 2-7. Now take a look at the customization options you find on this tab:

✔ You can change the sound that SmartCenter makes whenever you perform such actions as opening and closing drawers. Select the SmartCenter event — for example, opening a drawer — from the Event drop-down list. Then select from the Sound drop-down list the sound you want SmartCenter to play whenever that event occurs. You can preview the sound by clicking the button displaying the speaker icon.

✔ To silence the sound of a SmartCenter event, select None in the Sound drop-down list. (Sounds are cool, but some sounds can become annoying after a while.)

✔ By adjusting the Drawer Speed slider at the bottom of the Effects tab, you can change how fast the SmartCenter drawers open and close after you click a drawer. Drag the marker to the left to make the drawers open slower. (We don't know why you'd want to do that, but you can.) Drag the marker to the right to make the drawers open faster.

Figure 2-7:
The Effects tab controls sound effects in SmartCenter.

The Appearance tab of the SmartCenter Properties dialog box is where you can get fancy with your SmartCenter redecorating. SmartCenter provides many textures you can apply to your drawer buttons. To select a different texture, simply scroll down the list to see your options and click the one you like.

The Browser tab allows you to choose what browser you want to use to view the Web pages that you access through SmartCenter. You can select your system's default browser (that could be Internet Explorer, Netscape Navigator, or any other browser you choose) or SmartCenter's own browser.

After you make your choices in the SmartCenter Properties dialog box, click OK to apply the changes to SmartCenter.

Adding drawers and folders

So much for the cosmic effects; now to examine how to do something useful —
such as adding your own drawers and folders. After all, SmartCenter is
supposed to help you organize your work. For SmartCenter to succeed at
that goal, you must be able to adapt the feature to your own style and to the
projects on which you work.

To add a drawer to SmartCenter, click the SmartCenter Main Menu button
and choose New Drawer from the menu that appears. The New Drawer
dialog box appears. Type a name for your drawer in the Drawer Label text
box. Then select an icon for the drawer from the Drawer Handle drop-down
list box. After you click OK, the new drawer is added to SmartCenter.

Of course, an empty drawer doesn't do you much good. You want to put
something in the drawer. You start by adding folders to a drawer. To add a
new folder to the drawer you just created or to any of SmartCenter's existing
drawers, follow these steps:

1. **Right-click the drawer to which you want to add a folder, and choose
   New Folder from the pop-up menu that appears.**

   This action opens the New Folder dialog box, shown in Figure 2-8.

   The first step in creating the folder itself is deciding what type of folder
   you want. (Folder type is an important distinction, because the different folder types hold different kinds of information.)

2. **Choose the appropriate folder type by clicking its name in the Folder
   Type list.**

   The New Folder dialog box suddenly acquires some extra tabs. The exact
   nature of these tabs varies depending on the folder type you select.

Figure 2-8:
The New
Folder
dialog box
starts out
with a
single tab.

3. **Click the Next button to proceed to the next step in creating a new folder.**

For most folder types, the next step is the Basics tab, which is similar to the one shown in Figure 2-9.

Figure 2-9:
The Basics tab is where you label your new folder.

4. **Type a name for your new folder in the Folder Label text box.**

You can also choose a color and icon for the folder from the Color and Icon drop-down list boxes.

5. **Click Next to move on to the next step.**

The Step 3 and Step 4 tabs vary somewhat depending on what kind of folder you are creating. For a File folder type, for example, you need to specify whether you want to see large or small icons and whether the SmartCenter folder is linked to a Windows desktop folder; for an Internet Weather folder, you need to specify the location for which you want to receive weather reports and how often you want those reports updated.

6. **Fill in the information requested on each tab and click Next to move on to the next step (if you have one).**

7. **After you fill in all the information in the dialog box, click Done to create the folder.**

That's it! You created a new folder.

What can I put in a SmartCenter drawer?

The short answer to the question of what you can put in a SmartCenter drawer is — folders. The more pertinent question, however, is what can you put in a SmartCenter folder? The answer to that depends on what kind of folder you create.

Most of the folder types are designed to hold a specific kind of information. Address folders hold addresses, calendar folders hold appointments, and a dictionary folder provides access to the dictionary database built into SmartSuite.

The File folder type is a notable exception. This folder holds Windows shortcut icons. You can use file folders to hold shortcuts to programs (including non-SmartSuite programs) and shortcuts to files of all descriptions — even shortcuts to other Windows folders. Adding a shortcut icon to a folder is easy. All you need to do is drag a shortcut icon from your desktop or an Explorer window and drop it on an open SmartCenter folder. Press and hold the Ctrl key as you drag if you want to copy, instead of move, the shortcut icon. (See *Windows 98 For Dummies* for more information on working with shortcut icons.)

SuiteStart: A Tray Full of SmartSuite Programs

SmartCenter and the Start menu aren't the only ways to start SmartSuite programs. The standard SmartSuite setup also installs *SuiteStart,* a set of icons for SmartSuite programs that appear in the system tray — the expandable section at the right end of the taskbar that is home to the clock display and speaker volume control icon. (See Figure 2-10.)

To start a SmartSuite program by using SuiteStart, simply click the icon for the program you want to start. The program starts (almost) instantly. This method is by far the fastest way to start a SmartSuite program. Also, you can do the following with SuiteStart:

✔ If you decide that you don't want SuiteStart in your taskbar, you can temporarily remove the feature by right-clicking any of the SuiteStart icons and choosing Exit from the pop-up menu that appears. SuiteStart removes itself from the taskbar (but it returns when you reboot your computer).

✔ If you want to temporarily remove one of the program icons from SuiteStart, right-click the icon you want to remove and choose Remove (Program Name) Icon from the pop-up menu that appears. Poof, it's gone.

✔ You can add shortcuts to SuiteStart that open other non-SmartSuite programs and files. Simply right-click any SuiteStart icon and choose Add File from the pop-up menu that appears. This opens a standard Windows Open dialog box. Locate the file you want to add and click OK to add an icon for it to the System Tray along with the other SuiteStart icons.

Figure 2-10:
The
SmartSuite
icons in the
taskbar's
system tray.

Taskbar   System tray   SuiteStart icons

✔ If SuiteStart isn't running and you want to use the feature, click the Start button and choose Programs➪Lotus SmartSuite➪Lotus Accessories➪Lotus SuiteStart.

✔ If you don't want SuiteStart to appear in the system tray each time you start Windows, you must remove it from the Startup folder of your Windows Start menu. Ask an experienced Windows user to help you, or read *Windows 98 For Dummies* to discover how to do it yourself.

Chapter 3

Moving On

● ●

In This Chapter

▶ Getting help from SmartSuite

▶ Picking the correct program for the job

● ●

*F*iguring out how to get unstuck — that's what this chapter's all about. Whether you're having trouble using a particular feature in a SmartSuite program or you don't even know which program to use to do what you want to do, we show you the way.

Help! What Do I Do Now?

What's the scariest thing about using computers for most people? It's not the fear that you may get sucked into the darned thing like the guy in the movie *Tron*. If you're like most folks, you're more likely to worry that you may panic if you can't figure out how to perform a task that's necessary to your work. That's probably why you bought this book — for which we thank you profusely. This book can't cover every SmartSuite feature, however, or even all the possible ways to use the features it does cover. So where can you turn?

Good news! All the SmartSuite programs are chock-full of helpful instructions and sage advice that can be called on whenever you need them. You can also tap the treasure trove of information in SmartCenter's Suite Help drawer.

Hey! How about some help over here?

Most of the time, what you really need from SmartSuite's Help system is — help. Imagine that. You can get help in several ways, and the methods vary slightly among the SmartSuite programs, but you do have one consistent way to get the help you need in any SmartSuite program — by pressing F1

(the Help key). The F1 function key accesses *context-sensitive* Help — help that's relevant to what you're doing at the moment. Most of the time, the SmartSuite program you're using knows what you're trying to do and displays the appropriate Help screen. Amazing! Suppose, for example, that you're in Word Pro and you notice the Frame command on the Create menu. You can't remember — or never knew — how to create a frame, and you want to know how . . . now. Just choose Create⇨Frame, and then, when Word Pro opens the Create Frame dialog box, press F1. A Help window appears to instruct you on how to create a frame.

Your Help windows may be larger or smaller than the one shown in the figure. Just as you can resize other windows, you can resize Help windows by positioning the mouse pointer over one of the window's edges so that the pointer turns into a double-headed arrow; then hold down the left mouse button and drag the window's edge until the window becomes the size you want.

As you work with Help windows, remember the following points:

✔ Context-sensitive Help works for just about any menu command or dialog box option.

✔ More help for a topic is often available than can fit in one window. You may need to use the scroll bars to move down the window to bring the additional Help information into view.

✔ At the bottom of Help screens (you usually must scroll down to get there), you often find a small gray button beside some text such as See Related Topics. Click the button to view a list of related topics. Then you can select a topic from the list and click the Display button to view that topic. Don't be afraid to explore. In addition to the See Related Topics button, you sometimes see other buttons (such as See Details). Clicking these items takes you to related Help screens.

Finding help on a topic

If context-sensitive Help doesn't give you the help you need, you can usually find what you need by searching for that information. You can choose Help⇨ Help Topics or click the Help Topics button in most Help windows to open a dialog box similar to the one shown in Figure 3-1.

The Help Topics dialog box is another one of those tabbed dialog boxes. The three tabs give you three different ways to locate information in the Help file. The three tabs in the dialog box function as described in the following list:

✔ Perhaps the most useful of the three is the Index tab. This tab lists a program's Help topics in a format similar to that of the index in a book.

Figure 3-1:
Search for
help on the
topic you
need in the
Help Topics
dialog box.

To use the Index to search for information, type a word in the text box to display the portion of the list of Help topics that includes the word you want help with. Select a specific topic from the list by clicking the topic name and then click the Display button to display that Help topic in a Help window.

✔ The Contents tab of the Help Topics dialog box arranges the Help topics in a collapsible outline style similar to that of the table of contents of a book. If a topic displays a small, closed book icon next to its name, one or more subtopics are listed under the main topic. Double-click the book icon to view a list of those subtopics. (Guess what? Yep, the icon changes to an open book if the subtopics are visible. You can double-click the open book icon to hide the subtopics again.) If you see a Help topic listed with a question mark icon instead of a book, you can select that topic and click the Display button (or simply double-click the topic) to view its information.

✔ The Find tab of the Help Topics dialog box provides a more detailed search of the Help topics for a program. You can use this feature to search for topics that may contain key words or phrases anywhere in the text — not just in the topic title. Using the Find tab, however, is more time-consuming than using the other tabs, and you usually don't need to bother with such a detailed search. You can usually find what you need by using one of the other techniques.

The Help Topics dialog box disappears after you display a specific Help topic in its own window. You can access the dialog box again if you want to look for another topic; just click the Help Topics button located below the menu bar of the window displaying the current Help topic.

In case you're wondering what version of a particular program you own, you can choose Help⇨About (whatever program you're in) to open a dialog box containing that information. In Word Pro, for example, choose Help⇨About Word Pro to display a dialog box showing the release (or version) number of the program. By the way, this tip works for most Windows programs — not just for SmartSuite.

Taking in a movie

Some Help topics include prerecorded demonstrations to show you how to perform some action. You can recognize these demos, if they're available, because they're accompanied by a button displaying a movie camera icon. Just click the button to play the demonstration lesson.

We cover only the basics of getting Help in this chapter. The best advice we can give you is to explore the various Help facilities in the individual SmartSuite programs. In addition to the basic information available in all the SmartSuite programs, specific programs offer more ways to help you find out how to use their features. In Word Pro and 1-2-3, for example, you can choose Help⇨Ask the Expert and complete the sentence How do I . . . in the Ask the Expert bar that appears across the top of the workspace to get help on a feature or procedure. In Freelance Graphics, you can click the Guide Me button to get context-sensitive advice.

Reading manuals on-screen

Tired of having to go dig up the manuals if you need to look up something? Well, you may be able to find the information you need with just a few mouse clicks instead. A wealth of documentation for the SmartSuite programs is available for you to read on-screen. You find these on-screen manuals in SmartCenter's Suite Help drawer. Just open the DocOnline folder and double-click the icon for the manual you want to read. A special document viewer program opens and displays the book on your computer screen.

To save hard disk space, most of the SmartSuite installation options do not install the online document files on your hard disk. The document reader retrieves the files it needs from the CD-ROM disc as you view the online documents. Of course, that means you must have the SmartSuite CD-ROM disc available in the drive before you can read the online documents.

Help for converts from that "other" suite

Suppose that you used to use that "other" office suite, and now you've wised up and switched to Lotus SmartSuite; or perhaps you use a different word processor or spreadsheet program at work and use SmartSuite at home. Whatever your reason for doing it, Lotus tries to make the transition from another program to SmartSuite as easy as possible. Word Pro and 1-2-3 not only open and save documents using another program's file formats but also include special help features for users who may be accustomed to working with a competing product.

For example, in Word Pro, you can choose Help➪Microsoft Word Menu Help to display an extra menu bar across the top of your Word Pro document that looks just like it came out of Microsoft Word. When you choose a command from the Word menus, Word Pro pops open a Help window describing how to do the same thing in Word Pro. If the Help window doesn't contain instructions for the action you had in mind, check the space between the Word menus and the regular Word Pro menus for a list of other related topics. When you're through using the Microsoft Word Menu Help, click the Done button next to that list of related topics.

Word Pro includes special help for users making a transition from Ami Pro, Microsoft Word, and WordPerfect. 1-2-3 includes similar help for former Excel users.

Casting the Net

Another source of information about SmartSuite and the SmartSuite programs is the Internet. Lotus maintains Internet sites to provide information about the products, updates, and add-ons, as well as access to technical support.

One way to access help on the Internet is to open the Suite Help drawer in SmartCenter and then open the Lotus Online folder. The folder is a mini Web browser that automatically opens to the Lotus SmartSuite home page (provided you have your system configured to automatically access the Internet). From there, you can follow links to other helpful Web pages.

Most of the SmartSuite programs provide access to Internet-based help directly from within the program. Choose Help➪Lotus Internet Support and then choose Lotus Home Page for information via the Web, Lotus Customer Support for technical support, or Lotus FTP Site for access to files that update your SmartSuite programs.

Dealing with the year 2000 thing

No doubt, you've heard about the potential problem that some computer programs and computer-controlled equipment may have when trying to deal with dates in the year 2000 and beyond. Well, it's a very real problem, but you can relax and quit worrying about it — at least as far as SmartSuite is concerned.

The year 2000 date problem (sometimes called the Millennium Bug) is the result of using just two digits to represent the year. That's a convention that computer programmers and lots of other folks have used for decades. For example, if you enter a date as 8/24/95, computers and people alike understand that to mean a date in the year 1995. But what if the two-digit number used to represent the year is 05? Does that mean 1905 or 2005? That's the problem.

All the SmartSuite programs store date information internally by using a special format, called a serial date, that leaves no room for doubt about what century a year is in. You can format the date display to have two digits or four digits in the year, but that doesn't change the underlying data in the SmartSuite program, and it's the serial date that SmartSuite programs use in their calculations. So, if SmartSuite can handle dates after the year 2000, the only problem is properly interpreting dates that you enter or import from other programs.

When you enter a date by using a two-digit year, the SmartSuite program into which you enter the date must guess what century that year is supposed to be in. If you enter 5/3/29, humans can make an educated guess about whether that date is supposed to be in 1929 or 2029, based on whether the date represents the birthday of an older relative or the payoff date on a 30-year mortgage. Computer programs can't make that kind of educated guess, so they use rules. For interpreting two-digit years, the SmartSuite programs use a sliding window rule that assumes the date is somewhere in the 100-year span starting 80 years in the past and projecting 19 years in the future from the current year. (Organizer is the exception to this rule. It follows a similar rule that uses a 50-50 split — 50 years into the past and 49 years into the future.) So, in 1999, 1-2-3 and most of the other SmartSuite programs would interpret 5/3/29 as being in 1929 because that year ends in 29 and falls within the sliding window. Of course, if you really mean for the date to be in 2029, all you need to do is enter the four-digit year, and 1-2-3 will record the correct date.

You can get more information on how SmartSuite programs interpret two-digit years, including a full explanation of the sliding window rule, by choosing Help⇨Year 2000 in any of the SmartSuite programs where dates are an issue.

What Program Do I Use — and When?

Deciding which of the SmartSuite programs to use for a particular project is your first and often most difficult challenge. These applications offer some overlap in capabilities, so you can complete many projects by using any of the programs. Choosing the best one, however, makes the job go more smoothly and gives you greater flexibility to do the work the way you want.

Picking the correct program may seem just a matter of common sense — if working with words, use Word Pro; if manipulating numbers, use 1-2-3; if creating a presentation, use Freelance Graphics; if attempting complex database management, use Approach. You get the idea. You can't go too far astray by just following this line of reasoning. Because of the shared capabilities of the SmartSuite programs, however, the choice is not always quite that easy.

Often, projects need to include elements that are the forte of more than one of the SmartSuite programs. To create a report that contains some text but also includes several charts, for example, you have several options. You could create the text portion of the document in Word Pro and the charts in 1-2-3 or Freelance and then join them together. Or you could create the entire document in Word Pro because Word Pro also enables you to create charts. Or you could create the whole thing in Freelance Graphics, which can produce dandy charts and handles text elements reasonably well, too.

The following are a few examples of the SmartSuite programs your authors would choose for various kinds of activities:

- ✔ Word Pro makes putting together almost any written document a breeze. For business or personal letters, book-length manuscripts, memos, and annual reports, Word Pro is the SmartSuite program of choice.

- ✔ For household or company budgets, forecasts, and cash-flow analyses, 1-2-3 is our choice.

- ✔ For keeping track of inventories, maintaining a large customer database, processing sales orders, and performing other data-intensive work, we use Approach.

- ✔ Whenever we think of putting together the materials for making a presentation, whether in front of the board of directors or the local homeowners' association, we turn to Freelance Graphics.

- ✔ If we need to combine elements from more than one program, we usually use Word Pro to create the master document into which we insert tables and charts from 1-2-3, reports from Approach, or charts and graphics from Freelance.

Don't feel limited to using just one program to complete a project. The beauty of SmartSuite is that you can use elements from several programs and combine them in one glorious document.

You never really have an absolutely right (or absolutely wrong) program choice. In most cases, the decision on what program to use is simply a matter of personal preference. So don't let anyone — except maybe your boss — tell you anything different.

Part II
Take a Letter, Word Processor

The 5th Wave   By Rich Tennant

"It's a ten step word processing program. It comes
with a spell-checker, grammar-checker, cliche-checker,
whine-checker, passive/aggressive-checker, politically
correct-checker, hissy-fit-checker, pretentious
pontificating-checker, boring anecdote-checker and a
Freudian reference-checker."

In this part . . .

You may as well make friends with Word Pro — SmartSuite Millennium Edition's powerful word processing program. After all, if you're anything like most computer users, you spend most of your time working with words. Whether you need to write a simple letter or a hefty novel, this part covers all the basics you need to know to get started quickly and painlessly. We can't teach you to write well, but we do show you how to put Word Pro's tools to good use.

Chapter 4
Boot Camp for Word Pro

• •

• •

*A*nyone out there still using a typewriter? Man, was that white ribbon correcting stuff a pain (even though it had that liquid white-out stuff beat all to heck)! If you discovered one tiny little mistake after you took the paper out of the typewriter, trying to line the paper back up was virtually impossible. Those *weren't* the good old days! But we digress. If you're reading this book, presumably you own Lotus Word Pro word-processing software (and maybe even a computer), so you're hearing no more typewriter talk from us. Ever.

What's a Word Pro?

Un ami est quelqu'un que vous aimez et qui vous aime aussi. Oops, that was a flashback from high school French class. See, Word Pro used to go under the name Ami Pro, and Ami is a French word that means friend. And Word Pro is a word processor that wants to be your friend. (Is that cute enough for you?) But seriously, Word Pro is a really cool word processor that goes far out of its way to make your life easier. And that's what friends are for, *n'est-ce pas?*

A word processor, you're thinking. That means that I can type letters and reports and maybe even change the margins around and add such nifty stuff as footers, footnotes, and fonts. Yeah, sure. But hey, this is the information age. Technology is king and queen. You think Lotus is gonna give you a word processor that can't do anything but process words? No way!

Along with all the preceding, you can cook up some nifty tables and charts, add clip art pictures, draw your own pictures, and (as they say in the ad biz) do a whole lot more. So get with the program.

Starting Word Pro

Can't do much with Word Pro until you do something to get the program going. No problem — getting Word Pro to pop up on your screen is no biggie. Just make sure that Windows is running.

The easiest way to start Word Pro is from SuiteStart. If SuiteStart's running, all you need to do is click the Word Pro icon in the taskbar's system tray (that collection of miniature icons in the lower-right corner of your computer screen — next to the clock). Here's a clue to help you find the icon: As you hold the mouse pointer over the correct icon, a little tag appears that reads Lotus Word Pro. (Refer to Chapter 2 for more information on using SuiteStart.)

You can also start Word Pro from SmartCenter. Just open the SmartSuite drawer, open the Lotus Applications folder, and then double-click the Lotus Word Pro icon. For more information about SmartCenter, check out Chapter 2.

The other way to start Word Pro is from the Windows Start menu. Click the Start button in the taskbar, point to Programs, point to Lotus SmartSuite, and finally choose Lotus Word Pro from another cascading menu.

Welcome to Word Pro

After you first start Word Pro, a logo briefly appears, and then the program shows up on-screen with the Welcome to Lotus Word Pro dialog box open, as shown in Figure 4-1. The tabs and buttons in the dialog box give you the following options:

✔ The Open An Existing Document tab presents a list of documents you've worked on recently, in case you want to reopen one of them.

✔ The Create A New Document From A SmartMaster tab enables you to create a document based on a template. (We cover SmartMasters in Chapter 5.)

✔ The Create A Plain Document button does just what the name implies: creates a plain document, ready for you to start typing.

Figure 4-1:
The
Welcome
to Lotus
Word Pro
dialog box.

At this point, you probably don't have any existing Word Pro documents, and we haven't gotten to SmartMasters yet. So take the other document creation option in this dialog box by clicking the Create A Plain Document button. This action starts Word Pro with a simple, blank document — kind of like slipping a blank sheet of paper into a typewriter. (Yeah, that same typewriter we promised not to mention again. Ah, well. . . .)

Later, if you decide you want to create another new document, you can choose File⇨New Document to open the New Document dialog box, which, not coincidentally, is very similar to the Welcome to Lotus Word Pro dialog box. For more information on creating a new document, see Chapter 5.

If you installed the ViaVoice dictation program, it starts automatically when you open a new document in Word Pro. Don't let the extra toolbar at the top of the screen or the voice coming from your speakers startle you; that's just ViaVoice getting ready to take dictation. For now, just ignore ViaVoice. We show you how to use it in Chapter 7. If you want to get ViaVoice out of the way temporarily, choose Dictation⇨Stop ViaVoice to exit the dictation program. Don't worry. You can always restart it again later.

Making Friends with Word Pro's Screen

"Hullo, screen." "Hullo, *mon ami*." There. Now you're friends. But in any good relationship, you want to find out as much as possible about the other party. So in that spirit. . . .

The first time you start Word Pro, the Word Pro Preferences dialog box appears with the Personal tab displayed. That's Word Pro's way of getting to know you — by asking a few questions about your name and address and so forth. Then Word Pro can use that information to automatically fill in your return address on envelopes and stuff like that.

Right about now, your screen should look something like the one shown in Figure 4-2 (except without all the lines and words that tell you what all the different components are for).

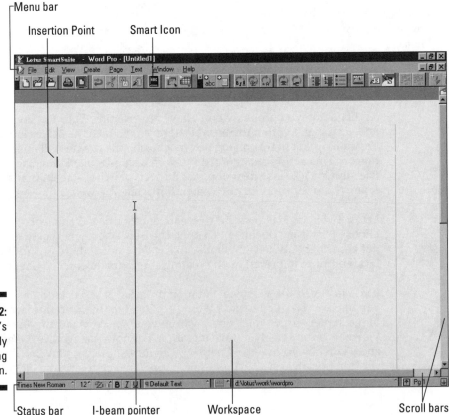

Figure 4-2:
Word Pro's
friendly
opening
screen.

The elements of the Word Pro opening screen are described in the following paragraphs:

- The white space in the middle of the screen represents a piece of paper where you type stuff. The vertical lines on the left and right sides of the "paper" indicate the margins. And the whole thing, including the gray area around the page, has its very own name — it's your *workspace*.

- The *insertion point* is that flashing line near the top of the left margin, and it marks where the text you type appears. As you type stuff, the text is inserted to the left of the insertion point, and the insertion point graciously moves over to make room.

- The thing that looks like a capital letter I is the *I-beam pointer*. The I-beam pointer is really just your regular old mouse pointer in disguise. Whenever you're somewhere in Windows where you can enter text, you get an I-beam instead of an arrow pointer.

- The Word Pro *menu bar* works just like any Windows menu bar. Click an item (or press the Alt key in combination with the underlined letter) to open the menu and then click one of the menu item names to make a choice from the menu itself.

- The cute little buttons with pictures on them, located just below the menu bar, are the *SmartIcons*. Just click one of these buttons to make something happen in Word Pro, such as saving or printing your document. SmartIcons provide a quick alternative to choosing commands from the menus.

  Unless you love surprises, you may want to know what is going to happen *before* you click a SmartIcon. If you hold your mouse pointer over a SmartIcon button for a fraction of a second or so, the button actually speaks to you. (Well, really the button "speaks" in the form of a bubble that appears right there on-screen and tells you what the button is for.)

- The *status bar* is a very cool place to hang out. Not only does this area give you all sorts of useful info, such as what page you're on and what font you're using, but the status bar also actually *does* stuff. After you type some text (see the next section for more on text entry), select it and click some of the status bar's buttons — such as the typeface, type size, or bold attribute button — and see what happens.

Entering Text

Entering text in Word Pro is easy. Just start typing and stop whenever you're tired, hungry, or done, whichever comes first. Ah, but what happens when you come to the end of a line? Keep typing (unless you're tired or hungry).

We're not talking typewriters here — you don't need to press Enter to move the text to the next line. Word Pro does all the moving for you. You see, word processors offer this cool feature called *word wrap*. If no more words can fit on a line, Word Pro automatically moves (or *wraps*) the text to the next line.

We get into all sorts of stuff you can do elsewhere in this chapter and in the other chapters of this part, but for now, here are a few rules of the road to send you merrily on your way:

- As you're typing along, sooner or later you're bound to make a mistake (or so we've been told). If you notice the error right away, simply press the Backspace key to get rid of the character you just typed. If you want to get rid of more than one character, just keep pressing the Backspace key. Backspace keeps deleting a character at a time as long as you keep holding down the key.

- But what about the Delete key? If the Backspace key deletes stuff, why do you need another key to do the same thing? We have our own conspiracy theory on this oddity — basically, we think that, at the beginning of computer time, the ubiquitous "they" decided to stick in two deletion keys just to make the rest of us feel dumb. Here's the scoop:

  - The Backspace key deletes the character to the left of your insertion point.

  - The Delete key deletes the character to the right of your insertion point.

- What if you don't notice a mistake until you've typed several more lines? Piece of cake. Move the I-beam pointer (remember that the I-beam pointer is your mouse pointer in disguise) to the place you want, and click the mouse to move your insertion point to the I-beam's new position. Now you can use the Backspace and Delete techniques just described.

- To start a new paragraph, press Enter. And that's the only time you're to press Enter — never, never, never press Enter just because you're at the end of a line; if you do, you end up with major headaches whenever you change your margins or make other formatting changes. See, Word Pro's pretty smart, and the program knows to wrap text to the next line as it reaches the right margin. If you change the margins, Word Pro stays right on top of the situation and rewraps all the lines to fit into the new margins. If you press Enter at the end of a line, Word Pro can't perform its word wrap magic.

- You don't need to do anything special after you get to the end of a page either. Word Pro automatically starts a new page for you. If you want to force Word Pro to start a new page at a spot other than where the program would automatically do so, choose Page⊅Insert Page Break from the menu bar.

> ✔ You can always tell what page you're on by looking at the status bar. (The page number is located at the far right of the bar, between the two arrow buttons.)

What's Your Mode?

Do you know what Word Pro *mode* you're working in? Did you know that Word Pro had modes? No? Well, Word Pro has the following three modes:

✔ In *Insert* mode, Word Pro inserts text to the left of your insertion point as you type, and the text pushes the insertion point over to the right. Insert mode is the default mode, meaning that unless you have changed your mode without telling us, you're in Insert mode right now. Insert mode is where you want to be most of the time.

✔ In *Typeover* mode, whatever you type replaces the text that's already there. For example, if you move the insertion point in front of the word *example* at the beginning of this sentence and turn on Typeover mode, the first letter you type replaces (or types over) the *e*, the second letter replaces the *x,* and so on.

✔ In *Markup Edits* mode, anything you add or delete is marked with a different color or text style so that you can tell what has been changed. This mode is handy if you're editing someone else's work or just trying to keep track of changes between drafts for your own stuff.

To switch between Insert and Typeover modes, press the Insert key. Before you do that, however, take a peek at the status bar. Notice the Document Info button? (The button probably shows the drive and folder name where you save your file.) Click that button and check out the items in the pop-up menu that appears. The second line should read Insert. That line tells you that you're in Insert mode. Click anywhere to close the info list and then press the Insert key. Check Document Info again, and you see that you're in Typeover mode.

To switch into Markup Edits mode, choose Edit➪Markup Edits from the menu bar. This command is a *toggle* command. Choose the command once to activate the Markup Edits mode. After the feature is active, a check mark appears beside the command name in the File menu. Choose the command again to turn off Markup Edits mode. (See — the command *toggles* from one mode to the other, hence the name of this type of command.)

Getting from Here to There on the Word Pro Screen (Wherever "There" Is)

After you enter a bunch of text on-screen, the fun has just begun. You get to rearrange your text, format the text (as described in Chapter 5), or even give your golden prose to your boss to hack to death (not the desired choice). Your first order of business, however, is simply moving around the screen — because how can you rearrange or hack up your text if you can't get to it? (Rhetorical question.)

We tell you earlier in this chapter that you can move your insertion point just by clicking at a new location on-screen. You can also use the up-, down-, left-, and right-arrow keys on your keyboard to move the insertion point (wow — what a concept!). The up- and down-arrow keys move you up or down one line at a time; the left- and right-arrow keys move you left or right one character at a time. Unless you're gunning for terminal tediousness, however, hang in there while we add to your navigational repertoire.

Keyboard kapers and shortkuts

Word Pro offers a bunch of keyboard shortcuts that keep you from having to press an arrow key 9,354 times. And we're going to tell you about them right here.

Time for a quick review here, however, just in case you're staring in glazed amazement at the following list. If we list something along the lines of *Ctrl+Home* (or tell you to *press* Ctrl+Home), we're actually telling you to press and hold down the Ctrl key while you press the Home key. Do not pass Go, do not collect $200, and *do not* release the Ctrl key until after you press and release the Home key. The plus sign (+) between the two keystrokes always means that you hold down the first key while you press the second key. Simple, eh? Carry on.

The following keystroke shortcuts enable you to easily move your insertion point around in Word Pro:

- **Ctrl+Home:** Moves the insertion point to the beginning of the document (or to the beginning of a division if you've broken your document into multiple sections).

- **Ctrl+End:** Moves the insertion point to the end of the document (or to the end of the current division).

✓ **Ctrl+Page Up** or **Ctrl+Page Down:** Moves the insertion point up or down a page at a time.

✓ **Page Up** or **Page Down:** Moves the insertion point up or down a screenful at a time.

✓ **Ctrl+↑** or **Ctrl+↓:** Moves the insertion point to the beginning of the current or next paragraph, respectively. If you're already at the beginning of a paragraph, Ctrl+↑ moves you to the beginning of the previous paragraph.

✓ **Ctrl+period:** Moves the insertion point to the beginning of the next sentence.

✓ **Ctrl+comma:** Moves the insertion point to the beginning of the previous sentence.

✓ **Ctrl+→ or Ctrl+←:** Moves the insertion point to the right or left one word at a time.

✓ **Home:** Moves the insertion point to the beginning of the current line.

✓ **End:** Moves the insertion point to the end of the current line.

Stupid mouse tricks

(Before you skip past this section, we'd better tell you that these really aren't *stupid* mouse tricks. That was just our lame attempt at a cute heading. These are *super-important* — dare we say even *brilliant?* — mouse tricks that are sure to cause your friends to gasp at the mere mention of them! Hmmm. Did we just go too far in the other direction?)

Earlier in this chapter, we tell you about the super-easiest mouse trick of all — just click anywhere in a document and your insertion point moves to wherever you click. Easy, yes. Efficient . . . not always. What if you want to move your insertion point somewhere that you can't see on-screen? Kind of hard to click something you can't see, and those brilliant keyboard short-cuts that we explain in the preceding section don't cover all the bases.

Ah, but that's what scroll bars are for. *Scroll bars* are those vertical and horizontal bars located along the right and bottom edges of your screen (see Figure 4-3). If you single-click the vertical scroll bar's up- or down-arrow button (located at the top or bottom of the bar, respectively), the document view moves up or down one line. And if you hold down the mouse button as you click the up or down arrow, the view keeps moving up or down until you release the button. The horizontal scroll bar functions the same way but moves side to side instead of up and down. Nothing too fancy so far.

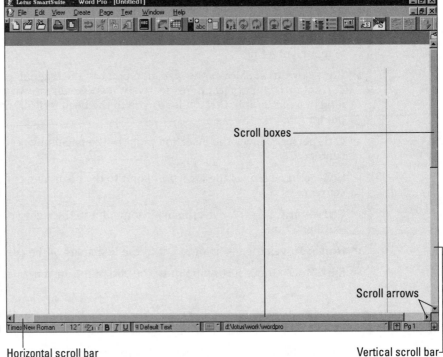

Scroll boxes ——————————————

Scroll arrows

Figure 4-3:
Use the
scroll bars
to move up
or down or
from side to
side in your
documents.

Horizontal scroll bar   Vertical scroll bar⌐

But take a look at the box or button inside each scroll bar. (By some strange coincidence, this item's called the *scroll box*.) That box is the key to scroll bar mastery. You can tell where you are in a document by looking at the scroll box. If the vertical scroll box is about halfway down the scroll bar, that means that what you're looking at on-screen is about halfway through the document. So what can you do with this information? Well . . .

- ✔ You can drag the scroll box up or down to move to a different relative location. If you want to move toward the beginning of the document, drag up; if you want to move toward the end, drag down.

- ✔ The size and position of the scroll box relative to the scroll bar vary to indicate the size and position of the current window relative to the entire document.

- ✔ You can also click the shaded area anywhere above or below the scroll box to move up or down a screenful at a time.

Repeat after me: Scrolling *isn't* clicking

So you think you're pretty cool and you've got this scrolling thing down. You started on the first page and, with a combination of the scroll arrows and the scroll box, you moved to just the right location on page eight. Yup, there it is — page eight, right in front of you. You start typing and — wait just one doggone minute! The stuff you typed ended up back on page one! What in tarnation happened?

What happened is that you forgot that moving to a different location by using the scroll bar doesn't do anything to change the position of your insertion point. Scrolling changes your view, but the insertion point stays where it was before you scrolled — until you click somewhere else in the document. As soon as you click, the insertion point moves to the place you click. The scroll bars are great for navigating vast distances, but just remember that final click.

Being Selective

Word Pro (and all the SmartSuite programs) enables you to do all kinds of things to text and other parts of a document. The other Word Pro chapters in this book talk about all the things you can do. But before you can do these things to text, you must find out how Word Pro knows which text you want to change. If you want to make some text bold, for example, you need to tell Word Pro *which* text you want to make bold before you apply the bold attribute.

This process is called *selecting.* Before you do just about anything to text, you select the text you want to affect. After the text is selected, you can delete that text, move it, copy it, or make the text look different. The following section talks about moving and copying text; to know how to *delete* selected text, however, you don't need an entire section of explanations — just press the Delete key.

You can use the mouse or the keyboard for selecting text; use whichever one makes more sense to you at the time. The simplest way to select text by using your mouse is just to place the insertion point where you want the selection to start and then hold down the mouse button while you drag the mouse over the text you want selected. As you drag, you highlight that text.

The *Shift+click* trick is a great way to select a bunch of text with precision. If you drag to select text, you must make sure that you release the mouse button at just the right place or you end up with more or less text selected than you want. And if you need to select text that starts on one page and ends on another, dragging can be a real . . . drag. The Shift+click trick is just what it sounds like. You click to place your insertion point at the beginning of the text you want to select. Then you scroll to the end of the text you want selected and hold down the Shift key as you click to place the insertion point there.

The following list describes a few other mouse-selection shortcuts:

- ✔ To select a word, double-click anywhere in that word.
- ✔ To select a sentence, press and hold the Ctrl key and then click anywhere in the sentence.
- ✔ To select an entire paragraph, press and hold Ctrl and then double-click in the paragraph.
- ✔ To select text a word at a time, double-click the first word you want; then, without releasing the mouse button, drag to the last word.
- ✔ To select text sentence by sentence, press and hold Ctrl and then click anywhere in the first sentence. Without releasing the mouse button, drag to the last sentence.
- ✔ To select text paragraph by paragraph, press and hold Ctrl and then double-click anywhere in the first paragraph. Without releasing the mouse button, drag to the last paragraph.

To select text by using the keyboard, just press and hold the Shift key and then press any of the arrow keys. Suppose, for example, that you want to select the word *word*. Put your insertion point in front of the *w* and press and hold the Shift key as you press the right-arrow key four times.

Amaze your friends with this little-known selection tip. Did you know that you can use any of the keystroke combinations that move your insertion point (the ones we talk about in the section "Keyboard kapers and shortkuts," a little earlier in this chapter) to select text? Well, you can. The trick is to press and hold the Shift key as you press the regular keystroke combination. Say, for example, that you want to select all the text from where your insertion point is to the end of the document. Press and hold Shift while you press Ctrl+End, which is the keystroke that moves your insertion point to the end of the document.

Don't get caught by the disappearing text gremlin. Whenever text is selected, the first thing you type *replaces* the selected text. So if you have two pages selected and then type a word, your two pages are gone and that one lonely little word is all that's left. A couple of things you can do may help you avoid this disaster. First, just be aware how this selection stuff works. Unless you want to get rid of the selected text, click anywhere to deselect that text before you start typing. Second, if you forget and wipe out the selected text anyway, you can always use Word Pro's Undo feature to nullify that last action (as described in the section "I Didn't Mean to Do It — So Now What?" later in this chapter).

Moving and Copying Text

One of the cool things about using a word processor instead of a typewriter is that text doesn't need to stay where you put the words initially. You can move or copy any amount of text from one place to another. You can keep juggling words and phrases around 'til the cows come home. Heck, you can even keep juggling after those cows have turned in for the night.

You already know how to do the most important part of moving and copying — you can select text. Remember that you first select and then you tell Word Pro what to do with the selection. With text selected, moving or copying that text anywhere else (even to another document or application) is a piece of gooey chocolate cake. The only problem is that, here again, Word Pro gives you too many choices. You can use the mouse or the keyboard; you can cut and paste, or you can drag and drop. Decisions, decisions.

But don't fret. Coming right up — the most straightforward way to move or copy stuff from one place to another: Just *drag and drop.* With your text selected, you just place your mouse pointer on the text and drag the selection wherever you want. As you drag, a fist clutching a note attaches itself to your mouse pointer and a small bar shows where the text you're dragging is going to land. After the mouse pointer is located at the place in your document to which you want to move the text, release the mouse button. That's the entire process. If you want to copy instead of moving the text, press and hold the Ctrl key while you drag the selection. (A plus sign appears below the fist to show that you're copying instead of moving the selected text.)

So what's the difference between moving and copying? If you move text, you actually delete the selected text from its original location and insert the selection in a new location. If you copy text, you leave the selected text where it is and insert a copy of the text in the new location. Got it?

Here's another way to move and copy text. Use this method if you want to make several copies of a block of text, move or copy text to another document or another application, or move or copy text to a distant location inside your document. Just follow these steps:

1. **Select the text you want to move or copy.**

2. **Click the Cut SmartIcon (that's the one displaying the scissors) to move the text, or click the Copy SmartIcon (the one with two little A's in boxes) to copy the text.**

   This action places a copy of the selected text in a special section of Windows memory called the Clipboard.

   Pressing Ctrl+X or choosing Edit⇨Cut from the menu bar is the same as clicking the Cut SmartIcon. Pressing Ctrl+C or choosing Edit⇨Copy from the menu bar is the same as clicking the Copy SmartIcon.

3. **Put your insertion point at the place in your document where you want to move the text.**

4. **Click the Paste SmartIcon (the one displaying the little paste pot).**

Pressing Ctrl+V or choosing Edit⇨Paste from the menu bar is the same as clicking the Paste SmartIcon.

The selected text stays in the Clipboard until you put something else there, so you can paste that same text in as many times as you want.

Moving or copying stuff to another application is just as easy as moving or copying stuff to another place in a Word Pro document. After you cut or copy text, that block of text ends up in the Windows Clipboard, where the poor thing just sits and waits for you. (Nothing waits forever, though; the Clipboard can hold only one thing at a time, so as soon as you cut or copy something else, the new stuff replaces whatever's already there.) For example, if you want to copy some text from Word Pro and paste that text into a 1-2-3 worksheet, all you need to do is select the text in your Word Pro document and copy the text to the Clipboard by clicking the Copy SmartIcon; then open 1-2-3, put your insertion point in the worksheet cell where you want to paste the text, and click the Paste SmartIcon. All SmartSuite applications (as well as most other Windows applications) use the same techniques for moving and copying, so you don't need to worry about memorizing a different method of working with text when you switch from one application to another. You can paste stuff into any SmartSuite program by pressing Ctrl+V, choosing Edit⇨Paste from the menu bar, or clicking the Paste SmartIcon.

I Didn't Mean to Do It — So Now What?

By now (provided, of course, you've looked at the other sections in this chapter), you know just enough to be really dangerous. You can type and select and move and copy. Terrific. But knowing how to do all that stuff also means that you can do things you didn't mean to do, such as moving something that should've stayed where it was or deleting a bunch of text that, as soon as you hit Delete, you realize is the most brilliant, incisive work you ever created. Are you panicking yet? If so, carry on for a few more seconds, just to get your heart pumping, and then read on.

If you do something you wish you hadn't done, just undo that action. Word Pro's Undo feature enables you to reverse your last action. In fact, you can reverse your last several actions, but that's a story for another time and place — or maybe for the section "Making Undo do its thing," a bit later in this chapter.

So how do you do this magical thing? Just choose Edit⇨Undo from the menu bar or click the Undo SmartIcon (the one with the arrows that can't decide which way to go). You can also press Ctrl+Z. Undo automatically does its thing.

 The Undo command on the Edit menu changes to reflect what action it can undo. The command may appear as `Undo Typing` or `Undo Drag & Drop` or some other variation. But the exact wording doesn't matter. You still use the command the same way to undo the last action you performed.

 Undo can even help save you from itself. If you undo something you didn't mean to undo, just choose Edit⇨Undo/Redo Special, choose the action you want to fix from the lists in the Undo/Redo dialog box, and click the Undo or Redo button (depending on which list the item is in).

What can Undo undo?

Undo can undo just about anything. If you type stuff you didn't mean to type, Undo can delete the unwanted text. If you delete stuff you want back, Undo can take care of that problem, too. If you make a formatting change and decide the new format stinks, just click the Undo SmartIcon.

What can't Undo undo?

Undo is a very cool thing, but the feature has its limits. Here are some things that Undo can't fix:

- ✔ If you closed your document since you did the thing you want to undo, you're out of luck.

- ✔ Undo can't undo anything if Undo's turned off. By default, Word Pro is set up to undo the last editing change. If you try Undo and nothing happens, some sneaky person or gremlin may have done something to your User setup. Read the following section so that you know how to foil that dastardly plan to confuse you.

Making Undo do its thing

You can set up Undo to reverse your last several editing changes. Sounds great, right? If Word Pro can do that, why on earth would anyone want to tell the program to undo only one or two levels or even — dare we say it — none?

We have two words for you: speed and memory. To keep track of the last several edits you've made, Word Pro must store information about *everything* you did, in case you decide to change any of it. The fewer levels of Undo you activate, the less stuff Word Pro has to think about, so the program can go about its business at a faster pace. The general rule is to activate as many levels of Undo as your computer can handle without slowing down. The more powerful your computer, the more levels of Undo your machine can handle gracefully.

To control the Undo levels, choose File⇨User Setup⇨Word Pro Preferences to open the Word Pro Preferences dialog box, as shown in Figure 4-4. The Undo Levels text box on the General tab shows how many actions Undo can reverse. Click the up or down increment arrow beside the Undo Levels text box to select the number of levels you want. (Select 0 if you don't want to use Undo at all.) After you're done, click OK. Your Undo levels are set.

Figure 4-4:
You can
change
Undo levels
(and other
stuff) in the
Word Pro
Preferences
dialog box.

Saving Your Work

If you've been typing anything other than practice garbage up to this point, stop immediately and read this section. And if you ever plan to type anything except practice garbage, stop immediately and read this section. In other words, if you ever type stuff that you don't want to lose, saving is a very good thing to know about. Until you give your document a name, all those glowing words exist only in your computer's temporary memory. So if you stumble over the power cord, pulling it out of its socket and breaking your leg in the process, you not only end up hobbling around in a cast, but you also must retype the whole stupid document. Wouldn't your mood improve as you're hobbling around if you knew that your document was waiting for you on your hard drive, all safe and sound?

So save your text. Now. And often. Here's how:

1. **Choose File⇨Save As.**

   The Save As dialog box appears.

   You can do a bunch of stuff in here, but all you need to know about for now is the File Name text box. Notice that the Save As Type box already has Lotus Word Pro (*.LWP) selected, which means that Word Pro automatically adds a period and the letters LWP to the end of the name you assign to your file. *LWP* is the *extension* (kind of like a last name) that Word Pro gives its documents. (Because LWP is already selected as the dialog box opens, all you need to do is start typing a document name; the name you type goes into the File Name text box.)

2. **Type a name in the File Name text box.**

   You can call a document just about anything you want. Word Pro supports Windows long filenames, which means that you can use any combination of letters, numbers, and spaces.

   Actually, your filename can be up to 255 characters long (including the drive, path name, and the period and extension Word Pro adds automatically). That's the theoretical limit, but you'd never really use that many characters in a filename. And, if you did, you'd have trouble viewing such monstrous filenames in most dialog boxes.

   If you need to swap documents and files with others, using long filenames for your documents may not be a good idea. Many other programs and networks are still restricted to filenames that are only eight or fewer characters. You may need to be creative to come up with a filename using only eight characters, but doing so can avoid a lot of hassles if your document file must go to someone whose program can't recognize long filenames.

3. **Click Save or press Enter.**

Your document's safe — for now. But as soon as you add more stuff to what you already saved, that stuff isn't safe until you save the document again. Save whenever you think about doing so — and save whenever you think about something else, too. Save, save, save! Have we made our point?

After you save a document the first time and give that document a name, you can save the file again without opening the Save As dialog box each time. Resaving a document with the same name is quick and easy. You can click the Save SmartIcon (the one with the arrow pointing down into an open file folder), choose File⇨Save from the menu bar, or press Ctrl+S. We like to use the keystroke shortcut Ctrl+S to save while working on a document. We've trained our fingers to start tingling if they haven't pressed Ctrl+S in more than a few minutes.

You can even sit back and have Word Pro do some of the driving for you by using its Auto Backup or Auto Timed Save options. These options are set in the Word Pro Preferences dialog box. (To open the dialog box, choose File⇨User Setup⇨Word Pro Preferences from the menu bar, just as you did to set Undo levels.) Check out the following options in the Word Pro Preferences dialog box:

✔ If you check the Auto Back Up Documents (.BAK) option in the Word Pro Preferences dialog box, you see that Word Pro makes another copy of your document every time you use any of the saving techniques. The program gives both of the copies the same name but adds the BAK extension to the backup copy. You can also tell Word Pro to put the backup copy into a different directory by clicking the Locations tab and entering in the Backups text box a path name (the drive and folder where you want Word Pro to put the files). (If you think a folder is just something you use to keep a bunch of papers together and a path is found only in the woods, *Windows 98 For Dummies,* by Andy Rathbone, published by IDG Books Worldwide, Inc., can set you straight.) We like Auto Back Up Documents a whole lot better than we do the Automatically Time Save feature — and we're just about to tell you why.

✔ You can click the check box for Automatically Time Save Every X Minutes and tell Word Pro how often you want to perform this procedure. If you type **5** in the text box, Word Pro automatically saves your document every five minutes to protect you against the whims of fate. Even if the power goes out or your cat jumps onto your keyboard and stands on the Delete key, you never lose more than five minutes of work because Word Pro saves your document for you. The problem with this option is that Word Pro saves your document on schedule, no matter what's happening. Here's the rub: Word Pro may save your document when you don't want the document to be saved. We'd rather control the process ourselves — but the earlier "save, save, save" advice still applies.

We're Off to See the Printer

You created this really cool document, and now you want to share your masterpiece with the world. So send the file to the printer already. What're you waiting for? Oh, we understand. You're waiting for us to tell you how. Okay. Follow these steps:

1. Click the Print SmartIcon (the one displaying the little printer).

You can also choose File⇨Print from the menu bar or press Ctrl+P.

The Print dialog box appears.

2. To print more than one copy of your document, type a number in the Number of Copies text box.

If typing a number is too hard, you can click the up or down increment arrow on either side of the box, and Word Pro automatically increases or decreases the number for you.

3. To print the entire document, just click Print or press Enter.

To print just the current page, click the Current Page radio button before you choose Print. To print some other grouping of pages, type or choose the page numbers in the From and To text boxes and then choose Print.

And that's all you do. Your document's on its way to the printer. Hooray! (Just make sure that your printer's turned on before you get too excited.)

Chapter 5

Format with Style

· ·

In This Chapter

▶ Formats for everything

▶ Making text **bold,** *italic,* and <u>more</u>

▶ Ruling your tabs and indents

▶ Left, right, or center (we're talking alignment — not politics)

▶ Changing line spacing

▶ Setting margins and borders

▶ Treating paragraphs with style

▶ Mastering SmartMasters

· ·

*I*f you just want to type a whole bunch of text and don't care too much what that text looks like, you may as well just use a typewriter. (Oh, oh — the dreaded T-word again!) Sure, a typewriter enables you to change your left and right margins and adjust your tab settings, but that's about all. For fancy formatting, however, nothing beats a word processor such as Word Pro.

Formatting Basics

Formatting is just a catch-all term for all the things that affect the appearance of your document. If you change the margins or add a border to a page, you're changing the document's format. Word Pro formatting falls into three categories: *text formatting, paragraph-level formatting,* and *document-level formatting.* The following paragraphs describe these three levels of formatting:

   ✔ If you apply features to one character or selected characters, you're applying formatting at the *text level.* Type styles and attributes such as bold and italic are examples of text formatting.

   ✔ If you add features that affect an entire paragraph or selected paragraphs, you're applying *paragraph-level formatting.* Line spacing, tab settings, and alignment are examples of paragraph-level formatting.

✔ If you add features that affect the whole document, that's *document-level formatting.* Paper size, headers and footers, and page numbering are all examples of document-level formatting. *Headers* and *footers,* in case the terms are unfamiliar, are those lines of text, numbers, and so on that appear at the top (the *head*) or the bottom (the *foot*) of a page. Don't you just *love* body part analogies?

Doing Stuff to Text

One of the simplest ways to add emphasis to a document is to add boldface, italics, or underlining to some of your text. Another way is to change the text's size or type style. If you need a quick refresher on selecting text for such changes, just review the pertinent sections in Chapter 4 before you move on, because all this text formatting stuff revolves around working with selected text.

Making text bold, italic, or underlined

We're lumping all these attributes together because you use exactly the same technique regardless of which attribute you want. Just select the text to which you want to add the attribute; then click the appropriate button on the status bar, make a choice from the Text menu, or use the keyboard shortcut, as described in the following list:

✔ To make text bold, click the Bold button on the status bar (the one with the big B — you can't miss it) or choose Text➪Attributes➪Bold from the menu bar. *Keyboard shortcut:* Ctrl+B.

✔ To italicize text, click the Italic button on the status bar (the one with the tipsy *I*) or choose Text➪Attributes➪Italic from the menu bar. *Keyboard shortcut:* Ctrl+I.

✔ To underline text, click the Underline button on the status bar (the capital U with a line under it) or choose Text➪Attributes➪Underline from the menu bar. *Keyboard shortcut:* Ctrl+U.

After you apply an attribute, notice that the text remains selected. You can continue to add more attributes without reselecting the text. If you want some text to be both bold and italic, for example, just select the text and click first the Bold button and then the Italic button. (Or vice versa, as you prefer. Doesn't really matter which is first as long as the text remains selected.) If you want to remove an attribute from some text, just select it and click the button (or you can choose the menu command or press the keyboard shortcut) for the attribute you want to remove. For example, to remove the bold attribute from some text, select the text and click the Bold button.

Changing the type style or size

SmartSuite comes with a whole bunch of type styles (a.k.a. *fonts*) that can be used in just about any size you want. Changing fonts is just as easy as adding attributes. Just follow these steps:

1. **Select the text you want to affect.**

2. **Choose Text⇨Font & Color from the menu bar to open the Text Properties InfoBox to its Font, Attribute, and Color tab, as shown in Figure 5-1.**

Font, Attribute, and Color tab

Alignment tab

Bullet tab

Lines and Border tab

Figure 5-1:
The Font,
Attribute,
and Color
tab of the
Text
Properties
InfoBox.

Style tab

You can also open the Text Properties InfoBox by right-clicking the selected text and choosing Text Properties from the pop-up menu that appears.

3. **Choose a type style from the Font Name list.**

In Figure 5-1, Times New Roman is selected. Notice that any change you make in the InfoBox takes effect immediately. You can see the result right there in your document.

4. **Select a type size from the Size list.**

If the size you want isn't listed, you can type a specific size in the Size text box, just below the Size list, or use the increment arrows next to the text box to choose a size.

5. **To add attributes to the text, select one or more attributes from the Attributes list.**

More attributes are included on this list than are available by clicking status bar buttons. For example, you can choose double underlines and superscript.

6. **To add color to the text, click the arrow button next to the Text Color box.**

   This action opens a palette of color choices. Click a color swatch to make that color appear in the Text Color box and change the text to that color. (Just remember that the color doesn't print unless you use a color printer.)

7. **Click the Close (X) button to close the InfoBox after you finish making your choices.**

Text sizes are specified by measuring the height of the characters in points. *Point* is a typesetting term for a measurement that equals 1/72 of an inch. So a 72-point font is about one inch high. (Fonts are measured from the top of the tallest capital letters to the bottom of the *descenders* — or tails — of letters such as *g*. A 72-point capital *M,* therefore, isn't really quite one inch high.)

Going overboard with type styles and text attributes is all too easy. Unless you're actually writing a ransom note, try to avoid using too many type styles and attributes on a page. A good guideline is to use no more than two type styles per page — one for headings and one for regular text. As far as the attributes go, remember that <u>underlining strictly for emphasis</u> is generally considered <u>tacky</u>. (It's a holdover from the days of typewriters when underlining was the only available substitute for italics.) Also remember that you use **bold** and *italic* type for *emphasis.* If **you** use them ***too much,*** the attributes *lose* **their *effectiveness.***

Getting rid of text formatting

Okay, so you're really upset and you dash off a nasty letter to your state senator. In the first paragraph, you use three type sizes, apply boldface to 15 words, and underline the bold words for additional emphasis. Then you cool down a bit and decide that the senator may be more open to your message if you tone the text down a bit (visually, at least). No problem. To remove all the text formatting at once, simply follow these handy steps:

1. **Select the text from which you want the formatting removed.**

2. **Choose Text⇨Normal from the menu bar.**

   You can also press Ctrl+N instead of using the menu commands.

And like magic, all the bold and underlining disappears! Ta daaaaa!

Adding Tabs and Indents

The simplest way to add a tab to your document is just to press Tab at the beginning of a paragraph to indent the first line. But this tab and indent thing has much more to it than that. As shown in Figure 5-2, Word Pro enables you to create four kinds of tabs. And for indenting the first line of each paragraph, Word Pro offers an Indentation feature that can automate the process for you.

Figure 5-2:
Different
types of tab
settings and
how they
appear in
Word Pro.

Left	Center	Numeric	Right
Tomfoolery	Tomfoolery	Tomfoolery	Tomfoolery
90210	90210	90210	90210
98.6	98.6	98.6	98.6
789.4321	789.4321	789.4321	789.4321
.02	.02	.02	.02
Neverland	Neverland	Neverland	Neverland
The End	The End	The End	The End

Notice the ruler at the top of the workspace, just below the SmartIcons. (What? The ruler isn't there? Then choose View⇨Show/Hide⇨Ruler to make it appear.) As the following section makes clear, the ruler enables you to easily set and adjust tabs in Word Pro.

Word Pro makes working with tabs easy, so you really have no excuse not to use them. Don't try to just hit the spacebar several times instead of using a real tab. That technique might have worked on a typewriter using a mono-spaced font, but it doesn't work on a computer with modern, proportionally spaced fonts. Using tabs gives you text that is neatly aligned, but your text never lines up quite right if you try to use spaces as an alignment tool.

Setting tabs

Word Pro comes with tabs preset every one-half inch. Unless you change the tab settings, the insertion point moves one-half inch to the right every time you press Tab. Here's how you change the tab settings for any given paragraph:

1. **If the ruler isn't visible on-screen, choose View⇨Show/Hide⇨Ruler from the menu bar or click the Show/Hide Ruler SmartIcon.**

   This SmartIcon looks, not surprisingly, like a little ruler.

2. **Right-click anywhere in the ruler and choose the kind of tabs you want to create from the pop-up menu that appears.**

   You can choose Left, Centered, Right, or Numeric (decimal) tabs. Whenever the pointer is over the ruler, a small arrow attaches itself to the pointer to indicate the kind of tab you're creating.

3. **To add a new tab stop, click the ruler at the location where you want the new tab to appear.**

   After you click the ruler, a new tab marker — a small arrow — appears. You can place several tabs just by clicking different locations on the ruler. You don't need to right-click the ruler to open the pop-up menu each time unless you need to change the kind of tab you want to create. Word Pro assumes that you want to continue creating the same kind of tab until you tell it something different.

   Moving a tab is exceptionally easy. Just point to an existing tab on the ruler. A small double-headed arrow attaches itself to the pointer to indicate that you are in Move Tab mode. Then you can simply drag the tab marker to a new position on the ruler. As you drag, a vertical line appears on your document page to help you see the tab position in relation to your text.

4. **To clear all the current tab settings, right-click the ruler and choose Clear <u>A</u>ll Tabs from the pop-up menu.**

   To delete a single tab stop, you just drag its marker off the ruler.

To quickly create a centered tab in the center of the page, right-click the ruler and choose Quick Center Tab from the pop-up menu. For a right tab on the right margin, right-click the ruler and choose Quick Right Tab from the pop-up menu. Cool shortcut, don't you think?

After you change tab settings, the new settings apply only to the paragraph your insertion point is in (or to any paragraphs you select before changing the settings). If you want to change tab settings for the entire document, do so from the Page Layout dialog box. Changing page layouts is covered in the section "Changing the Page Layout" (where else?), later in this chapter.

Tabs are great for lining up columns of stuff, but tables are even better. Tables are much easier to set up, provide a lot more options, and are covered in Chapter 6.

Changing indents

If you want to indent the first line of every paragraph, has SmartSuite got a feature for you! First, select the paragraphs you want to affect; then right-click the selected text and choose Text Properties from the pop-up menu that appears. The Text Properties InfoBox opens. Click the Alignment tab (the second tab from the left) to view the options shown in Figure 5-3. Notice the four buttons under the Indent label. To indent the first line of each selected paragraph, click the second button from the left. Below the Indent buttons you find the Indent From Margin text box. You use this setting to determine the amount in inches that the first line of the paragraph indents from the left margin. Type in a value or use the up and down increment arrows to adjust the setting. Close the Text Properties InfoBox by clicking the Close (X) button.

Figure 5-3:
Set Indents
in the
Alignment
tab of the
Text
Properties
InfoBox.

Word Pro offers you the following indent options:

 ✔ The All option (the first Indent button) indents every line in the selected paragraphs from the left margin.

 ✔ The First option (the second Indent button) indents the first line of each selected paragraph.

 ✔ The Rest option (the third Indent button) indents every line except the first line of each selected paragraph.

 ✔ The Both option (the fourth Indent button, at the far right) indents selected text from both the left and right margins. This style is often used to set off quotations.

All indents except Both measure from the left margin. So if your left margin is set at one inch and you specify a first-line indent of one-half inch, the first line of each paragraph will be indented one-half inch from the left margin, or one and one-half inches from the left edge of the page.

If you need more control over your indents, click the Options button at the bottom of the Text Properties InfoBox to open the Indent Options dialog box, where you can set each indent distance individually. To remove the indents from your paragraph, click the No Indent button at the bottom of the Text Properties InfoBox.

Lining Up Text

Take a look at this book. The text is all lined up at the left margin, but the right margin is uneven. Left alignment is considered somewhat informal, and that's why we use that variety — we want you to feel right at home. Check out Figure 5-4 for examples of this type of alignment and the other Word Pro alignment styles.

All the alignment options affect either the paragraph in which your insertion point is currently located or all selected paragraphs. You can set the alignment by clicking one of the alignment buttons on the Alignment tab of the Text Properties InfoBox, or you can use the shortcut keys or menu commands in the following list:

- ✔ To left-align text, press Ctrl+L or choose Text⇨Alignment⇨Left.
- ✔ To center text, press Ctrl+E or choose Text⇨Alignment⇨Center.
- ✔ To right-align text, press Ctrl+R or choose Text⇨Alignment ⇨Right.
- ✔ To justify text (line up the text on both the left and right margins), press Ctrl+J or choose Text⇨Alignment⇨Full Justify.

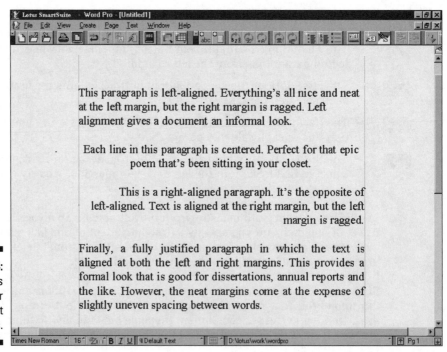

Figure 5-4:
Word Pro's
four
alignment
styles.

Individual SmartIcons for each alignment option are not part of the default SmartIcon palettes for Word Pro. One SmartIcon, however, enables you to cycle through the alignment options. Click the Cycle Alignment Options SmartIcon to apply the next option. Click the SmartIcon again to apply another alignment option. Continue until you reach the alignment option you want.

You can also change alignment settings by right-clicking the selected text and choosing Text Properties from the pop-up menu to open the Text Properties InfoBox. After the InfoBox opens, click the Alignment tab and then click one of the Alignment buttons. In addition to the four regular alignment options, the InfoBox contains a fifth alignment button that causes Word Pro to left-align text and aligned numbers according to the numeric alignment options. This setting is useful only within tables; you normally wouldn't use it on regular paragraphs.

Spacing Out

Need a triple-spaced draft that gives your boss room to mark up your text to the point of unrecognizability? No problem. Word Pro enables you to adjust line spacing just about any way you want. To change line spacing, just follow these steps:

1. **Select the paragraphs you want to change.**

   If you want to change the spacing for only one paragraph, you don't need to select that single paragraph — just place your insertion point anywhere in the paragraph.

2. **Right-click the selection and choose Text Properties from the pop-up menu to open the Text Properties InfoBox; then click the Alignment tab.**

   (Refer to Figure 5-3 to see this tab of the Text Properties InfoBox.)

3. **In the Line Spacing drop-down list box, select the line spacing you want or select Multiple, Leading, or Custom to specify nonstandard line spacing.**

   Selecting Multiple, Leading, or Custom opens a small dialog box for each specific selection. The Multiple dialog box enables you to enter nonstandard fractions of lines (2.75, for example) for line spacing. The Leading and Custom dialog boxes enable you to specify a unit of measure (inch, centimeter, point, or pica) and a specific measurement. Enter the desired line spacing in whichever dialog box you open and click OK to return to the Alignment tab of the Text Properties InfoBox.

4. **Click the Close (X) button to close the InfoBox.**

As with alignment changes, line spacing changes apply *only* to the paragraph you're in at the time you make the change or to any paragraphs you selected before changing the spacing.

You can change line spacing for an entire document by selecting the document first: Just press Ctrl+Home to get to the top of the document and then press Shift+Ctrl+End to select to the end of the document or choose Text⇨Select⇨Entire Document. Then follow the instructions for changing line spacing as described in the preceding steps.

Changing the Page Layout

The *page layout* consists of a whole bunch of stuff such as the tab settings, margins, and paper size. I explain earlier in this chapter how to change tab settings by using the ruler, but that's just one way of changing these settings. If you use the ruler, you're changing tabs only for the paragraph you're in or any paragraphs you select before you make your changes. To get to a place where you can make changes that affect the entire document, right-click anywhere in the workspace and choose Page Properties from the pop-up menu that appears. This action opens the Page Layout Properties InfoBox. Figure 5-5 shows the first tab (Size and Margin) of this InfoBox.

The first thing you should remember about this InfoBox is that the box itself is composed of several tabs. Notice that the Size and Margin tab is open in Figure 5-5. Well, if you click another tab, a whole new set of options appears.

To make changes in the InfoBox, all you need to do is select the options you want. You see the effect immediately (provided that you're in layout view). Experiment until you get the effect you want and then click the Close button to close the InfoBox after you finish. The following sections provide a quick rundown of what you can do in this InfoBox.

Figure 5-5:
The Size and Margin tab of the Page Layout Properties InfoBox is where you tell Word Pro what size of paper to use.

Size and Margin tab

Color, Pattern, and Line Style tab

Selecting pages

The Layout Type button that you select on the Size and Margin tab of the Page Layout Properties InfoBox determines which pages of your document you affect with the settings you choose in the Page Layout Properties InfoBox. The pages you choose here are the ones that your changes in this InfoBox affect, no matter which tab you're in at the time. Your choices include the following:

 ✔ Click the All Pages button (the one on the left) to apply your settings to every page in the document. The title bar of the InfoBox reflects your choice by showing `Page Layout - All Pages`.

 ✔ Click the Right/Left Pages button (the one on the right) to apply your settings only to odd-numbered (right) or even-numbered (left) pages. The title bar of the InfoBox reflects your choice by showing `Page Layout - Left Pages` or `Page Layout - Right Pages`, depending on whether the insertion point is currently located on a right or left page. If you want to adjust the setting for the opposite page, you simply move the insertion point to that page.

If you choose Right pages or Left pages and change some settings, you can click Mirror pages to have Word Pro reverse your new layout settings for the opposite type of pages (right or left). If your left margin is set at one inch and your right margin at two inches on *left* pages, for example, mirroring places the left margin at two inches and the right margin at one inch on *right* pages. This option is great for any material that you plan to print on both sides of the paper and then bind together, because you usually need a larger margin in the middle to leave room for the binding.

Setting page size and margins

The Size and Margin settings are shown in Figure 5-5 and function as described in the following paragraphs:

✔ Use the Page Size drop-down list box to tell Word Pro what size of paper you want to use. Word Pro comes with a generous selection of preset page sizes. If your paper doesn't fit any of the predefined settings, you can select Custom from the list and enter your own measurements in the dialog box that Word Pro opens.

 If your printer is already set up for the size of paper you want to use, check the Use Settings From Printer Driver option to instruct Word Pro to get the settings from your printer driver and apply them to the Page Size and Orientation settings in the InfoBox.

✔ Click one of the Orientation buttons to tell Word Pro how you want the text oriented on the page. Word Pro avoids the sometimes confusing Portrait and Landscape terminology by labeling the buttons with icons representing tall (portrait) or wide (landscape) pages.

✔ Change margin settings by typing numbers in the appropriate text boxes or by clicking the up or down increment arrows next to each box.

Adding lines

Impress your friends by adding a border around every page or maybe just a slick-looking line down the left margin. Click the Color, Pattern, and Line Style tab in the Page Layout Properties InfoBox to access these options, as shown in Figure 5-6.

Figure 5-6:
You can add borders or lines around your page by using this Page Layout Properties InfoBox.

The best way to figure out what you want to do here is just to play around. Click the different options and see what happens to the page currently on-screen.

To better appreciate the effects of page borders, make sure that you're in Layout view (by choosing View⇨Layout) and choose View⇨Zoom To Full Page to make the entire page visible on-screen.

Here's a rundown on the main options you find in this tab of the InfoBox:

✔ The Lines Around Page buttons offer a quick way to add a standard border to your page.

✔ For a fancy border, try one of the selections from the Designer Borders drop-down list box. If you don't like any of the choices you see in the list box, click Other for even more border choices.

✔ Choose the first Lines Around Page button — None — to quickly get rid of a border.

✔ The 12 drop-down list boxes below the row of Lines Around Page buttons enable you to fine-tune your border by changing such details as the thickness and color of the lines, drop-shadow effects, and whether the line should surround the page or appear on only one side.

Most computer printers incorporate what's called an *unprintable zone*. This zone is usually about a quarter-inch wide, all the way around the sheet of paper, but may be larger — especialy on inkjet-type printers. If your printer can't print all the way out to the edge of the page, your lines don't show up on the printout if you select Page edge in the Line Placement drop-down list box. You can choose View➪Set View Preferences and check the Show No-Print Zone option on the Show tab of the View Preferences dialog box; then click OK to close the dialog box. This instructs Word Pro to simulate on-screen how your printed page will look by not showing on-screen any text or lines that fall in the printer's no-print zone.

Inserting a page layout

If you modify the page layout, you change the entire document. If you want to change the page layout in the middle of a document (such as to set different margins for one section), choose Page➪Insert Page Layout from the menu bar to open the Insert Page Layout dialog box. This dialog box lists the existing page layouts in your document. You can choose one of the existing layouts from the list and click Insert to insert a new page with a copy of the existing page layout settings, or you can click Insert & Edit to insert a copy of the default page layout and open the Page Layout Properties InfoBox you're already familiar with. Then just make the changes you want there and close the InfoBox. Word Pro inserts a manual page break, and a small page icon appears in your text to indicate where page layout settings change.

To remove from your document a page layout that you inserted, you need to delete the page layout icon. Remember that because the page layout icon is also a page break, removing the page layout also removes the page break. The easiest way to delete a page break (whether or not it's also a page layout icon) is to position the text cursor just to the left of the page layout icon and then press Delete. Word Pro removes the page break icon, and the text from the next page jumps up to take its place. If you still want a page break there, you must insert one by choosing Page➪Insert Page Break.

You can insert as many page layouts in your document as you want. Here's what Word Pro does with these layouts: Word Pro uses the settings for the original layout until the end of the document or until the program encoun-ters an inserted page layout. Word Pro then uses the settings for that new layout until encountering yet another inserted layout (or until the program reaches the end of the document, whichever comes first). If you want to revert back to the default layout at any point in your document following an inserted page layout, you need to insert another page layout with a copy of the default layout.

Understanding Paragraph Styles

Paragraph styles are nothing mysterious. A *paragraph style* is simply a set of formatting information that is given a name. (This formatting information can include text formatting, such as font and size, and paragraph formatting, such as tabs and indents.) After you create a certain paragraph style, you can then apply that named style to a paragraph. When you apply a named style to a paragraph, you are applying to that paragraph all the formatting information recorded in that style — and you apply this formatting all at once instead of needing to apply each formatting option individually. Pretty handy, huh?

Perhaps an example can help you understand paragraph styles better. Suppose that you're writing a paper containing numerous quotes and you want the quoted material to appear in italics and indented from both left and right margins. You could select each quote, click the Italic button on the status bar to add the italic attribute, and then open the Text Properties InfoBox and go to the Alignment tab, where you could click the appropriate button to indent the paragraph from both margins. Or you could do all that once, save the paragraph's formatting as a named style, and then apply that same formatting to each subsequent quote by simply clicking anywhere in the paragraph, clicking the Named Style button on the status bar, and then selecting the style name.

Actually, you've been using styles all along and you didn't even know what you were doing. (Okay, maybe you did, but you didn't get the information from us.) Every time you start a paragraph in Word Pro, that paragraph starts out with a certain paragraph style. So far, we've been using the default settings for a plain document; the default paragraph style is called *Default Text*. That means that, if you don't do anything to change the style, you're using the Default Text style for each paragraph you create. This style provides default values for all the text and paragraph formatting options that Word Pro offers. You can override those settings by applying any other formatting that you want to a paragraph, but the paragraph style itself provides the starting point.

How do you know which paragraph style you're using? Just look at the status bar; the Named Styles button just to the right of the Attribute buttons displays the name of the current paragraph style.

In addition to the Default Text paragraph style, you may find that your Word Pro document contains predefined paragraph styles for headings, bulleted lists, numbered lists, and more. These styles greatly simplify the task of formatting your document.

To format a heading, for example, you may want to change the font and size, add the bold attribute to the text, and center-align the paragraph. Of course, you could do all that manually for each heading, but simply clicking the Named Styles button in the status bar (the button probably reads `Default Text` unless you've been playing with the styles while we weren't looking) and selecting the Heading style to make Word Pro apply all that formatting for you in a single stroke is much easier.

Whenever you create a new document, Word Pro bases that document on a specific SmartMaster template. (Even a plain document is based on a default template.) The SmartMaster includes a set of predefined paragraph styles you can use in your document. But you're not confined to those styles. You can redefine the styles and create new ones of your own.

You create new styles by example. Start by formatting a paragraph the way you want. Then right-click the paragraph and choose Named Styles⇨Create from the pop-up menu to open the Create Style dialog box.

Type in a name for your new style and, if you want, a description; then click OK. Word Pro adds the new style to the list that appears after you click the Named Style button in the status bar so that you can then apply that same new set of formatting to other paragraphs in your document.

To redefine an existing paragraph style, start by applying the style to a paragraph (or by selecting a paragraph that uses the style you want to change). Reformat the paragraph as needed and then right-click the paragraph and choose Named Styles⇨Redefine from the pop-up menu to record these changes. Changing the definition of the style changes the formatting of all the paragraphs that use that style. So, for example, if you change the typeface that you use for a heading and redefine the Heading style, you instantly change all the headings in your document to the new typeface.

Understanding SmartMasters

You don't need to know too much about SmartMasters to use them effectively in Word Pro. *SmartMasters* are simply templates that serve as patterns or molds for Word Pro documents. Every time you start a new document, Word Pro makes you choose a SmartMaster on which to base the document. (*Remember:* Even if you choose to create a plain document, Word Pro still bases that document on a default SmartMaster.)

At the very least, each SmartMaster contains a set of simple paragraph styles and settings such as page margins. The more elaborate SmartMasters also contain the skeleton of a document containing text, lines, and Click Here fields (fill-in-the-blanks) that enable you to get a head start on creating a finished document.

A simple memo SmartMaster, for example, may include the word *Memo* at the top of the page, plus the current date and all the normal To and From headers. If you start a new document based on that SmartMaster, all you need to do is just fill in the recipient's name, the subject, and the text of your memo to create a nicely formatted memo. You don't need to do any formatting to make the headers a different font or align the To and From names or add a line to separate the header area from the memo text. All of that is already taken care of by the SmartMaster. SmartMasters run the gamut from simple memos and letterheads to invoices, newsletters, and business cards.

Starting a new document based on a SmartMaster

To use a SmartMaster, you normally create a new document based on the SmartMaster of your choice. How do you start a new document by using a SmartMaster? Glad you asked. Just follow these handy steps:

1. **Choose File⇨New Document from the menu bar or click the Create A New Document SmartIcon.**

   This action opens the New Document dialog box. To create a new document based on a SmartMaster you used recently, simply click the SmartMaster file name from the list in the Create From Recently Used SmartMaster tab of the New Document dialog box. Word Pro displays a preview of the SmartMaster in the right side of the dialog box. Otherwise, proceed to Step 2.

2. **Click the Create From Any SmartMaster tab to display the SmartMaster selection options.**

3. **Choose a general category of SmartMaster from the Select A Type Of SmartMaster list on the left side of the dialog box; then select a variation or graphic treatment from the Select A Look list box.**

   Word Pro displays a thumbnail sample of your selected SmartMaster on the right side of the dialog box.

4. After you're satisfied with your selection, click OK.

Word Pro creates a new document based on the SmartMaster and opens that document in the workspace, ready for you to begin work. Depending on the SmartMaster you choose, you may see a blank document with only a few default formatting options, such as the margins and font selection determined by the SmartMaster, or you may see a nearly complete document in which you can simply fill in a few blanks to produce the finished invoice or other document.

Working with styles in a SmartMaster

A SmartMaster is, above all, a collection of predefined paragraph styles. After you create a new document based on a SmartMaster, you can override and revise those styles with your own formatting choices. You should, however, keep a few of the following points in mind in dealing with styles and SmartMasters:

✔ If you modify a paragraph style in a document, the new style settings take precedence over those of the original SmartMaster.

✔ Modified paragraph styles affect only the current document. If you start a new document by using the same SmartMaster, the paragraph styles revert to their original settings.

✔ If you change a bunch of paragraph styles and other settings in a document, you may want to save the settings in a new SmartMaster so that you can use them in other documents. Choose File⇨Save As to open the Save As dialog box, and then select Lotus Word Pro SmartMaster (*.MWP) from the Save As Type list box. Give your SmartMaster a name and click Save. Now, whenever you choose File⇨ New Document from the menu bar, your newly created SmartMaster appears in the list of available SmartMasters along with all the others that came with Word Pro.

Chapter 6

Polishing Up Your Word Pro Document

So you know how to do all sorts of stuff with words — put them in documents, save them, and change the way they look on the page. But what if you want to add some pretty pictures to your documents to illustrate a point or simply to give your document some pizzazz? Or maybe you want to add a table to support and clarify a portion of the text. (Hey, appearances count, and sometimes it pays to dazzle your readers a little.) And then comes the matter of finding all those words and making sure that they're spelled correctly. If any of this seems relevant, you've come to the right chapter.

It's a Frame-Up!

Yeah, yeah. You want to learn how to put pretty pictures in your documents. So what's this "frame" stuff? In real life, you can unroll a poster and thumbtack it to the wall — no frame required (just some bandages, maybe). But in the world of Word Pro, the picture must go into a frame.

A *frame* is just a place to put stuff that's not part of the regular document text. After you have a frame, you can move or size the frame without affecting the layout of the rest of your document. And frames are good for more than just pictures — you can put charts (perhaps from 1-2-3 or Freelance), Approach data, or even text into frames. But why would you want to put text in a frame if you have a whole document for that purpose? Well, suppose that you're writing a company newsletter and you want to include a plea for help with the upcoming demonstration against management. And you want to be absolutely sure that everyone sees the notice. Try putting the notice in a frame with a nice border — that sets that particular text off from the rest and helps ensure a higher level of participation in your demonstration (although management turnout may be rather sparse).

You can also use frames to link information from other SmartSuite applications (or even — dare we say? — from non-SmartSuite applications).

Creating a frame

Now that we've talked the concept of frames to death, shall we get to work and actually create one? Just follow these simple steps:

1. **Make sure that you're in Layout mode.**

   Choose View⇨Layout from the menu bar if you're not in Layout mode.

2. **Choose Create⇨Frame from the menu bar.**

   This action opens the Create Frame dialog box, as shown in Figure 6-1.

Figure 6-1:
The Create
Frame
dialog box.

3. **In the Width box, type or select a value to tell Word Pro how wide you want the frame.**

4. **In the Height box, perform the same action to tell Word Pro how tall you want the frame.**

   Don't worry too much about getting the dimensions exactly right — you can easily change them later. (And we even tell you how — also later, however.)

5. **Click OK.**

   You end up with an empty frame much like the one shown in Figure 6-2.

Handles   Frame   Anchor

Figure 6-2:
You now
have a
frame
in your
Word Pro
document,
and you can
size, move,
and put
stuff in the
frame.

If you prefer a more visual approach, you can create a frame without enter-ing any measurements. Just click the Create Frame Manually SmartIcon (the one that looks like a little picture frame) or choose the Size & Place Frame Manually button after you're in the Create Frame dialog box (as described in the preceding steps). Your mouse pointer turns into a little box. Position the box on the page where you want one corner of the frame, press and hold the left mouse button, and drag the mouse until the box is the size you want; then release the mouse button. By using this technique, you still end up with an empty frame similar to the one shown in Figure 6-2.

Doing stuff to frames

In Figure 6-2, you see an empty box with a bunch of markers at the corners and in the middle of each side. You probably figured out that the empty box is the frame, but what are all those other things? Well, those little markers are called *handles*. The visible handles tell you that this frame is selected; and, as you soon discover, you can also drag the handles somewhere else on-screen to change the size of the frame. A little anchor symbol gives the frame a home base in relation to the text on the page. You can define the frame's position on the page in relation to this anchor, which you can move around in your document as you do text. For example, the frame may fit flush with the left margin, immediately after the paragraph containing the anchor. As you add or delete text ahead of the anchor, the anchor moves with the surrounding text, and Word Pro moves the frame automatically to maintain the same relative position just below the anchor paragraph — even if the anchor has moved to another page in your document. You can also define a frame's position so that it remains anchored on the current page, appears on all pages, or appears on left or right pages.

The capability to select frames is important because you can't make changes to a frame unless you first select that frame. (You can find more information about selecting things in Word Pro in Chapter 4.) Here's some stuff you can do to a frame:

✔ To select a frame, click anywhere inside the frame. To deselect a frame, click anywhere outside the frame. (The handles disappear if you deselect a frame.) You must select frames before you can move, resize, delete, or modify them.

✔ To change the size of a frame, position your mouse pointer over one of the handles until the pointer turns into a double-headed arrow. Then drag the handle to make the frame larger or smaller. To change both the height and width at the same time, drag one of the corner handles.

✔ To move a frame, just put your mouse pointer anywhere on the outer edge of the frame (but not on a handle), click and hold the left mouse button, and drag. The pointer changes to a fist that "grabs" the frame to drag it. (Isn't that cute?) Just release the mouse button after the frame outline is positioned where you want the frame.

✔ To delete a frame, select the frame and then click its outer edge. The outer edge of the frame and the handles darken. Press Delete. (Bye-bye, frame.)

You can also change how a frame looks and how the frame works in relation to the rest of the document by changing various options in the Frame Properties InfoBox. To open the Frame Properties InfoBox, click the right mouse button (an action that's also called a *right-click*) anywhere inside the frame and choose Frame Properties from the pop-up menu that appears. (You can also select the frame and then choose Frame⇨Frame Properties from the menu bar to open this InfoBox.)

You can do lots of things to a frame (and its contents) by using the Frame Properties InfoBox. (See Figure 6-3.) For example, you can adjust the size of the frame, change the margin between the frame and whatever you put in it, and change the *padding* (which is the space between the frame and the text around it). You can add a border to the frame, just like you can to a page, and you can format the text within a frame so that it appears in columns instead of in one big chunk. All this stuff is pretty easy to do, especially because the Frame Properties InfoBox is so similar to the Page Properties InfoBox (and all the other InfoBoxes for that matter). So go for it! Make yourself a frame, open the Frame Properties InfoBox, and start experimenting. You'll have frames mastered in no time.

Graphic and Watermark Options tab

Size and Margin tab

Newspaper Columns tab

Placement and Anchoring Options tab

Tab Settings, Alignment, and Grid tab

Figure 6-3: The Size and Margin tab of the Frame Properties InfoBox.

Named Style tab

Color, Pattern, and Line Style tab

Putting stuff in frames

We start by putting some text inside a frame, because that action is the most straightforward one you can perform. And then we move on to the main attraction — pretty pictures.

Putting text in frames

Here's the deal: You're frantically trying to get out your year-end budget, but you just found out that you're missing some critical information. So, in your projected budget notice, you insert an APB (all points bulletin) for the missing data. Because getting the notice noticed is of prime importance, you put the notice in a frame to set its message off from the rest of the text. The result is as shown in Figure 6-4.

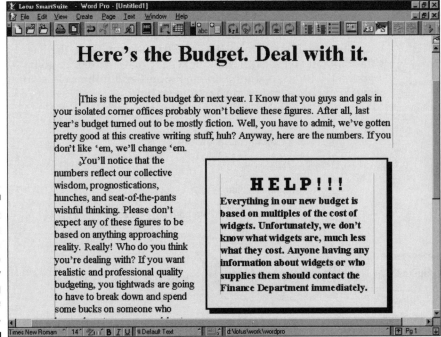

Figure 6-4:
You can
add extra
emphasis to
text by
putting
some inside
a frame.

So how is this accomplished? Simple. To put text in a frame, simply follow these easy steps:

1. Select the frame.

(You already know how to select a frame if you read this section on frames from the beginning. If not, meander back to the "Doing stuff to frames" section, earlier in this chapter.)

2. Start typing.

After you select the frame, an insertion point appears inside the frame, and you can type text inside the frame just as you can on the main page. If you type more words than can fit on one line, the text automatically wraps to stay within the frame. And if your text runs on too long to fit the frame, just drag one of the frame handles to enlarge the frame.

3. Format the text.

You can change the font or formatting by using any of the techniques we discuss in Chapter 4.

4. After you finish, click anywhere outside the frame.

Putting pictures in frames

Now that we've told you all about how to create frames, forget what we said. Yeah, you heard right. If you import a graphic image (picture) into a Word Pro document, you don't need to create the frame first — the frame is created automatically as you import the picture. But we really had a reason for going into all that frame stuff first — honest. Even though you don't need to actually go through the steps to create a frame, you still end up with a frame that you can move, delete, resize, and do all sorts of other things to. So everything you just read about frames is not for naught.

Where do you get pictures to put in your Word Pro documents? You have the following sources:

- ✔ Word Pro comes with a bunch of its own clip-art images you can use.

- ✔ You can use the graphics that come with some of the other SmartSuite applications.

- ✔ You can import drawings or charts from Freelance Graphics or 1-2-3 into Word Pro documents.

- ✔ If you use other drawing programs, such as CorelDRAW, Visio, or Adobe Illustrator, you can import their creations into Word Pro, too (although you may need to go through some extra steps to export drawings from those programs to a file format — such as EPS or Windows Metafile — that Word Pro understands).

- ✔ If you own or have access to a scanner, you can scan photographs or other images.

- ✔ You can buy commercial clip art and photographs from software stores.

To place a picture into your document, follow these steps:

1. **If you already have a frame into which you want to put the picture, select the frame.**

   The frame you select should be empty. If the frame contains another picture, the new picture replaces the previous occupant of the frame. If your frame contains text, Word Pro creates a frame within a frame to hold the picture. If you don't want to create a frame ahead of time, just skip to Step 2. Word Pro automatically creates a frame as the program imports the picture.

2. **Choose File⇨Import Picture from the menu bar.**

   This action opens the Import Picture dialog box, shown in Figure 6-5.

Figure 6-5:
The Import
Picture
dialog box.

3. **Make a selection from the Files Of Type list.**

This list displays all the different graphics file types that Word Pro supports. The pictures that come with Word Pro are in Word Pro Draw format (SDW).

4. **If necessary, select the folder and/or drive containing the picture you want to import.**

The current folder name appears in the Look In drop-down list box. (A folder is just another name for the directories you may be familiar with from DOS or earlier versions of Windows.) You can use standard Windows navigation techniques to select a different folder or drive. If you're not familiar with these techniques, check out *Windows 98 For Dummies,* by Andy Rathbone (published by IDG Books Worldwide, Inc.).

5. **Select the picture you want to use from the main list box in the middle of the dialog box.**

If the Preview check box is selected (the default), you see a preview of the selected picture in the box in the lower-left corner of the Import Picture dialog box. This preview enables you to make sure that you selected the correct picture before importing the image into your Word Pro document.

6. **Click Open to import the selected picture.**

In Figure 6-6, we add a picture to our budget document.

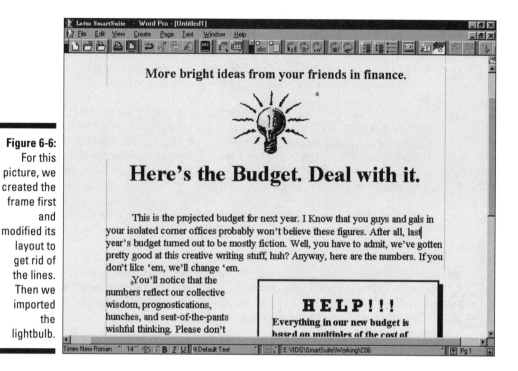

Figure 6-6:
For this
picture, we
created the
frame first
and
modified its
layout to
get rid of
the lines.
Then we
imported
the
lightbulb.

You can move or resize the frame containing the picture. You can also move or resize a picture inside its frame. Selecting just the picture, however, can be a bit tricky. As you first select a frame containing a picture, you see the thick border appear around the frame, indicating that the frame itself is ready to be moved. You need to double-click the picture to get rid of the thick frame marker and show just the frame handles. Next, you must click the picture again to select the picture instead of the frame. After you select the picture, handles (small black boxes) appear around the picture. (The handles appear inside the frame and border. Sometimes they are hard to see because they are partially cropped by the frame and appear as thin lines instead of square boxes.) You can drag these handles to resize the picture within the frame the same way that you drag frame handles to resize the frame. Clicking and dragging the center of the picture instead of the handles moves the picture within the frame.

Moving or resizing a picture so that some of its handles are outside the frame (making the picture larger than the frame, for example) can result in some bizarre and difficult-to-control behavior. You're best off to just stick with moving and resizing the picture within the confines of the frame.

If you press Delete with the frame selected, both the frame and the picture go away. You can't just delete the frame and leave the picture. You can, however, achieve a no-frame effect by telling Word Pro not to display the lines in the frame. Of course, you do that by adjusting the settings on the Color, Pattern, And Line Style tab of the Frame Properties InfoBox.

If you want to delete the picture and leave an empty frame, select the picture (as described in the preceding paragraphs) so that the handles appear around the picture inside the frame; then press the Delete key. That does the job. Given the hassle of selecting the picture inside the frame, however, you may find that just deleting the whole frame and then creating a new, empty frame is easier.

If your clicking finger's just too fast and you delete a frame and its contents without meaning to, just click the Undo SmartIcon right away (or choose Edit⇨Undo).

Printing documents containing lots of pictures can take a long time. You can speed up the printing process (which is especially useful for printing drafts) by telling Word Pro not to print the pictures. Just choose File⇨Print from the menu bar to open the Print dialog box, choose the Options button, and then choose Without Pictures in the Print Options dialog box and click OK to close the dialog box. Finally, click the Print button in the Print dialog box to start printing.

Tabular, Dude!

In this section, we show you how to create a simple table. Tables are great for organizing text and numbers into rows and columns. In Chapter 5, we show you how to line up text by using tabs, but tables are easier to work with and offer a lot more formatting options.

Even though Word Pro enables you to perform calculations and other fancy stuff in tables, you're really better off doing that kind of stuff in 1-2-3 and then pasting or linking the 1-2-3 data into your Word Pro document. Part III covers 1-2-3. Check it out for pertinent info.

In case you're beginning to wonder why Word Pro even has a tables feature, however, let us hastily amend our preceding caveat. Word Pro tables are great for organizing text items into a tabular format. The tables even work well as small numeric tables.

To create a table in Word Pro, follow these steps:

1. **Choose Create⇨Table from the menu bar.**

   This action opens the Create Table dialog box, shown in Figure 6-7.

Figure 6-7:
Use the
Create
Table dialog
box to
create a
table.

So that you can move the table freely within your document, put the
table in a frame. Before you open the Create Table dialog box, create a
frame and select that frame. As Word Pro creates the table, the program
puts the table in the selected frame. You can then work with the table
and its frame just as you can with any other frame and its contents.

2. **Type or select values in the Number Of Columns and Number Of
   Rows text boxes to tell Word Pro how many columns and rows you
   want and then click OK.**

Word Pro instantly displays the table on-screen.

After you click OK in the Create Table dialog box, Word Pro actually
adds a Table menu to its menu bar so that you can more easily work
with tables. Considerate little program, isn't it?

Here are a few points to remember as you work with tables:

- ✔ To enter text in the table, just put your insertion point in one of the
  little boxes (called cells) and start typing.

- ✔ To move to the next cell, press Tab.

- ✔ If you're in the last cell of a row, pressing Tab takes you to the first cell
  of the next row.

- ✔ Press Shift+Tab to move backward a cell at a time.

- ✔ Press Tab in the last cell of the last row to create a new row.

That default table with single lines is pretty boring. Fortunately, Word Pro
enables you to change the table's layout and formatting. To access Word
Pro's table layout options, choose Table➪Table Properties from the menu
bar to open the Table Properties InfoBox, shown in Figure 6-8.

The options available in the Table Properties InfoBox are similar to the
options available in the Frame Properties InfoBox (among others). You're
probably getting the hang of these InfoBox settings by now. The main thing
to remember about these settings is that they apply to the table as a whole.

Figure 6-8:
Use the
Table
Properties
InfoBox to
change a
table's
layout.

To adjust the formatting of certain cells in your table, select the cells you want to format (by dragging the pointer across the cells — just as if you were selecting text), and either choose Table➪Cell Properties or right-click a cell and choose Cell Properties from the pop-up menu. Either action opens the Table Cell Properties InfoBox, shown in Figure 6-9.

Figure 6-9:
The Table
Cell
Properties
InfoBox.

This InfoBox is where you adjust the settings for individual cells. For example, the table lines you see on-screen that separate the rows and columns aren't really lines. Well, they are lines, but they don't necessarily show up on the page if you print the table. The lines you see on-screen are just there to help you work with the table. If you actually want lines to appear in your finished table, click the Color, Pattern, And Line Style tab in the Cell Properties InfoBox and then make sure that the second Lines Around Cells button is depressed. This option prints lines that resemble those on-screen. If you want lines around only certain sides of the cells, choose some of the other options.

The Number Format (#) tab of the Table Cell Properties InfoBox (shown in Figure 6-10) is a little unusual. This tab enables you to configure cells to display numbers in consistent formats — automatically adding currency symbols and showing a certain number of decimal places and such. For example, if your cell contains the number 123, you could select Currency in the Format Category list and U.S. Dollar in the Current Format list to instruct Word Pro to display the number as $123.00.

Figure 6-10:
The
Number
Format tab
of the
Table Cell
Properties
InfoBox.

You can add columns or rows to your table by choosing Table⇨Insert⇨Row/
Column from the menu bar to open the Insert Row/Column dialog box, as
shown in Figure 6-11. This dialog box enables you to add multiple rows or
columns to your table.

Figure 6-11:
The Insert
Row/
Column
dialog box.

Here's some other table stuff you can do:

✔ To insert a single row into the table, right-click a cell in the row above
which you want to insert a new row and choose Insert a Row from the
pop-up menu that appears.

✔ To insert a single column into the table, right-click a cell in the column
to the left of which you want to insert a new column and choose Insert
a Column from the pop-up menu. Word Pro adds the new column to the
right of the column you clicked.

✔ To delete a row or column, right-click a cell in the row or column you
want to delete and choose Delete Row/Column from the pop-up menu.
Choose Row or Column in the dialog box that appears and click OK.

✔ To select the entire table, choose Table⇨Select⇨Entire Table from the
menu bar.

✔ To change the width of a column by using the mouse, place your mouse
pointer on the line that separates the two columns. After your mouse
pointer turns into a two-headed arrow, drag the line in either direction
to make the column wider or narrower.

Take a look at Figure 6-12 to see how a finished table can look in Word Pro
after you create and pretty the thing up some. Impressive, huh?

Figure 6-12:
A finished
table that
explores
some of the
Word Pro
table
capabilities.

Preliminary Budget Forecast		
Category	First Quarter	Second Quarter
Whopee Cushions	$4,332.00	$7,598.00
Pencils	$122.00	$50.00
Erasers	$1,075.00	$922.00

Finding and Replacing Stuff

Suppose that you have a document full of text. Then you remember that premium widgets aren't premium widgets anymore — their name got changed to *plenipotentiary* widgets in the middle of the project. You know that you talked about those stupid widgets a lot, but you're not sure whether you used the new name throughout the document. You could laboriously read through the widget document, line by line, eyes slowly glazing over, or you could use the Word Pro Find and Replace feature — not only to find all the places where you mentioned the widgets but also to replace any incorrect entries with the correct text. Here's how to use Find and Replace:

1. **Choose E̲dit⇨F̲ind & Replace Text from the menu bar (or press Ctrl+F).**

   You may expect this command to open a dialog box, but Word Pro has a surprise in store for you. The Find & Replace bar appears just below the menu bar and SmartIcon palette, as shown in Figure 6-13.

Figure 6-13:
The Find &
Replace bar.

? Find & Replace	Find: premium widgets ▾		Find	←	→	Done
Whole words only ▾	Replace with: plenipotentiary widgets ▾		Replace	Replace All		Options...

2. **Type the text you want to search for in the Fi̲nd text box.**

3. **If you want to replace the text with something else, type the replacement text in the Replace W̲ith text box.**

4. **Click the F̲ind button to locate the first place the search text occurs, or click Replace A̲ll to automatically replace all occurrences of the search text with the replacement text.**

If you choose Replace All, Word Pro goes through the document and does its thing without any input from you. Unless you're absolutely sure that you want to replace every single occurrence of the search text, you're usually safer to choose Find. That way you get to make decisions about what to replace as you go along.

In Figure 6-13, notice that the Find text is *premium widgets* instead of just *premium*. We chose to use both words because the word *premium* could easily be used in another context, and we wouldn't want to replace all occurrences of *premium* with *plenipotentiary.*

If you choose Find, Word Pro stops at the first place it finds the search text. Click the Replace button to replace this instance of the search text and search for the next occurrence. Click Replace All to replace this and all other occurrences without further input from you.

 5. **Click the Done button to close the Find & Replace bar after you finish searching for text.**

You can also use Find and Replace as a quickie way to delete text. Suppose that you find out that your boss, John Snowflake Adams, is terribly embarrassed by his middle name and begs you not to use it in the bio you just completed. Just do a search for *Snowflake*, don't put anything in the Replace With box, and choose Replace All. Word Pro replaces all occurrences of Snowflake with nothing. Now the only person left alive who knows John's middle name is you. Hmmm, with a little blackmail . . . er, that is, *subtle persuasion,* maybe you can finally get that corner office.

We've explained how to do a simple text search and replace. But, hey, Word Pro doesn't stop there. You can narrow down the search specifications, you can tell Word Pro in which direction to search and what parts of the document to search, and you can even search for styles and text attributes such as bold and italic type.

For quick, routine control over the search, you can perform the following actions:

 ✔ Click the left- or right-arrow buttons to tell Word Pro in which direction to search — toward the beginning of the document or toward the end.

 ✔ Specify whether Word Pro should look for the search word as whole words only or for words that begin with, end with, or contain the search term. Make your selection in the drop-down list below the Find & Replace title.

To specify more elaborate search preferences, choose the Options button in the Find & Replace bar. This action opens the Find & Replace Text Options dialog box, shown in Figure 6-14.

Figure 6-14:
The Find &
Replace
Text
Options
dialog box.

By using the options in this dialog box, you can perform the following search operations:

✔ Select Entire Document or Current Division (if you've divided your document into sections) in the Look In drop-down list box to tell Word Pro how much and what part of the document to search.

✔ Make selections in the Include drop-down list box to search all the text or just tables, headers, and so on.

✔ Select the Match Case check box to find text that matches exactly the upper- and lowercase letters of your search word or phrase; otherwise, a search for *the* finds *the, The, THE,* and even *tHe* or *thE.* You can choose the counterpart to this option — Exact Case — for replacement text.

✔ Select the Include Properties check box to find the search text only if that text uses a specific font or type size, or bold, italics, or another text attribute. If you choose this option, click the Text Properties button (the one with an A and a Z on it) next to this option and specify the text properties you want to match in the mini-InfoBox that appears. You can choose this option for both search and replacement text.

✔ Use the Special Characters Help drop-down list to find out how to specify special characters (such as tabs and returns) in the Find or Replace With boxes.

SmartCorrect Takes Shorthand

Do you repeatedly make common typographical errors, such as transposing characters (typing **teh** for *the* or **adn** for *and*)? If so, you're going to love the Word Pro SmartCorrect feature!

SmartCorrect watches as you type and, if the feature detects a common mistake, corrects the error automatically. But SmartCorrect can do more than just correct mistakes. The feature can also automatically expand abbreviations. You'd be amazed at how your typing speed picks up when you can type a few letters and have SmartCorrect replace them with an entire phrase. You may, for example, type **otoh** and have SmartCorrect replace this abbreviation with the full text *on the other hand.*

SmartCorrect works by keeping a list of mistakes and abbreviations as well as the corrected text with which to replace these errors (or their shorthand terms). SmartCorrect comes with a sizable list of common mistakes to seek out. To take full advantage of the SmartCorrect feature, however, you probably need to customize the list with your own entries.

Choose File⇔User Setup⇔SmartCorrect Setup to open the SmartCorrect dialog box, as shown in Figure 6-15. Here you can scroll through the list of SmartCorrect entries. After you click to highlight an entry, the replacement text appears to the side of the list.

Figure 6-15:
The
SmartCorrect
dialog box.

You can change the SmartCorrect entries by performing the following actions:

- ✔ To delete an entry from the list, click that entry and then click the Delete Entry button.

- ✔ To add your own entry to the list, click the Add Entry button to open the Add SmartCorrect Entry dialog box. Type the text you want to replace in the SmartCorrect Entry text box. Then, in the Replacement text box, type the text that you want to replace the original text and click OK. Word Pro adds the entry to the SmartCorrect Entries list.

 ✔ Select the Change Straight Quotes To Smart Quotes check box to automatically replace straight quotes (") with typographically correct curved quotes (").

 ✔ Select the Correct TWo INitial CApitals check box to instruct SmartCorrect to correct this common typing error.

 ✔ Select the Start Sentences With Capital Letters check box to have SmartCorrect automatically capitalize the first word of each sentence. (Just don't be surprised when SmartCorrect capitalizes the word following a terminal punctuation mark in the middle of a sentence, such as might occur in a quote.)

 ✔ If you select the Change Internet Address To Hyperlink check box, SmartCorrect automatically transforms any Internet address that it recognizes into a clickable hyperlink within your document.

Spelling Words Correctly

All the SmartSuite applications use the same dictionary for spell-checking purposes, and you use the same basic techniques to run a spell-check in each application. We describe spell-checking in SmartSuite in general in Part I, but in this chapter, we cover some options that are unique to Word Pro.

 Here's a quick reminder on how to start a spell-check: Click the Check Spelling SmartIcon (a little book marked with ABC) or choose Edit⇨Check Spelling from the menu bar or press Ctrl+F2. In other SmartSuite programs, this command opens a dialog box, but in Word Pro, the same command opens the Spell Check bar, shown in Figure 6-16.

Figure 6-16:
The Word
Pro Spell
Check bar.

The Spell Check bar may look different from the usual dialog box, but this feature works much the same as a dialog box. The bar arrangement just keeps a dialog box from covering up the text you're working with.

One interesting button on the Spell Check bar is SmartCorrect. Clicking this button adds the currently selected misspelled word (and its suggested replacement text) to the SmartCorrect Entry list. The next time you make that error, Word Pro corrects the error automatically; you don't need to use the Spell Check bar to make the correction.

Actually, the Spell Check feature is active all the time in Word Pro (or, at least, you can set the feature to remain active). Word Pro checks each word as you type and highlights any words the feature doesn't recognize. Choose View⇨Show/Hide⇨Misspelled Words to display the light blue highlights that mark misspelled words. Choose the same command again to suppress the highlights if you find them distracting.

Here, too, are a couple of points concerning the use of the status bar in spell-checking:

✔ Click the Check Spelling button on the status bar (it's in the middle and looks like a book marked with ABC) and then choose Show Misspelled Words or Hide Misspelled Words from the pop-up list to display or hide the highlighting that marks misspelled words. (Note that this button is the one on the status bar, not the Check Spelling SmartIcon.)

✔ Click a misspelled word and then click the Check Spelling button in the status bar for quick access to the basic Spell Check commands without opening the Spell Check bar. A pop-up menu appears displaying a list of options that vary depending on the circumstances. For example, for a simple misspelling, you see such commands as Add to Dictionary, Skip, and Replace, along with a list of suggested replacement words (one of which is highlighted).

After you open the Spell Check bar, Word Pro starts at your insertion point position and jumps to the next misspelled word. Click the Options button to give Word Pro specific spell-check instructions. The Spell Check Options dialog box opens, as shown in Figure 6-17. By using the various options in the Spell Check Options dialog box, you can tell Word Pro to check or not check specific types of text, and you can identify the User Dictionary (which is the list of names and other words you previously identified as being spelled correctly) that you want to use.

Figure 6-17:
The Spell
Check
Options
dialog box.

Spell Check Options

- ☑ Check for repeated words
- ☑ Check words with numbers
- ☑ Check words with initial caps
- ☐ Include user dictionary alternatives

Color for unrecognized words:

User dictionary(s) to use:
✔ d:\lotus\compnent\spell\ltsuser1.udc

OK
Cancel
Help
Clear Skipped Words
Edit Dictionary...
New Dictionary...
Choose Dictionaries...

If you select Check For Repeated Words in this dialog box, the spell-check stops upon finding the same word twice in a row and asks what you want to do. You can either replace the word with something else or ignore the repeated word and move on. You may think that selecting the Check Words With Numbers check box is a good thing — and using this option usually is.

After all, a slip of the finger can easily turn *steam* into *st3eam*. But what if your document contains a whole bunch of part numbers such as *CSP432a9z765?* If that's the case, you can save time and aggravation by turning off number checking.

Unless you have a particular reason not to, you should probably go ahead and select Check Words With Initial Caps. With this option selected, Word Pro stops at every questionable word that begins with an uppercase letter (proper names, place names, product names, and so on). This stop-and-go procedure can become annoying, but we figure that spending a little extra time going over a handful of additional words is better than missing those few words that really are misspelled.

If you add words to your user dictionary during a spell-check (by clicking the Add To User Dictionary option on the Spell Check bar after Word Pro stops on a word), you can tell Word Pro to include words from your customized word list in the list of alternatives Word Pro gives you to choose from. (In other words, selecting the Include User Dictionary Alternatives check box in the Spell Check Options dialog box is usually a good idea.)

Make sure that you save your document after you run a spell-check. Until you do so, none of the changes made during the spell-check are safe, and you could lose all the corrections if your system suffers a power surge or your dog chews through the power cord at that particular moment.

Using Thesaurus for the Perfect Phrase

Is that perfect word on the tip of your tongue but nowhere in sight of your typing fingers? Try Word Pro's thesaurus. (And, no, you didn't see one of those in *Jurassic Park!*) Just use the closest word you can think of and have the thesaurus give you some help. To use the thesaurus, follow these steps:

1. **Place your insertion point in the word you want to check.**

2. **Choose Edit⇨Proofing Tools⇨Check Thesaurus from the menu bar.**

   Word Pro selects the word and opens the Thesaurus dialog box, shown in Figure 6-18.

3. **If the word you want appears in the Synonyms For list, select the word and click Replace or just double-click the word.**

4. **If none of the words work for you, try clicking a different word in the Meanings For list.**

   For each word in this list, you get a different set of synonyms; if you spot the one you want, select that word and click Replace.

Figure 6-18:
Don't know
the right
word?
Thesaurus
to the
rescue.

5. **If one of the words in the Synonyms For list is close but no cigar, try selecting that word and clicking Lookup.**

   Word Pro uses the selected word as a new jumping-off point and presents you with a new list of synonyms for that word.

6. **If you haven't found a word you want to use, you can terminate the Thesaurus session without making any changes by clicking Cancel or pressing Esc.**

Keeping Track of Revisions

You compose a document. Next, you read through the document once to make sure that you typed what you intended; then you check the spelling, print the document, and send your masterpiece out. Ahh, don't you wish that life was as simple as that? In the real world, however, several other people usually need to review the document (and probably suggest changes) before your work is ready to go.

Fortunately, Word Pro includes some features to make collaborative editing a little easier (if not more fun). Word Pro can keep track of editing changes in a document. The program can show edits on-screen, with additions and deletions marked with distinctive colors and fonts. Then you can review the edits and decide whether to accept them or revert to the original text.

Marking edits

If you want Word Pro to keep track of editing changes as you make them and display those changes on-screen, choose Edit⇨Markup Edits to turn on the feature. While the feature is active, a check mark appears beside the command on the Edit menu. If you delete text, Word Pro changes that text's color and marks the deleted text with a strikethrough line. If you add text, the additions appear in italics of a different color. If you want to disable the Markup Edits feature, simply choose the command again.

Reviewing marked edits

Before you begin reviewing marked edits, you need to prepare yourself for the task. Take a deep breath. Now imagine that your ego is a jacket. Remove the jacket and hang it outside in the hall. Leave the garment there until you finish reviewing the marked edits. (In extreme cases, removing the ego jacket may not be enough. You may need to don an imaginary asbestos suit as well.) There — now that you're adequately prepared, you can get started.

After your team members edit your document (using the Markup Edits feature, of course), you can review the changes they make and decide whether to accept or reject them (the edits, not your coworkers).

Open the document and choose Edit⇨Review Marked Edits. Word Pro opens the Review bar, shown in Figure 6-19. You can move through the document, finding editing changes, by clicking Next Edit or Previous. (The Next Edit button is initially labeled Find Next.) After you locate a change, Word Pro shows who made the change and the date.

Figure 6-19:
The Review bar enables you to review marked edits.

The buttons on the Review bar enable you to perform the following actions:

✓ Clicking the Version button opens the Version For File dialog box, where you can select a previous version of the document you're editing or create a new version of the document so that you can make changes freely in the new version and still go back to the previous version if you change your mind.

Oh, did you know that Word Pro can store more than one version of a document in a single file? Well, now you do.

✓ Click Accept Edit to make the suggested change and remove the editing markup.

Depending on the kind of edit that is highlighted, the Accept Edit button may be labeled Accept Insertion, Accept Deletion, or something similar. The Reject Edit button changes in a similar manner.

✓ Click Reject Edit to revert to the original text and remove the suggested text.

✔ Click Accept All Edits to automatically accept all the suggested changes and remove the editing markups.

✔ Click Reject All Edits to automatically remove all the suggested changes and revert to the original text.

✔ Click Clear Tags to remove the editor's initials that Word Pro adds to the duplicate paragraphs that result from comparing two documents. (Comparing documents is a somewhat advanced feature of Word Pro. If you haven't used the Compare feature, the Clear Tags button doesn't do anything.)

✔ Click Done after you finish reviewing marked edits.

(You can retrieve your ego from the hall now.)

Chapter 7

Word Pro Final Touches and Shortcuts

*N*ot only can Word Pro create great-looking letters, but the program can also create form letters, address envelopes, and even take dictation. That's right, you talk to your computer, and Word Pro turns your words into text so that you don't have to wear your fingers to the bone by typing. Although none of the features described in this chapter are necessary to use Word Pro, these features can make Word Pro much easier to use. Unless you enjoy doing things the hard way, take a look at these fancy features that take the burden of entering text off you and put that weight on the computer, where the pesky thing so obviously belongs.

Caution — Merge Ahead

Suppose that you want to type the same letter over and over again, except that you want to address each nearly identical letter to a different person. The hard way is to type each letter separately and hope that you don't make a mistake. The easy way is to make some minimum-wage coworker do the work for you so that you have someone to blame if something goes wrong. If neither approach is feasible, the computer solution is to make Word Pro type these letters for you automatically. To do so, you must create the following two separate documents:

✔ A form letter

✔ The merge document

The *form letter* contains the text you want to send to everyone. The text in a form letter never changes from one letter to another. To tell Word Pro where to plug in personalized information, you must create certain elements called *fields*. Often, these fields appear at the top of your letter, as in the following example:

<First_Name> <Last_Name>
<Address>
<City>, <State> <Zip>

Dear <Title> <Last_Name>,

Thank you for your recent inquiry on our latest best-seller, *Atom Bomb Testing For Dummies.* The book is being sent separately, and you should receive your copy within one week from the receipt of this letter. We thank you for your business and hope that you may be interested in our other titles, such as *Chain Saws For Dummies, Artillery Spotting For Dummies,* and, of course, our perennial best-seller, *Tax Evasion For Dummies.*

In the preceding example, *<First_Name>* is a field because that information tells Word Pro: "Hey, this spot is where you insert a person's first name."

The *merge document* contains the information that you want inserted into a form letter, such as each person's name and address. For example, the Word Pro data file may contain the following information:

Mr. John Doe
123 Main Street
New York, NY 10012

Ms. Mary Jane
8763 Average Avenue
Fairmont, CO 30302

Word Pro actually stores the data in a funky, hard-to-read format with each record (address) on a single line and the fields separated by the tilde (~) character. But you don't need to worry about having to work with the merge data directly. Word Pro is the only one that needs to read this data. You can create and edit the data file by entering text in a dialog box.

If you tell Word Pro to create form letters for you, Word Pro grabs the document containing your merge data and plugs it into the gaps left vacant in your form letter to create a "personalized" letter, such as the following example:

John Doe
123 Main Street
New York, NY 10012

Dear Mr. Doe,

Thank you for your recent inquiry on our latest best-seller, *Atom Bomb Testing For Dummies.* The book is being sent separately, and you should receive your copy within one week from the receipt of this letter. We thank you for your business and hope that you may be interested in our other titles, such as *Chain Saws For Dummies, Artillery Spotting For Dummies,* and our perennial best-seller, *Tax Evasion For Dummies.*

Creating a form letter from scratch

To create both a form letter and a merge data file from scratch, open a plain, blank document in Word Pro and follow these steps:

1. Choose Text ➪Merge➪Letter from the menu bar.

The Mail Merge Assistant dialog box appears, as shown in Figure 7-1. The first step is to specify a data file to use.

Figure 7-1:
The Mail
Merge
Assistant
dialog box.

2. Click the Create New button to begin the process of creating a data file.

The Create Data File dialog box appears, as shown in Figure 7-2.

3. Type a field name (such as First Name **or** City**) in the Field Name text box and then click Add to add the field to the Fields For New Data File list.**

Repeat this step for each field that you want to create.

Figure 7-2:
The Create
Data File
dialog box.

You can save some typing by selecting a field name from the Commonly Used Fields list and then clicking Add to add this field name to the Fields For New Data File list.

4. **Arrange the fields in the Fields For New Data File list in a convenient order by clicking a field name and then clicking the up- or down-arrow buttons to move the field name up or down in the list.**

5. **After the list of field names is complete, click OK.**

   Word Pro displays an Edit Data File dialog box, shown in Figure 7-3, showing the fields that you created accompanied by empty text boxes in which to type your merge data.

Figure 7-3:
The Edit
Data File
dialog box.

6. **Click any field text box and then type the appropriate data in the field text box. Fill in all the fields and then click Add Record after you finish adding data for one record.**

   Repeat this step until you've entered all the merge data you want to create.

7. Click the Close and Save Data File button after you finish creating your merge data.

Word Pro displays a dialog box asking whether you want to save your newly created merge data.

8. Choose Yes.

A Save As dialog box appears.

9. Type a name for your file and click Save.

The Mail Merge Assistant dialog box reappears. The icon beside Step 1 in this dialog box displays a check mark to indicate that the step is complete and the options in Step 2 are now available.

10. Click Use Current to tell Word Pro that you want to create your form letter in the current (blank) document.

Word Pro displays your blank current document in the workspace and opens the *Merge bar* across the top, just below the menu bar and SmartIcon palette, as shown in Figure 7-4.

Figure 7-4:
The Merge
bar.

11. Type your form letter; whenever you want Word Pro to insert data stored in your merge data file, click the field name in the Merge bar's list and then click Insert Field.

Figure 7-5 shows one possible result.

12. After you finish creating your form letter, click the Done button in the Merge bar.

The Mail Merge Assistant dialog box reappears with the Step 2 icon checked off and Step 3 (Merge, View and Print) available.

13. Click Merge.

The Merge, View and Print dialog box appears, as shown in Figure 7-6. You can choose the following options for what items to print and how Word Pro prints the merge letters:

- *All Records* prints a merge letter for each record in the merge data file.

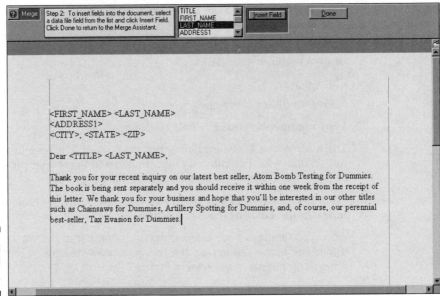

Figure 7-5:
A typical
form letter.

Figure 7-6:
The Merge,
View and
Print dialog
box.

- *Selected Records* enables you to specify what records to use for merge letters. Click the *Set Conditions* button to open a dialog box where you can specify the selection criteria (such as State=CA) for which records to print by making selections from a set of drop-down list boxes.

- *View On Screen Before Printing* gives you a chance to view your form letters before printing so that you don't print lots of form letters only to find that the formatting is wrong.

- *Send Directly To Printer* does exactly what you think — this option tells Word Pro to print the merge letters immediately without previewing each one on-screen first.

- *Print To File* does not print your form letters but saves the letters as a Word Pro document. If you choose this option, type a filename for your document in the Save As dialog box that appears. You can then skip the rest of these steps. You're done!

14. Turn on your printer and click OK.

If you select the View On Screen Before Printing option in the preceding step (highly recommended), Word Pro displays on-screen the first form letter with all the merged data in place. The Merge bar appears across the top of the workspace with a different set of buttons than those you use to create a form letter. The following buttons in the Merge bar enable you to preview the form letters and control printing:

- *Print and View Next* prints the current form letter and then displays the next variation with new data in place.

- *Skip and View Next* discards the current version of the form letter and displays the letter with data from the next merge data record.

- *Print All* automatically prints all the form letters — one for each selected record in the merge data file — without previewing each one on-screen.

- *Print Rest* automatically prints all remaining form letters. Use this button when you have printed some form letters individually and want to switch to automatic printing (like Print All) without reprinting the form letters you've already done.

If you select Send Directly to Printer, Word Pro cheerfully prints out your form letters with your merge data typed in the fields that you specified without requiring you to preview the letters first.

15. Choose File⇨Save to save your form letter.

A Save As dialog box appears.

16. Type the filename for your form letter and click Save.

If your merge document is missing data, such as someone's last name or address, guess what? Word Pro cheerfully shoves a blank space in the form letter where the last name or address is supposed to go. Before printing a lot of form letters, first use the View On Screen Before Printing option of the Merge, View and Print dialog box to view your completed form letters.

If you save your form letter, you can always open the letter later to make changes. Until you specify otherwise, Word Pro assumes that you always want to merge your form letter with the last merge document you used with that particular form letter.

To edit information stored in a merge document (to update the names and addresses, for example), follow these steps:

1. Open the form letter document you want to edit.

2. Choose Text⇨Merge⇨Letter to open the Mail Merge Assistant dialog box.

(Refer to Figure 7-1 if you don't recall what this dialog box looks like.)

3. Click the Use Existing button to open the Browse dialog box; then locate and select the merge data file you want to edit and click Open.

4. Click the Edit button in the Mail Merge Assistant dialog box to open the Edit Data File dialog box.

The Edit button appears after you select a Word Pro merge data file.

(Refer to Figure 7-3 if you don't recall what the Edit Data File dialog box looks like.)

5. Click the Delete Record or New Record button to delete or add a new record; to edit a record, click a tab or use the arrow buttons in the lower-right corner of the dialog box to select the record, type your changes, and then click the Update Record button.

6. Click Close And Save Data File after you're done.

A dialog box appears asking whether you want to save your changes in the file.

7. Click Yes.

The Mail Merge Assistant dialog box reappears. At this point, you can click Done to close the dialog box, or you can continue with the process of creating a merge letter, as described in Steps 10–16 of the steps on creating a form letter from scratch, a bit earlier in this section.

Creating a form letter by using an Approach database

If you have information stored in an Approach database using the dBASE format, you can merge the data into a Word Pro form letter. To link a Word Pro form letter to an Approach database, follow these steps:

1. Open an existing form letter document or a blank document.

2. Choose Text⇨Merge⇨Letter to open the Mail Merge Assistant dialog box.

(Refer to Figure 7-1 if you don't recall what this dialog box looks like.)

3. Click the Use Existing button beside the Step 1 icon to open the Browse dialog box.

4. Click the Files Of Type list box and select dBASE/ASCII (*.DBF).

5. **Click the name of the Approach database file that you want to use from the list of files and then click Open.**

   You may first need to change drives or folders to find the database you want.

   The File Type dialog box may appear. If it does, select dBASE/ASCII from the list to confirm the file type, and click OK.

   The Import dialog box appears.

6. **Click the Entire File radio button and then click OK.**

   The Mail Merge Assistant dialog box reappears with the Step 1 icon checked off.

7. **Follow Steps 10 through 16 of the first set of steps in the section "Creating a form letter from scratch," earlier in this chapter.**

The Envelope, Please

Obviously, Word Pro enables you to write letters. (Duh!) You can write individual letters or use Word Pro's merge capabilities to write dozens of letters. And, of course, letters need envelopes. You may be accustomed to addressing envelopes by hand or using an old-fashioned typewriter (there's that T word again) because properly formatting and printing an envelope with some word processors and printers is such a hassle. Well, no more! Word Pro handles envelopes like a real pro, so you can, too.

If you need to create an individual envelope, just follow these simple steps:

1. **Start by opening the letter document for which you need an envelope.**

   Actually, you don't have to start with a letter; you could start with a blank document on-screen if you want. However, if your letter contains the recipient's name and address, Word Pro can get the address information from the letter, which means that you won't have to retype it for the envelope.

2. **Select the recipient's name and address in the heading of the letter.**

   This step isn't always necessary. If you don't select the address from the letter, Word Pro automatically selects it for you. However, Word Pro isn't always successful at finding the correct address in your letter. Selecting the name and address manually ensures that the correct information is available for use on the envelope.

3. Choose Create⇨Envelope.

Word Pro adds a page to your document, formats that page as an envelope, and displays the Envelope bar just below the SmartIcon palettes near the top of the Word Pro window. (See Figure 7-7.) If you selected an address before creating the envelope, or if Word Pro was able to identify an address in your letter, that address appears automatically on the envelope.

4. Click the Return Address button in the Envelope toolbar to open the Return Address dialog box, shown in Figure 7-8.

Surprise! Your return address is already listed in the Return Address dialog box — or at least it is if you filled in the information that Word Pro requested on the Personal tab of the Word Pro Preferences dialog box that appeared when you started the program.

5. Select a return address from the Available Return Addresses drop-down list and click OK to close the dialog box and add the return address to the envelope.

Word Pro keeps track of the return addresses that you use frequently on your envelopes. If the return address that you want to use isn't listed, type the address in the Current Return Address field and type a name for that address in the Available Return Addresses box. Then click the Add To List button to add the new address to the list so that it will be available the next time you create an envelope.

Figure 7-7:
Word Pro provides a special toolbar to make working with envelopes easy.

Figure 7-8:
Word Pro
remembers
return
addresses
for future
use.

6. **If necessary, repeat Steps 4 and 5 for the Send To address.**

If you don't plan to use a return address or a Send To address again, you don't need to go through the respective Envelope toolbar buttons and dialog boxes to enter the addresses on the envelope. You can simply click the return address or Send To address areas of the envelope (indicated by margin lines) and type the address directly into the text boxes you find at those locations.

7. **When your envelope is complete, click Print to open the Print dialog box. Adjust the settings in the dialog box if necessary and then click Print to print the envelope.**

Make sure that your printer is ready with the envelope properly inserted and prepared to print before you click the Print button.

8. **Click Done to close the Envelope toolbar and return to your letter document.**

After you create an envelope, it remains a part of your letter document and becomes an extra page tacked on at the end. If you need to reprint the letter in the future, you won't have to re-create the envelope.

If you used Word Pro's merge capabilities to create a bunch of letters from a merge database, you can use the same data file to address the envelopes for your mailing. Simply choose Text➪Merge➪Envelope and work through the steps in the Mail Merge Assistant dialog box. The process is nearly identical to the procedure for creating a merge letter, except that an envelope doesn't require nearly as much text as a letter, so the envelope is usually easier to set up.

Becoming a Dictator

Just imagine being able to dictate to your computer and having it transcribe your words into text. You speak your thoughts into a microphone and watch as your words magically appear on-screen in a word processor document. Sounds great, huh? If you don't type very well or you suffer from repetitive stress injuries from typing way too much, this dictation capability lets you use your voice rather than your fingers to enter text into your computer.

The futuristic capability of dictating text with your voice instead of typing it on the keyboard is exactly the capability that voice-recognition software promises to deliver. Voice-recognition capability is now an add-on feature of Word Pro. And, guess what? It works — sort of. Actually, it works reasonably well, provided that your computer is powerful enough to get the job done and you're willing to spend the time to properly set up the voice-recognition software to recognize your voice.

Working via voice

Word Pro alone isn't capable of transcribing text from your voice input. For that, it needs the help of the IBM ViaVoice voice-recognition software. A special version of ViaVoice, designed to integrate with Word Pro, is included with SmartSuite Millennium Edition. However, although ViaVoice comes with SmartSuite, it's a separate program and is *not* installed as part of the default SmartSuite installation. If you want to use Word Pro with ViaVoice, you must install the ViaVoice add-on software separately.

Do you have what it takes to run ViaVoice?

Voice-recognition is a very difficult task for a computer, so a program like ViaVoice requires a fairly powerful computer. If you plan to use ViaVoice, your computer must meet at least the following specifications:

- 150 MHz Pentium processor with MMX (or faster)
- 32 MB RAM (48MB for Windows NT)
- 125MB hard disk space
- A good-quality sound card (Creative Labs SoundBlaster 16 or compatible)
- A CD-ROM drive
- A good-quality noise-canceling microphone
- Windows 95 or 98 (or Windows NT 4.0)
- Word Pro already installed

Notice that these requirements are considerably more stringent than the requirements for the rest of the SmartSuite programs. Also remember that these are just the minimum specifications. To get the kind of speed and performance that makes dictation a practical alternative to typing, you need a faster computer (at least a 200 or 233 MHz Pentium) and more RAM (say 64 MB). The microphone is a critical component of the voice-recognition system. A desktop microphone, or one that clips to your monitor, simply won't do, because they pick up too much background noise. You need a headset-style unit that allows you to position the microphone close to your mouth, and you must be very careful to wear the microphone in precisely the same position each time you use it.

Installing the ViaVoice software

ViaVoice is a separate add-on program, so it isn't installed along with the rest of the SmartSuite programs. A dialog box appears at the end of the regular SmartSuite installation to give you the option of installing ViaVoice and a couple of other add-ons. However, if you didn't take advantage of that option when you first installed SmartSuite, going through the entire SmartSuite installation just to get to that dialog box isn't really practical.

If you want to add ViaVoice to an existing SmartSuite installation, the simplest way to do it is to insert the SmartSuite CD in your CD-ROM drive, click the Start button in the Windows taskbar, and choose Run to open the Run dialog box. Type **x:\Extra\ViaVoice\Setup.exe** in the Open box (substitute the letter of your CD-ROM drive for x:) and then click OK to start the ViaVoice installation program. From there, you simply follow the on-screen instructions. The ViaVoice installation process seems a little disjointed because it's actually installing a couple of separate components, but you'll be fine if you just go along with what the installation program suggests. The one exception to the "go along" rule is the new-user enrollment. You can do the enrollment later (and we explain how in the next section of this chapter); you aren't required to complete a new-user enrollment when you install ViaVoice.

Enrolling as a ViaVoice user

Before ViaVoice can do a decent job of taking dictation, you must first teach the program how to understand your spoken words. But don't worry, because you don't have to teach ViaVoice the entire English language from scratch. The program already knows how to recognize normal speech. It just needs to learn the peculiarities of your voice and speech patterns. (But ViaVoice's recognition accuracy will be very poor until it does.) This learning process is called *enrollment*.

You can do your initial new-user enrollment with ViaVoice when you install the program, or you can do it later, but you *must* do it. It's a good idea to get the enrollment chore out of the way before you start using ViaVoice in Word Pro for the first time. The new-user enrollment process takes about one hour, and sitting and reading aloud to the computer can be tedious. But you need to think of that time as an investment in the software that will pay off later in the convenience of being able to dictate text into Word Pro.

If you didn't do the new-user enrollment during installation, you can start the process by opening the Windows Start menu, choosing Programs↔ IBM ViaVoice↔Tools↔Microphone Setup, and following the on-screen instructions to set up your microphone and adjust its volume. After you finish that, you can begin the enrollment process by choosing Start↔Programs↔ IBM ViaVoice↔Tools↔Enrollment. Select your name from the list in the IBM ViaVoice Enrollment dialog box and click Enroll. In the next dialog box, select First Enrollment and click Start. Then follow the instructions on-screen to give the program a sample of your voice by reading the words and paragraphs as the computer prompts you.

After the first 50 paragraphs, ViaVoice pauses to analyze those speech samples. The analysis may take several minutes, and you have the option to exit the enrollment process and start using ViaVoice when the analysis is done. Resist the temptation to abandon the enrollment at the first opportunity. Continue the process by reading the remaining 215 paragraphs. Completing the entire enrollment process is necessary to give ViaVoice enough speech samples to accurately recognize the words you speak during dictation. By the way, be prepared for the tongue twisters near the middle of the enrollment process. Be careful to speak distinctly, but as naturally as possible, when you read them. (Stumbling and stammering is normal. Just stop and then restart the sentence if you fumble too badly.)

It's important to conduct the ViaVoice enrollment in the same conditions you'll be in when you're dictating. Obviously, your microphone and other equipment setup should be the same, but also pay careful attention to room noises such as fans and office machines because they can make a significant difference, too. Also, if your voice changes (such as when you have a head cold), you need to redo the enrollment to teach ViaVoice how to recognize your new voice.

Word Pro, take a letter

After you install ViaVoice and go through the lengthy enrollment process, you're finally ready to actually use ViaVoice to dictate text into Word Pro. The fun part — at last!

Normally, you don't have to do anything special to start ViaVoice. After you've installed the program, it starts automatically when you start Word Pro and open a document. (If ViaVoice doesn't start automatically, you can start the program by choosing Dictation↔Start ViaVoice.) The only extra thing you must do is be patient because the ViaVoice program takes a while to load. When ViaVoice is ready to run, you see the ViaVoice toolbar at the top of the screen (as shown in Figure 7-9), and a voice welcomes you to the program. Yes, ViaVoice speaks to *you*. Isn't that too cute?

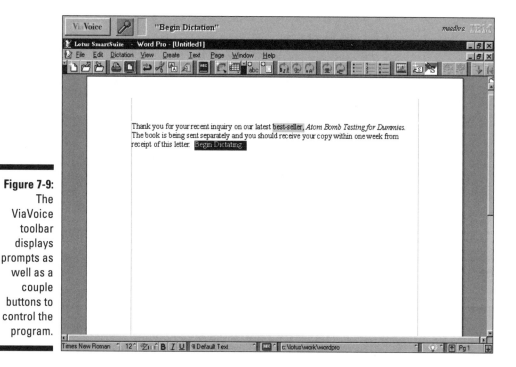

Dictating text

Dictating text into a Word Pro document using ViaVoice is really a simple and straightforward process, as the following steps illustrate:

1. **Click your Word Pro document to move the text insertion point to the location where you want to insert the text you will dictate.**

2. **Make sure that the microphone is turned on and then say, "Begin dictation."**

   The microphone button in the ViaVoice toolbar turns green to indicate that the microphone is on and ready to accept dictation. Clicking the button turns the microphone on or off.

   When you give ViaVoice the "Begin dictation" voice command, the program's voice responds by saying "Begin dictating," and Begin dictating text appears in your document.

3. **Begin dictating — speaking the words that you want to appear in your document.**

ViaVoice is a continuous speech dictation program, which means that you can speak naturally, in complete phrases and sentences, when you are dictating. You don't need to pause between each word. Speak clearly and distinctly, but don't exaggerate the enunciation of your words. Be sure to pronounce all punctuation marks such as comma, period, and question mark. To start a new paragraph, simply say "new paragraph."

As you dictate, ViaVoice transcribes your words and inserts them into your Word Pro document. However, the words don't appear immediately after you say them. You may notice a delay of several seconds while ViaVoice analyzes your speech and converts it into text. If you pause in the middle of a sentence, ViaVoice often does not display the last few words you spoke until you begin speaking again. If ViaVoice makes a mistake and mistypes something you said, just keep dictating. You can correct the errors later.

4. **When you're through dictating, say, "Stop dictation."**

The program voice acknowledges your command, and ViaVoice switches out of dictation mode — meaning that it no longer transcribes everything you say nor inserts the text into your Word Pro document. When it's not in dictation mode, ViaVoice ignores anything you say except the command to begin dictation and a few other control commands. (Say "What can I say?" to have the program display a list of those commands.)

While you're dictating, you can't use the normal mouse and keyboard controls in Word Pro. As soon as you stop dictating, Word Pro returns to normal, and your mouse and keyboard function as usual.

That's not what I said

Have you ever misunderstood what someone said to you? Of course you have. It happens a lot. Well, sometimes ViaVoice misunderstands what you say when you're dictating. So you need a way to correct errors, and ViaVoice obliges. Just follow these steps to correct your dictation errors:

1. **When you find an error in the dictated text, select the word or phrase by dragging the mouse pointer across it while holding down the left mouse button.**

You cannot edit or correct text while you are dictating. Finish dictating first, exit dictation mode, and then go back and make any necessary corrections to the dictated text.

2. **Right-click the selected text and choose** <u>C</u>**orrect Error from the pop-up menu that appears.**

ViaVoice responds by opening a small correction box similar to the one shown in Figure 7-10.

Figure 7-10:
The
ViaVoice
correction
box lets you
correct
dictation
errors.

3. **Select the correct word from the list at the bottom of the box, or type the correct word in the text box at the top of the correction box and then click OK.**

ViaVoice responds by replacing the selected text with the correction. The correction box also allows you to delete the selected word or click Options to display a cascading menu of formatting commands such as Capitalize, Lowercase, Uppercase, Numeric, and Spell Out.

As you correct dictation errors by selecting words from the list in the correction box or typing corrections in the text box at the top of the correction box, ViaVoice learns from those errors and uses that information to update its vocabulary and to improve recognition accuracy in the future. If you use the formatting commands in the correction box to change the capitalization of a word or change a number from numeric to spelled-out form, that doesn't change the information in the ViaVoice vocabulary.

If you're looking over your dictated text and you find some words or phrases that ViaVoice recognized correctly but that you want to change, be sure to use the normal Word Pro editing techniques to make the change. In that case, you should *not* use the ViaVoice correction box to make the changes because then the program would try to learn to match the wrong text to the words you spoke. Future recognition accuracy would suffer.

Read that back to me

ViaVoice not only converts speech into text but also converts text into speech. As a result, you really can have ViaVoice read something back to you.

ViaVoice can "read" text in two different ways. The first form of reading isn't really a text-to-speech conversion at all — it's simply a playback of your own speech that ViaVoice recorded while you were dictating. You can select a passage of text that you dictated and then choose Dictation⇨Playback to instruct ViaVoice to play the recorded speech. This comes in handy when ViaVoice has misrecognized some text and you don't remember exactly what you said. What better way to jog your memory than to check the words that came out of your own mouth?

The second form of reading is a true text-to-speech conversion. You simply select a passage of text and choose Dictation⇨Begin Reading. ViaVoice opens a small window containing an animated face and begins sounding out the words in the text selection using a synthesized voice. This text-to-speech conversion capability could be a real boon to users with vision difficulties and may also be useful for applications such as proofreading.

Getting Help for ViaVoice operations

As you may notice, even though ViaVoice is a separate program, it has its own menu in Word Pro. One of the commands that you'll want to check out on that menu is Dictation⇨Help Topics. Choosing this command opens a standard Help window similar to the ones in the SmartSuite programs and most other Windows programs, except that the help topics concern ViaVoice operations.

Closing ViaVoice

Just as ViaVoice starts automatically when you start Word Pro and open a document, ViaVoice closes automatically when you exit Word Pro. However, you don't have to exit Word Pro to close ViaVoice. If you want to continue using Word Pro and you know that you're not going to need ViaVoice for a while, you can shut down the ViaVoice program by choosing Dictation⇨ Stop ViaVoice. ViaVoice takes a while to load, and it takes a while to exit the program as well. Just be patient. Word Pro will be unencumbered shortly.

Part III
Spreadsheets As Easy As, Well — 1-2-3!

The 5th Wave   By Rich Tennant

"NIFTY CHART, FRANK, BUT NOT ENTIRELY NECESSARY."

In this part . . .

Time to put away your abacus. Whether you're scared
or excited by the prospect of diving into the numbers-
oriented world of spreadsheets, this part should allay
your fears and heighten your excitement. Get ready to
discover what all the spreadsheet fuss is about. These
chapters describe what spreadsheets are good for and
how they can make your life easier — or at least less
dependent on your pocket calculator. And, thank goodness, you don't need an MBA to put 1-2-3 to work. In fact,
if you understand fourth-grade math (or know some
patient fourth-graders who can help you), you're all set.

Chapter 8

Boot Camp for 1-2-3 (a.k.a. Basic Training by the Numbers)

· ·

In This Chapter

▶ Understanding spreadsheets

▶ Starting 1-2-3 by various methods

▶ Navigating in 1-2-3

▶ Entering data into a worksheet

▶ Copying data

▶ Calculating with formulas

▶ Assigning names to ranges of cells

▶ Printing

· ·

Are you tired of scribbling numbers on scraps of paper and then finding that not enough light is left for your solar calculator to calculate? If you're ready to move from that trusty old pocket calculator to the brave new world of computer number crunching, you should find this transition as easy as 1-2-3. NOT! But never fear. Although Lotus 1-2-3 may not be quite as easy as . . . er, well, 1-2-3, we intend in this part to make finding your way through the thicket of spreadsheet technobabble as painless as possible. So relax. After all, we haven't lied to you yet, have we?

Hey, Sarge, What's a Spreadsheet?

Spreadsheet. To the nontechnophile, the term may conjure up images of freshly washed bed linens drying on a clothesline or perhaps a bed turned back, all comfy and inviting. Well, computer spreadsheet programs aren't nearly so romantic. They are, however, more practical if you want to put a bunch of numbers and text in neat rows and columns. Spreadsheets can even calculate the numbers and turn them into dazzling charts and graphs.

Lotus 1-2-3 is rooted in laziness

Laziness is oft said to be the true mother of invention. This adage was proven correct again in 1978, when a couple of Harvard Business School students, Dan Bricklin and Bob Frankston, with too much homework and too little time (what with all their parties and carousing and all), decided to put their new-fangled personal computers to work to ease their burdens.

Most of their homework time was spent recalculating all the formulas in huge financial models as assumptions changed. Even with pocket calculators, the job was tedious and time-consuming. Perhaps, they reasoned, they could write some software to turn their computers into big ol' calculators. Yeah, they thought, *that's* the ticket! So the two created the first spreadsheet, called *VisiCalc*, which was short for "visible calculator." Most computer historians credit VisiCalc with starting the personal computer revolution (or at least kicking it into high gear).

A few years later, one of Dan and Bob's employees, Mitch Kapor — who had created a graphics program to work with VisiCalc, called VisiTrend/Plot (you gotta love that name) — decided to go off and start his own software company. The company . . . Lotus. The product . . . 1-2-3. And that's how the story all began. . . .

Think of a spreadsheet as the electronic equivalent of an accountant's ledger paper — the stuff with the grid lines that help line up all the rows and columns of numbers. And 1-2-3 enables you to create multiple worksheets in a file, so using the program is like having a whole ledger book (which 1-2-3 calls a *workbook*) in one file.

An electronic workbook actually contains thousands of rows and columns. If you just *must* know the nitty-gritty details, each spreadsheet page in a Lotus 1-2-3 workbook has a total of 65,536 rows and 230 columns, and a workbook can contain up to 255 worksheets.

By the way, even though the terms *spreadsheet* and *worksheet* are often used interchangeably, *spreadsheet* usually refers to the computer program, and *worksheet* refers to the actual document you create by using the spreadsheet program. Clear? Well, sorta?

Okay, we hear you asking: "But what are these spreadsheet things really good for? You know, for *humans,* not you techno-dweebs." All right, the following are just a few examples of what spreadsheets such as 1-2-3 are commonly used for:

✔ **Creating budgets.** This use is probably the most common spreadsheet task. Whether you're putting together a household budget that reflects some reasonable facsimile of reality (and that you can actually stick to this time) or a multiyear budget for a multibillion dollar, multinational corporation, a spreadsheet makes its creation easy. Well, at least a spreadsheet makes entering and calculating the numbers easy. Picking the *right* numbers . . . that's another matter.

✓ **Figuring out loan payments (or how long you're going to need to pay off that loan).** With 1-2-3's financial functions, tasks such as this one are a piece of cake.

✓ **Creating financial statements.** You can bet that 1-2-3 doesn't look like an accountant's ledger for nothing. (Or does it . . .?) You can create any sort of financial statement or accounting document that you can imagine. Even if you can't imagine one, 1-2-3 can probably create it anyway.

✓ **Performing statistical analyses.** You can use 1-2-3 to find, for example, the average, maximum, and minimum price for a gallon of gas.

Although 1-2-3 can create and manage lists of data, such as to-do lists, lists of appointments, and so on, you are usually better off turning to more specialized database tools for these types of tasks. Fortunately, you have two terrific database tools available to you right here in SmartSuite Millennium Edition: Approach and Organizer, which are covered in later parts of the book. You also soon discover that 1-2-3 provides a dizzying variety of options for turning your numbers into persuasive charts and graphs (also known as *pictures*). A picture is, after all, worth a thousand words (in the immortal words of someone or other). But keep in mind that SmartSuite also includes Freelance Graphics, which is specifically designed for creating charts. Explore both tools before deciding which tool is better for a particular job.

Starting 1-2-3

Wouldn't life be easy if you had only one way to start 1-2-3? No such luck. As with just about everything else in SmartSuite, you have myriad ways to kick off 1-2-3. The good news is that starting 1-2-3 works just the same as does starting any of the other SmartSuite programs. Following are a few options for bringing 1-2-3 to life:

✓ If SuiteStart is running, click the 1-2-3 icon in the taskbar's system tray. The icon is easy to spot — it's the one that reads 1-2-3 (of course).

✓ If SmartCenter is running, open the SmartSuite drawer by clicking the drawer front, click the Lotus Applications folder, and then double-click the 1-2-3 icon. If neither SuiteStart nor SmartCenter is running — why the heck not? Check out Chapter 2 for details on getting SmartCenter running.

✓ Click the Start button in the Windows 95 taskbar, point to Programs, point to Lotus SmartSuite, and then choose Lotus 1-2-3.

Friendly ol' 1-2-3 starts and greets you with the Welcome to 1-2-3 dialog box (unless you previously told 1-2-3 not to bother you with the welcome stuff anymore). From here, you get to make another choice. (Oh boy! *More* choices, you mumble sarcastically.) You get to decide whether to create a new workbook or work on an existing workbook file. The dialog box displays several recently used files (if someone has been sleeping in your bed, er . . . using your copy of 1-2-3 before). To open one of them, simply click the filename and then click OK. To open a file that isn't on the list, click the Browse For More Workbooks button to open the Browse dialog box, from which you can locate a file anywhere on your disk or network.

To start creating a new worksheet, just click the Create A New Workbook Using A SmartMaster tab to have 1-2-3 display the next page of the dialog box containing — you guessed it! — still more choices (see Figure 8-1).

Figure 8-1:
The
Welcome to
1-2-3 dialog
box with a
SmartMaster
highlighted.

To create a plain worksheet, you can take a shortcut and just click the Create A Blank Workbook button. To create a worksheet based on a SmartMaster template, such as the Loan Amortization SmartMaster, click the SmartMaster you want in the SmartMaster Templates list and then click OK. SmartMasters are great, by the way, and come complete with all the formulas and formatting already in place; all you need to do is supply the numbers, and you end up with a completed worksheet in no time.

You can skip the Welcome to 1-2-3 dialog box if you want. If you decide to bypass the Welcome dialog box, 1-2-3 whisks you straight to a new 1-2-3 workbook. To disable the Welcome to 1-2-3 dialog box, choose File⇨ User Setup⇨1-2-3 Preferences to open the 1-2-3 Preferences dialog box. In the Other Options list of the General tab, click the Show Welcome Dialog item (so that the option's *not* checked) and then click OK.

After you wade through these choices, you reach the initial 1-2-3 screen. Unless you chose to create a worksheet based on a SmartMaster, the 1-2-3 window contains a blank worksheet just waiting for you to fill it in, as shown in Figure 8-2. The worksheet includes the following elements:

- ✔ The area of the window containing all the cells is called the *Worksheet window*.

- ✔ The worksheet is made up of vertical *columns* (which are lettered A, B, C, and so on) and horizontal *rows* (which are numbered 1, 2, 3, and so on).

- ✔ The intersection of a column and a row is called a *cell*. Cells are where you enter information — numbers, text, and formulas.

- ✔ The *Selection Indicator* displays the address of the current cell (the one that the cell pointer is on). A cell's *address* is its column letter followed by its row number (which is explained in detail in the "Correctly addressing 1-2-3" section later in this chapter). For example, the cell in the first row of column A is cell A1.

- ✔ The *cell pointer* is the rectangle that surrounds the current cell.

- ✔ The *Navigator button* enables you to move to a named range or other named object in a file. A *named range* is simply a group of cells to which you assign a more meaningful name. *Objects* are items such as charts or graphics.

- ✔ The *@Function Selector* enables you to insert one of 1-2-3's zillions of functions. *Functions* are predefined procedures for various types of calculations.

- ✔ The *Edit line* shows the contents — if any — of the current cell (the one surrounded by the cell pointer, remember?).

- ✔ The *Worksheet tab* shows which worksheet you're currently working with. If you see multiple worksheet tabs, you have multiple worksheets in the workbook file.

The menus, SmartIcons, and scroll bars all work the same as these features do in the other SmartSuite programs.

If you need more details about SmartIcons, check out Chapter 1.

If you aren't sure what a particular SmartIcon button does, just point to the icon briefly with the mouse pointer (without clicking) to display the button's Bubble Help description.

┌Cell pointer
┌Worksheet tab
┌Selection Indicator   @Function Selector button
┌SmartIcon   Navigator button   Mouse pointer   Columns   Edit line   Worksheet window ┐

Figure 8-2:
The initial
1-2-3
screen with
a blank
worksheet
awaiting
your input.

└Status bar
└Rows

Scroll bars ┘

Classic, dude

Some people just don't want to do things the new way. New Coke bombed, classic cars are all the rage, and classical music (not to mention classic rock) remains as popular as ever. If you like doing things the old (comfortable?) way and you're familiar with an older, DOS version of 1-2-3, you may be pleased to know

that you can use 1-2-3 just as though nothing's changed — almost.

Just press the slash key (/) to display the Classic 1-2-3 menu. These menus are just like the ones in 1-2-3 Release 3.1 for DOS. If your 1-2-3 experience takes you back even farther than

3.1, you still find these menus remarkably similar to the menus in the very oldest releases.

We recommend that you not rely on the Classic menus too much or for too long. You're going to need to bite the bullet sometime and get up to speed with the Windows 95 and Windows 98 ways of doing things — the way all the other SmartSuite programs, as well as other Windows programs, work.

If you inadvertently summon the Classic menu and want to get out of the old thing, press the Esc key. If you find yourself knee-deep in Classic menus — several levels in — you can press Esc several times to get out or just press Ctrl+Break. The Break key is the one on your keyboard (usually near the top right somewhere) that has the words Pause and Break printed on it.

Getting Around

Before you can enter anything in your worksheet, you need to move the *cell pointer* to the cell into which you want to enter data. If the cell pointer is close to the cell you want to get to, moving to the target cell is simple; just click the cell that you want to go to or use the arrow keys to reposition the cell pointer. If the distances are greater, however, you may want to use more efficient alternative modes of transportation.

If you're creating a new worksheet and want to start working in the upper-left corner of the worksheet after starting 1-2-3, you don't need to go anywhere. You're already there. That's the default location of the cell pointer in a new, blank worksheet. After you start working with larger worksheets that span distances far greater than what you can see on a single screen, however, you need to know how to get from one location in the worksheet to another.

Correctly addressing 1-2-3

Even Carl Sagan may have trouble navigating the *bill*-ions and billions of cells in a 1-2-3 file. Okay, 1-2-3 files don't really have billions of cells, but they do have millions. And that's plenty mind-boggling for pea-brained authors such as us. Good news! Each cell has its own address to help you keep track of that particular cell. A cell's *address* is its column letter followed by its row number. So the address of the cell at the intersection of column C and row 12 is C12. Simple. When you go beyond 26 columns, 1-2-3 just adds another letter, as in AA, AB, AC, and so on. But wait! If you're using several worksheets in a workbook file, each cell address also includes the sheet letter followed by a colon. The sheets are lettered A, B, C, and so on. So the address of cell C12 in sheet D is D:C12.

If you use multiple worksheets in your workbook files, you can give them names that are more meaningful than the letters that 1-2-3 assigns them. (Gee, you'd be hard put to come up with *less* meaningful names.) Just double-click the sheet tab. 1-2-3 enlarges the tab and creates a text box where you can type the name you want to assign that sheet (and then press Enter). You can use up to 15 characters for each sheet name. After you assign a name to a worksheet, you can refer to that worksheet by either its name or its letter.

You don't need to worry about the sheet letter if you're working with a single-sheet workbook or just moving around in the current worksheet.

You can always figure out what the current cell or range is — and locate the cell pointer — by looking at the Selection Indicator area (at the left end of the line just below the menu bar). This area shows you either the worksheet name, the cell address, or the name of the range in which the cell pointer is located. (Range names are covered in the section "Naming Ranges," later in this chapter.)

Beam me up — or over

After you know where you want to go in a 1-2-3 file, getting there is a piece of cake. Our pal 1-2-3 provides a veritable plethora of navigation shortcuts for both keyboard peckers and mousers.

If you know the cell address or range name that you want to move to, you can use the Go To command or the Navigator button. Choose Edit⇨Go To (or press Ctrl+G) to display the Go To dialog box, shown in Figure 8-3.

To jump to a specific cell, just type its address in the text box below the Type Of Object drop-down list box and press Enter. If you have named ranges in your worksheet, these ranges are listed in the Names list box in the Go To dialog box. (We show you how to define named ranges later in this chapter.) You can double-click the one you want. 1-2-3 highlights the entire range and positions the cell pointer in the first cell of the range.

Figure 8-3:
The Go To
dialog box
enables you
to go to a
single cell
or a multi-
cell range.

The *Navigator button* is another quick way to move to and select a named range (or at least it will be a quick way to navigate around your worksheet after you create some named ranges). Click the Navigator button (located just to the right of the Selection Indicator area on the Edit line) to display a drop-down list of named ranges. Then click the named range that you want to select. 1-2-3 highlights the range and moves the cell pointer into the first cell of the range just as if you had chosen the range in the Go To dialog box.

For more random roaming, use scroll bars or one of the keyboard shortcuts, as described in the following list:

✔ Press the Tab key to move one screen to the right.

✔ Press Shift+Tab to move one screen to the left.

✔ Press Page Down to move down a screenful of rows.

✔ Press Page Up to move up a screenful of rows.

 Use the scroll bars to scroll vast distances. Using the scroll bars doesn't move the cell pointer, just the portion of the worksheet that's visible in the worksheet window.

 You can move to the beginning of a worksheet simply by tapping the Home key. If you want to move to the last cell containing data in the worksheet, press End, Home. (That's the End key followed by the Home key.)

Entering Labels and Values

Entering data into the cells of a worksheet is pretty straightforward. Just move the cell pointer to the desired location and start typing. Sound simple? It is.

Of course, 1-2-3 really understands only two kinds of information: *labels,* which are any sort of text entry, and *values,* which are any number or formula. Why the brain trust at Lotus came up with the terms *labels* and *values* instead of just calling these info types *text* and *numbers* is anybody's guess. You just have to deal with their terms.

Before you make a cell entry, 1-2-3 should be in *Ready mode,* meaning that the program isn't busy performing calculations. How can you tell that 1-2-3 is in Ready mode? Take a look at the *Mode indicator* at the right side of the status bar — that's down in the lower-right corner of the screen. If 1-2-3's in Ready mode, that's just how that area of the status bar reads (refer to Figure 8-2).

Just follow these easy steps for making any cell entry:

1. **Move the cell pointer to the cell into which you want to enter data by using any of the techniques described in the preceding section.**

   Make sure that the Mode indicator on the status bar tells you that 1-2-3 is in Ready mode. If the Mode indicator doesn't read Ready, clicking another cell or pressing the Enter key should solve the problem.

2. **Start typing whatever you want in the cell.**

   As soon as you start typing, the Mode indicator changes to either *Label mode* or *Value mode*, depending on the first letter of your entry. If your entry begins with a letter, 1-2-3 swings into Label mode. If your entry starts with a number or any character that could start a formula, 1-2-3 switches to Value mode. Formulas are covered in the section "Doing the Math — the Formula for Calculating in 1-2-3," later in this chapter.

3. **Confirm the entry by pressing Enter or moving the cell pointer to another cell.**

   If you decide that you don't want your new cell entry after all, you can instead press the Esc key.

After making a cell entry, remember that you can easily replace the cell's contents by creating another entry right over the unwanted one. If you just want to blast a cell's contents out of existence, however, press Delete. Poof! (But make sure that your cell pointer is in the cell that contains what you want to delete before you make the entry go poof.)

The instant you start typing, whatever was in the cell vanishes. Omigosh! You can avert disaster by pressing Esc before confirming the new entry. If you're too late for that and you haven't made another entry since confirming the new one, choose Edit⇨Undo, or just click the Undo SmartIcon — the one that looks like a couple of curved arrows. (Remember that you can locate the SmartIcon you're looking for by reading the icon descriptions in the little balloons that appear after you position the mouse pointer over them.)

After making some entries, you may notice that your labels start at the left edge of the cell and expand to the right, while values start out at the right and expand to the left. Nope, you didn't do anything wrong — those Lotus wizards just decided that most folks would want their labels left-aligned and their values right-aligned. The alignment for both labels and values can be changed, of course. The steps for changing alignment are spelled out in Chapter 9.

Don't worry if some of your entries seem to be chopped off in the middle. The entries didn't really change; they are all still right where you typed them. This abbreviated appearance is just something 1-2-3 does with entries if the program can't fit an entry in the cell. Chapter 9 gives you the lowdown on formatting your worksheets, including how to adjust column widths to make everything in a cell fit like a glove.

Makin' Copies

Most of what you discovered about copying (and moving) data in Word Pro applies to 1-2-3. (Check out Chapter 4 for more information.)

In addition to the basic stuff, 1-2-3 actually adds intelligence to some of its copy procedures. (They don't call the thing *Smart*Suite for nuthin'.) If you type **January** in cell B1, for example, you probably don't want to put *January* in C1, D1, and E1. Sure would be great if 1-2-3 knew that you wanted *February, March,* and *April* in those other cells. Well, guess what? The program does just that. Yippee!

To get 1-2-3 to do its smart copying, position the mouse pointer in the lower-right corner of the cell you want to copy. You know the pointer's in the right spot if it has two little extra arrows pointing down and two more pointing to the right. After you see these arrows, you can drag down, to the right, or both.

Drag down to increment down the column, or drag to the right to increment across the row. (*Incrementing* just means increasing the cell value by a specified amount.) If you enter **Monday** in a cell, for example, incrementing enters Tuesday, Wednesday, Thursday, and so on in the succeeding cells. You can make 1-2-3 increment numbers and days of the week as well as months.

Copying *formulas,* however, is an entirely different animal. Check out how to perform this action in the section "Copying formulas," later in this chapter.

Doing the Math — the Formula for Calculating in 1-2-3

If you view 1-2-3 as a really expensive pocket calculator — except that the program doesn't fit in your pocket — you're partly correct. Math is at the heart of 1-2-3. If not for its math capabilities, 1-2-3 wouldn't have much of a reason to exist. Oh sure, you can do zillions of things with 1-2-3 that don't involve those nasty, nerve-wracking calculations. But you know that their number-crunching capabilities are what make spreadsheet programs sizzle.

Unfortunately, 1-2-3 can't read your mind. So you must tell the program what numbers you want to crunch and how you want to crunch those numbers. You perform this task by entering a *formula* into a particular cell. A formula is nothing more than a mathematical equation that usually uses cell addresses — for example, B5 + B6 or B5 – B2.

Suppose that you want to find the answer to the burning question "What is 2 × 2?" You can go to any cell and type **2*2**. (The asterisk is the symbol for multiplication in 1-2-3.) As soon as you confirm the cell entry, 1-2-3 dutifully answers 4. Cool! And typing **4/2** (4 divided by 2) returns the answer 2. For addition and subtraction, you use the plain old plus and minus signs (+ and –).

By the way, after 1-2-3 completes its calculations, the answers appear in the cell that contains the formula. If you enter a formula in cell B3, the answer appears in B3. (The formula appears in the Edit line in case you need to refer to it or edit the formula.)

As swell as 1-2-3's capability to perform these math tricks is, its real math power comes from its capability to reference other cells in the worksheet that contain values. So, instead of entering **2*2** in a cell, you can enter a formula in cell B5 that multiplies B3 times B4. That way, if you change the values in B3 or B4, the result in B5 (the formula cell) is automatically updated.

This formula may come in handy, for example, in a weekly report worksheet that figures out how much money your company made in the sale of various products. Suppose that you sold eight items for $50 each. If you multiplied 8 by $50, you'd get the correct answer, but the formula would change every week based on which items you sold. If the formula referred to the cells that contain the quantity and the price, however, you'd always have the correct answer no matter how often you changed the numbers.

To create a formula in B5 that multiplies B3 by B4, follow these steps:

1. **Move to cell B5 and type + (the plus sign).**

   As far as 1-2-3 is concerned, formulas are just regular old values. If you start by typing B3, 1-2-3 thinks you are entering a label instead of a value. Starting with the + puts 1-2-3 in Value mode. Actually, you can use any mathematical operation symbol. Starting with = (the equals sign) works just as well and might even be easier to remember — especially if you've ever tried to use another spreadsheet program.

2. **Type B3 or click cell B3.**

   Clicking cells as references is often easier than typing the cell names. When you click a cell while entering a formula, the pointer changes to an arrow pointing to a box to indicate that you are building a formula and not selecting a new cell to work in.

3. **Type * (the asterisk).**

4. **Type B4 or click cell B4.**

5. **Press Enter.**

   The result of the formula instantly appears in B5. The formula in the *Contents area* of the Edit line should appear as follows: +B3*B4. The Contents area is on the Edit line — which itself is just below the menu bar — to the right of the buttons.

Because of the way 1-2-3 normally displays information, you can't see which cells contain formulas and which contain only numbers. The Contents area of the Edit line is the giveaway. If the cell pointer is positioned on a cell containing a formula, the Edit line displays the formula in all its gory . . . er, *glorious* detail.

If you want 1-2-3 to indicate which cells contain formulas, you can tell the program to display a small dot in the lower-left corner of those cells. Choose <u>V</u>iew⇨Set View <u>P</u>references to open the Workbook Properties dialog box. On the View tab, select the Formula Markers check box and click OK.

While you're looking for dots in cells, you may notice a small red dot in the upper-left corner of a cell. That indicates that someone attached a comment to the cell. You can use comments to make notes about your assumptions, the source of your numbers, or anything you like. To create a comment, right-click the cell and choose Cell Comment from the pop-up menu that appears. This action opens the Range Properties InfoBox with the Comment tab selected. Just type your comment into the Cell Comment text box and then click the Close button to close the InfoBox. 1-2-3 marks the cell with a red dot to indicate that this cell now has a comment attached. To read a comment, open the InfoBox just like you did to create the comment in the first place.

Be very careful not to delete cells that contain formulas — doing so can really ruin your day. (If you do accidentally wipe out a formula, click the Undo button before doing anything else. The day is saved.)

Entering formulas incorrectly is all too easy (for us, at least), so proofreading your worksheet to see whether the numbers make sense is very important. If you have a formula that should be multiplying 5 by 100 and the answer you get is 48,673, something is obviously wrong.

Copying formulas

If you're going to use the same formula to calculate several different values in your spreadsheet, you don't need to keep typing that formula over and over. Instead, just copy your formula from one cell to another.

The procedure for copying formulas is generally the same as for copying any other sort of data. If you copy formulas, however, 1-2-3 understands that you normally want the copies to be relative to their new location.

Suppose, for example, that the numbers in B3 are the number of hours your employees worked last month and that the numbers in B4 are their wages in dollars per hour. The formula in B5 to calculate how much the employees earned is +B3*B4. If you copy the formula to cell C5, you want it to change to +C3*C4. Good news. That's exactly what 1-2-3 does.

Yes, 1-2-3 uses *relative referencing,* so as you copy a formula, 1-2-3 copies the *logic* of the formula rather than the formula itself. The logic that 1-2-3 uses as you copy +B3*B4 from B5 to C5 is "Multiply the contents of the cell two rows up by the contents of the cell one row up." (Pretty logical, huh?)

Attaining functional literacy

Four-function math got you down? Having a hard time using addition, subtraction, multiplication, and division to create formulas for statistical analysis? Looking for easier ways to get the answers you need from your worksheet data? Feeling tired, irritable, and frustrated? Take heart — 1-2-3 *functions* can solve most of your problems. We know that we don't feel as tired, irritable, and frustrated since we started using functions.

Our friend 1-2-3 provides *functions* to solve virtually any math or data problem you can imagine. Functions are like preconstructed formulas that you can use simply by inserting their names into a cell in your worksheet. Want to find an investment's internal rate of return or future value? Use a function. Want to find the largest or smallest value in a range? Well, 1-2-3 has functions for that, too. Functions even exist for simple little things such as adding up a range of cells.

The reason to use functions instead of creating your own formulas is to make your life easier. We know that some folks like doing things the hard way. Not us. If an easier way is available, let us at it.

To use a function, start by typing the *at* symbol (@). Then type the function name — for example, **SUM**. Don't put a space between @ and the function name. Finally, in parentheses, enter the values, *operators* (the math symbols), and cell references that you want the function to work on. (All the stuff in parentheses is called the function's *arguments*.) You use two periods to separate the first and last cell addresses. For example, the formula to calculate the sum of the values in cells A1 through A9 would be @SUM(A1..A9).

Better yet, you can just click the @ button on the Edit line (the @Function Selector button, remember?) to open a drop-down list of some of the more common 1-2-3 functions. If the function you need isn't in the list, click List All to display the @Function List dialog box, shown in Figure 8-4. Just select All @functions from the Category list, select the function you want from the @Functions list, and that function appears on the Edit line. Look, Ma, no typing!

Figure 8-4:
The
@Function
List dialog
box enables
you to scroll
through
a zillion
functions.

The All @functions list is a long list. If you select a more limited category, such as Financial or Engineering, from the Category list box, you don't need to wade through so many @Functions to find the one you want.

Suppose, for example, that you want to find the average value of a range of cells. One of 1-2-3's functions is @AVG, which finds averages (what else?). To create a formula by using @AVG, follow these steps:

1. **Click the cell that is to contain the formula (the one in which the answer is to appear).**

 2. **Click the @Function Selector button on the Edit line to display the list of common functions and then click AVG in the list.**

   @AVG(list) appears in the formula cell and on the contents portion of the Edit line with the list placeholder highlighted. The range of cells for which you want to average the contents replaces the word "list" after the formula is completed.

3. **Point to the first cell in the range that you want to average, press and hold the left mouse button, and then drag until the entire range is selected.**

   The first and last cell addresses of the range, separated by two periods, replace the word list in the parentheses. If the range is C3 through C22, for example, the formula appears as @AVG(C3..C22).

The two dots between the first and last cells of a range indicate that all the cells from the first to the last are included.

4. Press Enter to complete the formula using the @AVG function.

The answer appears instantly in the cell you clicked in Step 1.

If you need additional help with a particular function's usage and *syntax* (its correct construction), the function Help screens are particularly useful. Suppose that you want to use the @AVG function to find the average value in a range, but you don't know exactly how to use this function. Just type **@AVG** in a cell and press F1. An @Function Help screen appears to enlighten you, as shown in Figure 8-5.

If the functions on the @Function Selector list aren't the ones you normally use, you can modify the choices to suit you. Click the Menu button in the @Function List dialog box to expand the dialog box to include additional buttons and list boxes. In the @Functions list, click the function that you want to add to the @Functions Selector button menu, and then click the >> (Add) button. To remove a function, click the function in the Current menu list, and then click the << (Remove) button.

That's SUM function

Creating a formula to add a row or column of numbers is easy enough. You want to add B2 and B3? No sweat. The formula is +B2+B3. But if you're working with a long column of numbers (a couple of dozen numbers or so), building the formula required to add each of those cells individually becomes tedious.

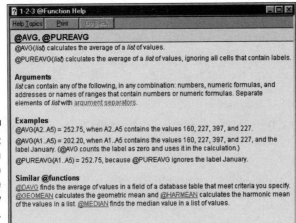

Figure 8-5:
@Function Help screens are actually helpful.

The easy way around this mess is to use the SUM function. In fact, 1-2-3 makes using the SUM function completely automatic. Just move the cell pointer to the cell directly below a column of numbers that you want to sum or to the right of a row of cells that you want to sum, and click the SUM SmartIcon button — the one that appears to be adding 1+2. (The button's description, seen in the Bubble Help description after you pause the mouse pointer on the SmartIcon, is Sum Values Above or to the Left.) That's all you do! Using the SUM function can be just that easy. (If you use the SUM SmartIcon in a cell where you have numbers in the column above and also in the row to the left, 1-2-3 assumes that you want to sum the column, and it ignores the row.)

Look at the Contents area of the Edit line to see that the function is entered just as though you typed the thing yourself.

One situation in which you may *not* want to use the SUM SmartIcon to enter the SUM function automatically is when the range you want to sum isn't adjacent to the formula cell — the cell where you want the answer to appear. In that case, you can enter the @SUM function manually, just as you can any other function, by typing the @SUM function into the formula cell and entering the range of cells that you want to sum between the parentheses.

 Here's a slick way to enter @SUM functions even more easily. Go to the blank cell at the bottom of a column of numbers (or several adjacent columns of numbers) and then move one cell to the left. Type **Total** into that cell and press Enter. Magically, 1-2-3 sums each column of numbers for you. Can you beat that? Sometimes 1-2-3 can read your mind. Oh, by the way, the same trick works with rows of numbers. The cells where the sums appear must be to the right of the numbers and must start out blank, and the word *Total* goes in the cell above.

Naming Ranges

Assigning names can make finding portions of a large worksheet much easier. Figuring out where your budget's 1999 income area is located, for example, is a whole lot easier if the section of the worksheet is called *Income 99* instead of *F22 through J43*.

To assign a range name, follow these steps:

1. **Select the range of cells that you want to name by dragging the mouse over them while holding down the left mouse button.**

   The address of the range is displayed in the Selection area of the Edit line.

2. **With the mouse pointer anywhere in the selected range, right-click to display the selection's pop-up menu and choose Name.**

   The Name dialog box appears, displaying any range names that are already assigned.

3. **Type a name (up to 15 characters) for the selected range and then click OK.**

You can use the Navigator button to jump to a named range. Click the Navigator button on the Edit line and then click the range name you want to go to in the list that 1-2-3 opens. You see the entire range selected.

In using functions, you usually find that named ranges are far easier to use and far more understandable than are ordinary cell references. If the cells containing your company's 1999 income are in the range F22 through J43, for example, you could name the range Income 99. (Hmmm, where have we heard that before . . . ?) Then, instead of a hard-to-understand formula such as @SUM(F22..J43), you could simply use @SUM(Income 99).

Printing Your Worksheet

Prognosticators have been hailing the coming paperless office for years. Is the great event here yet? We don't think so. And until it arrives, you need to get your worksheets on paper.

To print a worksheet, make sure that your printer is turned on, is online, and has paper loaded. Then follow these steps:

1. **Click the Print Preview SmartIcon button or choose File⇨Preview & Page Setup.**

   1-2-3 opens a Print Preview window beside the window containing your worksheet. The Preview & Page Setup InfoBox also appears, as shown in Figure 8-6.

   Now the fun begins.

2. **Change the options in the various tabs of the InfoBox and edit your worksheet as desired.**

   You see those changes reflected instantly in the Print Preview window.

3. **After the Print Preview looks the way you want, click the Print SmartIcon or choose File⇨Print.**

   The Print dialog box appears.

Figure 8-6:
The 1-2-3
Print
Preview
window is
interactive.

4. **Click the Current Sheet, Entire Workbook, or Selected Range radio button.**

   The Selected Range option makes sense only if you selected a range before opening the Print dialog box.

5. **Click Print.**

   Your masterpiece should start spewing from your printer momentarily.

You find more information on 1-2-3 printing options in the next couple of chapters.

Chapter 9

I Feel Pretty (Adding Style to Your Worksheet)

*D*ahling, you look mahvelous! If that's not the reaction your 1-2-3 worksheets are getting, time to get with the program. You can pour hours of blood, sweat, and tears into creating an accurate and informative worksheet, but if the thing doesn't *look* good, who cares? Who's even going to read your masterpiece? Not us. Figure 9-1 shows a dull, drab, unformatted worksheet. Pretty uninspiring, huh? Figure 9-2, however, is the same worksheet with some nifty formatting added. Ah, that's better.

Figure 9-1:
An icky old unformatted worksheet that wouldn't even get a CPA excited.

Figure 9-2:
Wow! The same worksheet with pizzazz! What a difference a bit of formatting can make.

	January	February	March	Totals
Classes	16500	17800	18300	$52,600
Textbook Sales	4500	5000	5500	$15,000
Total Income	**21000**	**22800**	**23800**	**$67,600**
Rent	1400	1400	1400	**$4,200**
Salaries	3500	3500	3500	**$10,500**
Materials	1100	1250	1300	**$3,650**
Total Expenses	**$6,000**	**$6,150**	**$6,200**	**$18,350**

Changing various formatting attributes (how text and numbers are displayed) can change a dull, lifeless worksheet into a powerful persuader. And persuasion, after all, is often what worksheets are designed for. You want your boss to approve your budget proposals, and a beautiful worksheet gives the boss the impression that you gave your work more thought. You *did* give the budget work *some* thought, didn't you?

Formatting Numbers

Why can't 1-2-3 just leave my numbers the way I enter them? Seems to me that, if I enter **300.50**, that's just how the number should look in the cell. But noooooo! Headstrong 1-2-3 decides that I don't really need that last zero and drops the extra digit — without even asking! And suppose I enter **1,000,000,000**. Well, 1-2-3 changes *that* to $1.0E+009$. What's 1-2-3 up to? Generally speaking, the problem is *General formatting*.

Unless instructed otherwise, 1-2-3 uses its General formatting rules to mess up... er, display your numeric entries. Trailing decimal places that don't fit in the column are arbitrarily discarded as cavalierly as a recruit's hair at Marine boot camp. Numbers that are too big to fit in the column are changed to the indecipherable *Scientific Notation (Exponential) format,* such as $1.2E+008$. Ouch! Our brains hurt from even looking at numbers formatted like that.

Contrary to what you may be thinking, General formatting's mission isn't to mess up your worksheets but to try to make big numbers fit in little columns. Ignoring leading and trailing zeros, dropping trailing decimal places that don't fit, converting huge numbers to scientific notation — all of these tricks are among 1-2-3's efforts to make big numbers fit into narrow columns. And 1-2-3's default column width is only nine characters. Without 1-2-3's heroic measures to scrunch your numbers, you'd often have to take heroic measures of your own just to keep your numbers visible.

If you're worried about how all this number scrunching may affect calculations, don't give the idea a second thought. No matter how your numbers are formatted, 1-2-3 stores the actual number. Formatting affects only how the numbers appear on your computer screen.

If you don't want General formatting to make decisions for you, be specific. Either enter numbers in a way that enables 1-2-3 to figure out your formatting intention (see the next section, "Formatting automatically — sometimes"), or choose the number formatting you want, as discussed in the section "Changing number formats," later in this chapter.

Formatting automatically — sometimes

Now, 1-2-3 really does have *some* smarts in the area of formatting numbers. The program tries to figure out by the way you enter your numbers how you really want those numbers to look. If you enter **$100.00**, for example, 1-2-3 automatically applies the *U.S. Dollar format* so that the number appears exactly the way you entered it. 1-2-3 even retains the dollar formatting if you enter a different number in the cell. Enter **200** in the cell, and the number's formatted as $200.00.

So how far do the 1-2-3 mind-reading powers go? The following are some examples of numbers on which 1-2-3 can perform its automatic formatting wizardry:

✔ **Numbers with comma separators.** Enter **1,000** and 1-2-3 applies the comma format and displays the number just as you entered it.

✔ **Numbers entered as percentages with a percent sign.** These are formatted as percents. Enter **10%** and that's just what 1-2-3 displays. (Of course, 1-2-3 records the value as 0.1.)

✔ **Numbers entered as dates.** You can enter dates by using just about any of the 1-2-3 date formats. All the following are acceptable date formats: April 22, 1998; 22-Apr-98; 22-Apr; Apr-98; and 4/22/98. Well, 1-2-3 alters some of these entries just a bit. For example, 4/22/98 is formatted as 04/22/98. You can enter the years as two-digit numbers (such as 98 for 1998) or as four-digit numbers (1998). Just be forewarned that 1-2-3 uses the sliding window rule, which we explain in Chapter 3, to interpret any two-digit year you enter. 1-2-3 assumes that any two-digit year is in the 100-year span starting 80 years before the current year and extending 19 years into the future. For years outside that range, you must use four-digit years.

 ✔ **Numbers entered as times.** As with dates, you can enter times in a variety of formats: 1:42, 1:42 PM, 13:42, and just about any other time format that makes sense are acceptable to 1-2-3.

If you're concerned about the actual number that 1-2-3 stores, place the cell pointer in the cell in question and take a gander at the Edit line. The real number — the one that 1-2-3 uses for calculations — appears there. For example, 1-2-3 stores 1,000.00 as 1000 and stores 10% as 0.1.

Dates and times are the exceptions to the previous rule. If you format dates and times as dates and times, that's how they appear on the Edit line as well as in the cells. 1-2-3, however, stores dates and times as serial numbers. For dates, the numbers represent the number of days after January 1, 1900. For example, 1/1/98 automatically appears in the cell *and on the Edit line* as 01/01/98. The number that 1-2-3 actually uses for calculations, however, is 35796 — 35,796 days past January 1, 1900.

After 1-2-3 automatically changes the formatting of a cell or range of cells, the name of the new formatting style appears in the Number format button in the middle of the status bar.

Some date formats just don't work at all. For example, 12/6 looks like 12 divided by 6 to 1-2-3. If you use the slash (/) in dates, make sure that you include the month, day, *and year* so that 1-2-3 doesn't get confused. After you format a cell as a date, however, you can safely enter 12/6 without 1-2-3 arguing about whether the thing's a date or a division formula. Also, remember that 1-2-3 interprets two-digit years as being in the 80/20 sliding window, so be sure to use four-digit years for the years outside that range.

Changing number formats

So now you know what 1-2-3 does with your numeric entries. But what if you're tired of 1-2-3 pushing you around, and you want to change the formatting of one or more cells? No problem. To change number formatting, follow these steps:

1. **Move the cell pointer to the cell you want to format, or select the range you want to format.**

2. **Click the Number Format button in the middle of the status bar.**

   A pop-up list of number formats appears, as shown in Figure 9-3.

3. **In the pop-up list, click the number format that you want to use.**

   1-2-3 instantly formats the contents of the cell or range with the style you select.

Figure 9-3:
All the number formats are visible in the status bar's pop-up Format list.

4. **If the number format is one that enables you to choose the number of decimal places, click the Decimal button in the status bar (the box just to the right of the Number format button) and choose a number from 0 to 15.**

The Decimal button is available only if you choose a number format that supports decimals (Comma, or a currency format, for example). Otherwise, the button appears as a blank box.

Another way to change number formats is by right-clicking the selection and choosing Range Properties from the pop-up menu that appears. The Range Properties InfoBox appears. Click the Number Format (#) tab and then select a format from the list boxes. The worksheet changes immediately to reflect your selections. The status bar method is faster, however, so why bother with the dialog box?

Line 'em Up: Aligning Your Cell Entries

You've probably figured out by now that text entries align to the left edge of the cell and number entries align to the right. Why? To quote Tevye in *Fiddler on the Roof,* "Tradition." That's the way the alignment was done in the very first spreadsheet — VisiCalc — so that *must* be the right way to set up alignments.

Don't be a slave to convention. Be bold and daring. No real reason exists to keep text and numbers in their default alignment. In fact, more often than not, having text and numbers more in alignment with each other makes more sense, stylistically speaking. You have no right or wrong way to align your entries. Just do what looks best.

To align the contents of a cell or range of cells to the left, right, or center, the easiest way is to use another of those slick little status bar buttons. The *Alignment button* (the third button to the right of the Number format button) gives you a choice of five standard alignments: left, right, centered, evenly spaced, and the default left-aligned text with right-aligned numbers.

If you want to get a little fancier and experiment with some of the other alignment possibilities, however, right-click the selected cells and choose Range Properties from the pop-up menu. This action opens the Range Properties InfoBox. Click the Alignment tab and make your choices from the options shown in Figure 9-4. (For some really wild effects, check out the options in the Orientation drop-down list box.)

Figure 9-4:
The
Alignment
tab of the
Range
Properties
InfoBox.

Figure 9-5 shows examples of some of the more — and less — popular alignment options. The following paragraphs describe a few of the more — and less — useful alignment options.

Figure 9-5:
Alignment
chaos.

Centering a label entry across several columns is a snap if you use the Align Across Columns check box on the Alignment tab of the Range Properties InfoBox. Suppose that you want to center an entry in row 1 of columns A through D. Make the entry in A1 and then select A1 through D1. Right-click the selection and choose Range Properties to open the InfoBox, and then click the Alignment tab. Then click the Center alignment option button and the Align Across Columns check box and — *voilà!*

To make a multiword cell entry that spills into the next column fit into its own column, click the Wrap Text In Cell check box in the Alignment tab of the InfoBox. The row height adjusts to accommodate the text. (Using the Wrap Text In Cell option is a much easier way to enter column headings than is entering each word in its own row.)

Sometimes, *rotating* a cell entry provides just the effect you need. To change the orientation of a cell's contents, choose one of the options in the Orientation drop-down list on the Alignment tab of the InfoBox. If, for example, you choose the Angled Orientation option, another drop-down list box appears, from which you can specify the number of degrees of rotation or accept the default 45-degree angle.

The Evenly Spaced option, found in both the Alignment selector on the Status Bar and the Alignment tab of the InfoBox, enables you to spread out all the letters of an entry so that the letters are evenly spaced across the cell. (Seems like kind of a dumb idea to us, but you can use that option if you really want.)

Using Fonts to Spruce Things Up

Nothing does more to add pizzazz to your worksheet and ensure that your readers perceive your work the way you intended than using the right fonts. (A *font,* if you don't know by now, is a typeface in a particular size. We discuss fonts in more detail in Chapter 5.)

To change fonts, select the cell or range of cells to which you want to apply the new font and then right-click the selected cells; choose Range Properties from the pop-up menu that appears. After the Range Properties InfoBox appears, click the Font, Attribute, and Color tab, as shown in Figure 9-6.

You can also choose fonts from the Font and Point Size buttons at the left end of the status bar. The Font button displays the name of the typeface — such as Arial or Times New Roman — in the active cell. The Point Size button displays a number — such as 10 or 12 — indicating the size of the font. Using the InfoBox is a better method, however, because all the font selection options are right there together — you don't need to keep opening selector menus to try different combinations of fonts, sizes, and attributes.

Figure 9-6:
The Font,
Attribute,
and Color
tab of the
Range
Properties
InfoBox.

Click the name of the font you want in the Font Name list of the Range Properties InfoBox and then select a point size from the Size list. If you like, you can also apply attributes from the Attributes list and select a color from the Text Color drop-down list.

The status bar includes buttons for the **bold,** *italic,* and <u>underline</u> attributes. To apply any of these attributes, select the cell or range to which you want to apply the attribute and then click the appropriate button. You can reverse an attribute by clicking the button again. If, for example, you click the Bold button to make a cell's contents bold, you can "unbold" the contents by clicking the Bold button again.

You can also change the color of your font by clicking the Text Colors button (located between the Point size and Bold buttons) in the status bar and choosing the desired color from the color palette that appears. Remember, however, that your worksheet doesn't print in color unless you have a color printer.

Changing Column Widths and Row Heights

The 1-2-3 default column width is nine characters. That's a fine number to use as a default but is often too small to fit the wider entries you need to make and wastes space if you have a column of only one- or two-character entries. Fortunately, changing column widths is easier than changing your socks — and certainly easier than learning Swahili.

Although you can specify a new column width in characters, you can more easily make the change visually by dragging with the mouse. Just move the mouse pointer to the right border (next to the column letter) of the column

We are the world — so give global formatting a chance, man

If you know in advance that you want a particular font, color, number format, column width, or alignment for most of the entries in a worksheet, you can make your life easier by changing the default for these formatting options.

Choose Sheet⇨Sheet Properties from the menu bar to open the Sheet Properties InfoBox, and then specify the desired format changes you want to make on the various tabs. The changes that you enter here become the defaults for the entire worksheet.

for which you want to change the width. The mouse pointer assumes the shape of a double-headed horizontal arrow. Click and hold down the left mouse button. Drag right to increase or left to decrease the column's width. As you drag, a vertical guide line helps you see your new column width, and a small box pops up to display the number of (standard-width) characters that the column holds at that width. After you release the mouse button to set the new column width, all the columns to the right shift left or right to accommodate the revised column.

You rarely need to change row heights, because 1-2-3 automatically adjusts row heights to accommodate their contents. If you change to a larger-sized font or rotate the text in a cell, the row height increases to fit the font size.

If you do need to adjust a row's height for some reason, click the mouse pointer over the row border, just below the row number, so that the pointer assumes the shape of a double-headed vertical arrow. Hold down the left mouse button and drag down to increase row height or up to decrease row height. 1-2-3 moves all the rows below to make room. Simple, no?

If you want to change the column width of several columns at the same time, select the columns and perform the column-width changing procedure just described. Ta daaa! All the selected columns change to the new width. (You can select multiple columns simply by dragging the mouse over the column letters you want to select.) The same trick applies to adjusting the height of multiple rows.

If you feel that you simply must tell 1-2-3 in more precise terms how wide a column needs to be, right-click the column (or selected range of columns) that you want to change and choose Range Properties from the pop-up menu to open the Range Properties InfoBox. Click the Basics tab and, in the

Column area, click the Width radio button, and enter the number of characters your new column width can hold in the adjacent list box. The Basics tab also contains options for automatically adjusting the selected columns to fit the widest entry (the button beside the Width list box), resetting them to the worksheet default columns widths, hiding the column, and forcing a page break at the column, plus similar options for row heights.

A slick way to quickly adjust column widths to accommodate the largest entry, without resorting to the Range Properties InfoBox, is to double-click the mouse on the right border of the column, right next to the column letter. 1-2-3 adjusts the column width automatically. If you select multiple columns and double-click the right border of the columns, 1-2-3 automatically adjusts the width of all the selected columns.

Adding Lines, Borders, and Frames

The *grid lines* that normally appear on-screen help you see just where the cells are. Usually, you don't print the grid lines (although you can if you want). But 1-2-3 enables you to add all sorts of lines to your worksheet — and have plenty of control over how the lines look. Adding lines or borders can greatly enhance the appearance of your worksheet, as you can see in the example in Figure 9-7.

Figure 9-7:
Lines and
borders
can make
entries look
even more
important
than
they are.

	January	February	March	Totals
Classes	16500	17800	18300	52600
Textbook Sales	4500	5000	5500	15000
Total Income	21000	22800	23800	67600
Rent	1400	1400	1400	4200
Salaries	3500	3500	3500	10500
Materials	1100	1250	1300	3650
Total Expenses	6000	6150	6200	18350

To add lines, borders, or frames, follow these steps:

1. **Select the cell or range of cells that you want to format with lines, borders, or frames.**

   Remember that you select cells by dragging the mouse over them while holding down the left mouse button.

2. Right-click the selection and choose Range Properties from the pop-up menu to open the Range Properties InfoBox; then click the Color, Pattern, and Line Style tab.

The Color, Pattern, and Line Style tab of the Range Properties InfoBox is shown in Figure 9-8. By using the Border options, you can choose which sides of the selected cells get borders and the style and color of the border lines. You can fill a cell or range of cells with a color and/or pattern by making selections in the Interior area of the dialog box.

Figure 9-8:
The Color, Pattern, and Line Style tab of the Range Properties InfoBox gives you myriad options for changing your worksheet's appearance.

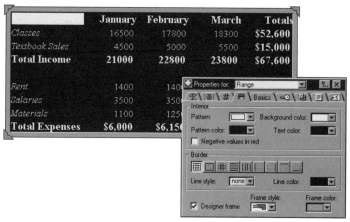

3. In the Border area, click the button to designate where to apply borders and, if you like, choose a Line Style and a Line Color from the drop-down palettes.

4. If you want to add a designer frame, click the Designer Frame check box and choose a Frame Style and Frame Color from the drop-down palettes.

You can see the effect of your selections immediately.

You can more easily determine what your lines, borders, and frames are going to look like on the printed page by getting rid of the grid lines that normally appear on-screen. To make these grid lines disappear, choose View➪Set View Preferences, click the View tab in the Workbook Properties dialog box, and then deselect the Grid Lines check box. This procedure affects only the display, not how the worksheet prints. If, on the other hand, you want to print the grid lines that you see on-screen, choose File➪Preview & Page Setup, click the Include tab in the Preview & Page Setup InfoBox, scroll down the Show list box, and click Sheet Grid Lines so that a check mark appears beside the option.

To remove lines from a selected range of cells, just select none in the Line Style drop-down list in the Border area of the Color, Pattern, and Line Style tab of the Range Properties InfoBox. And deselect the Designer Frame check box, too.

If the Line Style list box is blank in the Color, Pattern, and Line Style tab of the Range Properties InfoBox, the selected range contains mixed line types. In other words, the lines in the selection aren't consistent — for example, some may be single lines, and others may be double lines. You can still make a selection from the drop-down list if you want to override the previous settings for the entire selection.

Chapter 10

Charting Your Course

- -

In This Chapter

▶ Getting to know charts

▶ Creating quick charts

▶ Changing your charts

▶ Printing charts

▶ Choosing the best chart type for your purpose

- -

Explaining things and persuading others that you're headed in the right direction is usually easier if you chart your course. And because, as we all know by now, a picture is worth a thousand words (at least), using charts can make you seem that much more convincing. Of course, the idea that people with a lot to say must know what they're talking about is a given . . . right?

Figure 10-1 shows some dreary old sales numbers on the left side of the worksheet. Yawn. The same numbers, however, are represented by an attention-grabbing chart on the right side of the worksheet. See the difference?

Figure 10-1: Sleep-inducing numbers are magically transformed into a really cool chart.

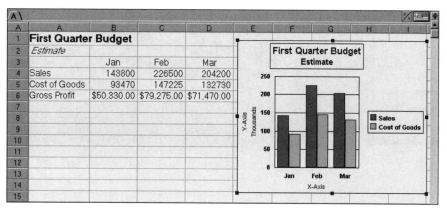

Chart Chat

Thankfully, 1-2-3 enables you to create gorgeous charts (or ugly ones, if you choose) to graphically represent the numbers in your worksheets. As with every other aspect of 1-2-3, you may find the vast number of charting options available to you somewhat overwhelming. But take heart — after you enter your data in a worksheet, creating a chart is just a matter of telling 1-2-3 which information you want to use, what type of chart you want, and where you want to put the chart. You don't even need to know much charting lingo to create charts, although familiarity with a few terms and what goes into a typical chart does help keep you on the right track. Check out Figure 10-2 to see the parts of a typical 1-2-3 chart.

All charts contain at least one data series. A *data series* is just a set of values for a particular category. Sales figures, for example, comprise one data series. The figures for the Cost of Goods are another data series. Each data series is represented on a chart by a line, a group of bars, a series of dots, or pie slices.

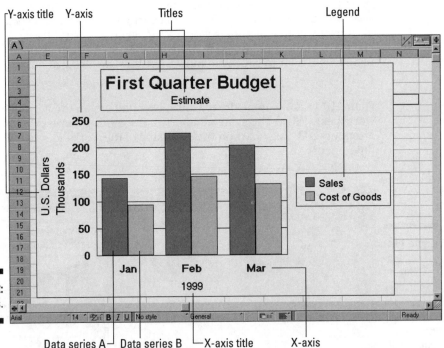

Figure 10-2:
Chart parts.

Most charts have an x-axis and a y-axis. Don't get freaked out by the terminology — the *x-axis* is the chart's horizontal plane, and the *y-axis* is the
vertical plane. (I hope that's plane . . . er, plain enough.) The way most data
is set up in a worksheet is that the x-axis (sometimes called the *category*
axis) plots the data series over time. The y-axis (sometimes called the *value*
axis) plots the amount of the numbers.

Keep in mind, too, the following points in considering charts:

✔ You can create 1-2-3 charts most easily if you enter your data in normal
table format, using contiguous rows and columns. Don't insert any
blank rows or columns into the table.

✔ Charts are based on numbers stored in your worksheet. If you change
any of those numbers, 1-2-3 automatically updates the chart to reflect
the new numbers.

✔ Although you have no practical limit to the number of data series you
can include in a 1-2-3 chart (well, okay, maybe a couple dozen), you're
better off keeping this number to a minimum to avoid creating a chart
that's chaotic and confusing. The practical minimum varies, too,
depending upon the chart type. A bar chart, such as the sample shown
in Figure 10-2, may start to look crowded with six or seven data series.
See the section "Choosing the Chart Type That Makes Your Point," later
in this chapter, for some insight into other chart types.

✔ 1-2-3 stores — and displays — your charts right on the worksheet. You
can have as many charts on your worksheet as good taste (or printer
memory) dictates. See the section "Printing Charts," later in this
chapter, for information on resolving printer problems.

✔ You can change, customize, and fiddle with every part of a chart until
its appearance suits you perfectly.

✔ You can use the data in 1-2-3 to create charts in other SmartSuite
programs, such as Freelance or Approach. You discover, as you explore
all the SmartSuite programs, that no one right program exists for
creating charts. (Chapter 3, however, provides some hints on how to
choose the right program for the job.)

Creating Charts the Quick and Dirty Way

Nothing is easier than creating a chart in 1-2-3. Okay, maybe getting someone else to provide the charts is easier, but we digress. Here are the steps
for creating a quick and dirty chart from the data in a worksheet. (You find
out how to clean up the chart in the section "Editing Charts," later in this
chapter.)

1. Select from your worksheet the data you want to chart.

The selection can include all the values and labels you want in your chart. In the example shown in Figure 10-3, we selected all the data in the worksheet. (Remember that you select cells by dragging the mouse over the cells while holding down the left mouse button. You can also select entire columns by clicking the column letter or select entire rows by clicking the row number.)

2. Click the Create a Chart SmartIcon — the one near the middle of the second palette of SmartIcons, displaying a picture of a bar chart; you can also choose Create⇨Chart.

After you click the Create a Chart SmartIcon, the mouse pointer turns into a crosshair pointer. The title bar displays the message Click Where You Want to Display the Chart.

If you click the Create a Chart button without first selecting the chart data, 1-2-3 displays the Chart Assistant dialog box, from which you can specify the data range and then continue to Step 3.

Figure 10-3:
After selecting the data, you need to define where you want the chart.

3. **Move the mouse pointer to the point in the worksheet where you want the location of the upper-left corner of the new chart, and then click the mouse button.**

   As soon as you click the mouse button, the new chart appears on-screen.

   If you don't want to use 1-2-3's default chart size, you can create the chart by dragging the mouse to specify the size of the chart. Just position the mouse where you want one corner of the chart, press and hold the left mouse button, and then drag diagonally until the outline is the desired size. After you release the mouse button, the chart appears. Cool!

Whenever 1-2-3 creates a default chart, the program makes the following assumptions — some of which may accidentally (er, actually) be correct:

✔ 1-2-3 always creates a bar chart. We describe how to change to other chart types in the section "Choosing the Chart Type That Makes Your Point," later in this chapter.

✔ 1-2-3 assumes that any text in the upper-left cells of the selected data is the chart title (or titles).

✔ 1-2-3 uses the first column for x-axis labels — if the column contains labels. If the first column contains values, 1-2-3 treats the contents of this column as chart data and inserts placeholders for the x-axis labels.

✔ 1-2-3 automatically figures out how large the y-axis needs to be to accommodate the values you're charting and adds labels, if necessary, to indicate the magnitude of these values.

✔ 1-2-3 inserts placeholder x-axis and y-axis titles, a legend, and a title.

As soon as 1-2-3 creates the chart, the program also selects the chart, and selection handles (those little black squares at the corners and in the middle of each side of the chart box) appear around the chart. You can manipulate the various elements of the chart by double-clicking the element and then making the appropriate choices in the InfoBox for that element's properties. (See the section "Editing Charts," later in the chapter, for more details.)

✔ After you (or 1-2-3) select a chart, the chart's name appears in the selection indicator (the left end of the Edit line). The default chart names are CHART 1, CHART 2, and so on. You can change the default name of a selected chart to something more meaningful. For example, for a pie chart comparing costs for your restaurant's hamburger ingredients, you may use the name *Cow Pie*. To change a chart name, double-click the chart background and click the Basics tab in the Chart Properties InfoBox. Then enter the new name in the Chart Name text box.

Identifying the chart background can be a little tricky. Basically, the background is anything inside the chart that isn't something else, such as a title, legend, plot area, bar, and so on. The tricky part is that the plot area of the chart is its own element and some other chart elements are bigger than you may think. The title, for example, usually encompasses a good-sized block of space above the plotting area, even though the text may not occupy all that space. Selecting the chart background, however, is not such a difficult issue. The pointer changes as it passes over the various chart elements (the pointer for the chart background is an arrowhead with a small black square), and clicking anywhere in the chart creates selection handles. If the handles appear around the title or some other element, instead of the entire chart, you know that you selected the wrong thing. If you do happen to double-click the wrong chart element and open its InfoBox instead of the Chart Properties InfoBox — no problem. Just select Chart from the drop-down list in the title bar of the InfoBox to display the correct set of options.

✔ Changing a chart's name (the one that appears in the Selection Indicator and on the Basics tab of the Chart Properties InfoBox) doesn't change the chart's title — just the name 1-2-3 uses to refer to the chart.

✔ Notice that, after you (or 1-2-3) select a chart, a Chart menu (which has commands for working with charts) replaces the Range menu (which includes commands for manipulating data ranges), and the default Chart SmartIcon palette replaces the default Worksheet palette.

Editing Charts

You soon discover that 1-2-3 gives you endless options for changing your charts. Charts consist of many elements that can be selected and manipulated individually. As a general rule, to manipulate a particular chart element, you can double-click the element to display an InfoBox relevant to that particular element. You can also right-click an element to display the object's pop-up menu and choose (Element) Properties from the menu to open the InfoBox, but double-clicking is faster and works on almost every chart element. (By the way, double-clicking some other frequently formatted objects in this, and other, SmartSuite programs opens the related InfoBox, but switching to text-editing mode is a more common result of double-clicking something.)

The following are some examples of chart elements that you can easily change:

✔ **Chart titles in the chart data range:** For the chart titles (the chart title and subtitle), 1-2-3 uses the contents of the labels in the upper-left cells of the chart data range. You can edit chart titles by editing the contents of those cells. As soon as you change the contents of the cells, the titles in the chart change.

✔ **Custom chart titles:** If you don't want to use the contents of the cells as the chart titles, you can edit the titles by double-clicking one of the chart titles to display the Title Properties InfoBox and then clicking the Options tab. Deselect the Cell check box next to the Line 1, Line 2, and Line 3 text boxes and then type new text into each of the text boxes. You can also have 1-2-3 use the contents of other cells for the titles by selecting the Cell check boxes and entering the appropriate cell addresses in the text boxes. Clicking the button that appears between the checked Cell check box and the text box for a title line enables you to select a cell simply by clicking that cell instead of typing the cell address into the text box.

✔ **Legends:** To change the text for the legend, you must do things just a bit differently. If you double-click the text of the legend, you open the Legend Properties InfoBox, in which you can control the positioning of the legend and the formatting of the text and such — but not the text of the legend itself. You need to double-click the color key box in the legend or one of the bars (or lines, or whatever) of the data series to open the Series Properties InfoBox to the Options tab. Near the bottom of this tab is where you find the Legend Label text box. Select the Cell check box and enter into the text box the cell address of the cell containing the legend text. Or you can deselect the Cell check box and type your new text for the legend into the text box.

✔ **Chart size and position:** You don't need to settle for the default chart size or the position you originally chose. You can select the chart and then just drag the entire chart to a new location. (Just make sure that you click and drag the chart background and not one of the chart elements, or you move the chart element instead of the chart.) You can resize the chart by first positioning the mouse pointer over one of the chart's corner selection handles so that the pointer turns into a four-headed arrow. Press the left mouse button and drag the mouse until the dotted box that appears is the desired size; then release the mouse button.

✔ **Deleting a chart:** To delete a chart, or any chart element, select the chart or element and press Delete. It's outta here!

Try double-clicking various chart elements to see what happens. You are likely to stumble upon all sorts of unexpected editing options. Sometimes just poking around — especially with visual objects such as charts — is the best way to learn. Explore. Have fun. (Really.)

Printing Charts

Great news! You don't need to know anything special to print charts. Because charts sit right on your worksheet, just include the chart in the range you want to print and let 'er rip. Check Chapter 8 for specific printing instructions.

If you want to print only the chart, select the chart and then choose File⇨Print. 1-2-3 automatically chooses the Selected Chart option button in the Print area of the Print dialog box. Just click the Print button, and the chart prints. Actually, you should make a habit of clicking Preview & Page Setup first to get an on-screen preview of how your chart will print. If you like what you see on the preview, go ahead and print it.

Of course, the beautiful color charts you see on-screen don't print in color unless you own a color printer.

Choosing the Chart Type
That Makes Your Point

Good ol' 1-2-3 enables you to create all kinds of different types of charts, from bar charts to pie charts to amazing 3D charts that really impress your boss. Changing the chart type is a snap. Just select the chart and then click the SmartIcon that displays the picture of the kind of chart you want. The default Chart SmartIcon palette includes buttons for some of the most popular chart types.

If you can't find a SmartIcon for the chart type you're thinking of, that doesn't mean 1-2-3 can't create that kind of chart. Just select the chart and click the Change Chart Type SmartIcon (the one with a picture of four chart types) to open the Chart Properties InfoBox with the Type tab displayed, as shown in Figure 10-4.

Figure 10-4:
The Type tab enables you to choose from 12 chart types.

You can choose a basic chart type from the Chart Type list on the left. Then you can select from a variety of styles within each chart type by clicking one of the option buttons for the chart type. The available options are represented by buttons on the right. Figure 10-4 shows the line chart styles.

As described earlier, the default chart type is a standard bar chart. You can, however, present your data by using any of about a zillion different chart types. Yes, 1-2-3 doesn't give you a mind-boggling variety of chart types just for fun. Sure they're a bunch of fun-loving guys and gals out there in Lotus land, but sometimes they do things for a reason.

In this case, the reason is that some chart types are better than others for presenting some types of data. This book isn't big enough to describe all the nuances of all the various chart types, but here are some basic rules of thumb for the common chart types:

- *Bar charts,* the 1-2-3 default chart type, often are used for comparing two or more related data series at a specific point in time or comparing a small amount of data over time. The bar chart works for the example back in Figure 10-1 because we were creating two data series (sales versus cost of goods) over time (a three-month period).

- *Pie charts* are great for displaying proportional relationships among data items, such as the share that each month's sales contributes to the sales for the quarter. Pie charts' primary limitation is that they can display only one data series, so a pie chart wouldn't work for the example in Figure 10-1.

- *Line charts* are used to emphasize the continuity of data over time. These charts are also a good choice for showing trends. They are especially useful for showing large sets of data, such as monthly sales of a product over a five-year period.

- *Area charts* are essentially line charts with the spaces between the lines filled in. You use area charts for the same kinds of data for which you use line charts. The only difference is aesthetic.

You can also choose among several mixed charts, which combine line and bar charts for data that could benefit from both chart types.

Many of the chart types, including several of the SmartIcon chart type options, are available in a 3D style. 3D just gives you a different look. Use 3D if you like it.

No hard and fast rules exist about which chart type is best to use in each situation. What we provide here are just general guidelines. Experiment to find the chart type that conveys your message the way that you — or your boss — want it conveyed.

Chapter 11
Final Touches and Shortcuts for 1-2-3

In This Chapter
▶ Using the 1-2-3 drawing tools
▶ Spell-checking your spreadsheet

As if doing calculations, formatting worksheets, and creating dazzling charts weren't enough, 1-2-3 packs enough other features into the program to make you think you may never discover everything 1-2-3 has to offer, let alone figure out how to use all its features. Relax! You don't *need* to know everything about 1-2-3 to use the program effectively. In fact, after you read this book's 1-2-3 chapters, you'll be able to accomplish great things with 1-2-3, but you can do scads more with 1-2-3 than we have room to cover in this book. This chapter introduces you to some of the niftier things hiding under 1-2-3's hood.

Enhancing Worksheets and Charts by Using the 1-2-3 Drawing Tools

Do you have a hankering to express your artistic creativity but don't think that a spreadsheet program is the best place to express yourself? Well, you're right. But you can still do some pretty fancy doodling in 1-2-3. In addition to all its standard spreadsheet text, number, formula, and charting capabilities, 1-2-3 includes a bunch of neat drawing tools to give you something to do if you don't want to concentrate on your real work — I mean, er, if you want to *enhance* your worksheets and charts. Yeah — that's the ticket! *Enhancement.* A wonderful concept. . . .

Figure 11-1 shows you just one example of some of the things you can do by using 1-2-3's drawing tools, even if you have no artistic talent whatsoever.

Almost all the major SmartSuite programs have pretty much the same drawing capabilities — and drawing in all those programs works pretty much the same way. So you don't need to use a specific SmartSuite program just to do some doodling. If you're in Word Pro, draw in Word Pro; if you're in Freelance Graphics, draw in Freelance. You get the idea. (Organizer, however, doesn't "do" drawings. I guess Lotus figures that, if you really want to get organized, you shouldn't be wasting your time doodling.)

Common SmartIcon palettes provide buttons for several of the more common drawing objects, including arrows, ellipses, and text blocks. These drawing SmartIcons are shown in Figure 11-1.

In addition, after you select any drawn object, 1-2-3 displays the default Arrange SmartIcon palette, which includes buttons for manipulating selected objects in the following ways:

Figure 11-1:
Aren't you just drawn to this stuff (ahem)?

✔ **Flipping objects.** To flip an object horizontally, click the Flip Selected Objects Left to Right SmartIcon. To flip an object vertically, click the Flip Selected Objects Top to Bottom SmartIcon.

 ✔ **Sending objects to the back or bringing them forward.** To bring selected objects forward so that they sit atop other objects that you may have drawn later, click the Bring Selected Objects to the Front SmartIcon. To send selected objects to the back, click the Send Selected Objects to the Back SmartIcon. Keep in mind that you can't send an object behind a cell's contents. All drawing objects float on top of the worksheet. You can only send objects behind other objects. On the left side of the worksheet shown in Figure 11-2, for example, notice that the ellipse is behind the rectangle. On the right side, the ellipse is in front of the rectangle.

 ✔ **Grouping or ungrouping selected objects.** To group selected objects so that you can size, move, and otherwise manipulate the objects as a group, click the Group or Ungroup Selected Objects SmartIcon. If you find that you need to manipulate one of the objects in a group independently, click the Group or Ungroup Selected Objects SmartIcon again to ungroup the objects for individual attention.

Figure 11-2:
Front-to-back and back-to-front placement of selected objects.

All the drawing tools that aren't available from the SmartIcon palettes are conveniently available from a secondary Drawing menu. Choose Create➪ Drawing to display this Drawing menu, as shown in Figure 11-3.

You can use all the drawing options to annotate and add emphasis to worksheet data and charts. You can also use these options to create your own drawings for any purpose you can imagine. Your options are limitless.

Figure 11-3:
Yet more
drawing
options are
available on
the Drawing
menu.

Moving and resizing objects

To move a drawn object (or a group of objects), click to select the object. (If the object you're trying to select is filled with a color or pattern, you can just click anywhere on the object to select it. However, for lines, arrows, hollow objects, and text boxes, you must click on the line for the edge of the object to select it.) Then position the mouse pointer over the object (but not over a sizing handle). After the pointer changes into a hand, you can drag the object to a new location on-screen.

To change the size of an object, you must first select that object. Then position the mouse pointer over one of the selection handles (after which the pointer changes into a double-headed or four-headed arrow) and drag the handle toward the center of the object to make the object smaller or drag away from the center to make the object larger. Dragging a corner handle changes both height and width. To change the size of the object proportionally, hold down the Shift key as you drag a corner handle. Dragging a side handle enables you to change the height or width of the object without affecting the other dimension. (Remember that the selection handles are those little squares that surround a selected object.)

Changing an object's attributes

You can also change a drawn object's attributes, such as line widths, interior patterns, and colors. You change these attributes in — you guessed it! — the Draw Object Properties InfoBox. You open this InfoBox by double-clicking the object, by right-clicking the object and choosing Drawing Properties from the pop-up menu, by selecting the object and choosing Drawing➪ Drawing Properties from the menu bar, or by pressing Alt+Enter. After the InfoBox opens, click the Color, Pattern, and Line Style tab to access the options shown in Figure 11-4.

Figure 11-4:
The Color, Pattern, and Line Style tab of the Draw Object Properties InfoBox for a text block.

The available options vary depending on the particular object you want to manipulate. If, for example, you select a text block (which you use to add to worksheets any text elements that you don't want to be constrained to a range of cells), you see the version of the Color, Pattern, and Line Style tab shown in Figure 11-4. This version includes options for designer frames, borders, interior patterns, and so on. If you select an arrow, you lose the borders and some other options on the Color, Pattern, and Line Style tab, but you gain options that enable you to put an arrowhead at either end of the line — or both ends — as shown in Figure 11-5. If you select a text object, the Draw Object Properties InfoBox includes a Font, Attribute, and Color tab and an Alignment tab as well.

Figure 11-5:
The Color, Pattern, and Line Style tab of the Draw Object Properties InfoBox for an arrow.

So why draw?

Some legitimate uses exist for using drawing tools in worksheets — not that playing around isn't legitimate, of course. One of the more common uses for spreadsheet drawings is to emphasize and call attention to the portions of the worksheet or chart to which you want the reader to pay special attention. You may, for example, draw an arrow to point to an important number or chart element. Figure 11-6 shows a chart on a worksheet with some drawing enhancements.

Be careful not to go overboard placing drawing objects on your worksheet. A few objects, tastefully placed, can enhance your message and help get your point across. Too many just add clutter and distract from your message.

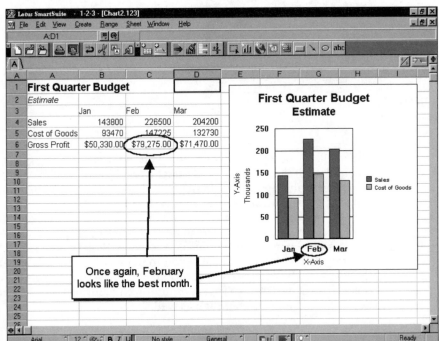

Figure 11-6:
Oh, so that's the point.

Using Spell Check

If you thought a spelling check was just for word processing, think again. If you read the preceding part of this book on Word Pro, you know how to use Spell Check to help rid your word-processing documents of misspellings and typos. The idea is for your readers to think that you know what you're talking about — that you actually put some thought into the document (and, of course, you *did* — right?). Well, having readers of your worksheets think you know what you're talking about with your figures and charts is just as important — and maybe more so. After all, if the boss thinks the worksheet is sloppy and therefore doesn't approve your budget proposal, you're sunk.

Fortunately, checking the spelling in 1-2-3 worksheets is just about as easy as checking spelling in word-processing documents. The only difference is that 1-2-3 doesn't highlight misspelled words for you before you start to check spelling, as Word Pro does (sigh). To start checking spelling in your worksheet, you must choose Edit⇨Check Spelling. The Check Spelling dialog box appears, as shown in Figure 11-7.

Figure 11-7:
1-2-3's
Check
Spelling
dialog box.

To begin checking all the worksheets in the entire file, make sure that you have Current Workbook selected in the dialog box's Look In drop-down list box, and then click Start. To check just the current worksheet, select Current Sheet in the drop-down list. You can also check a selected range or all linked workbooks.

After you begin spell-checking, you use the Check Spelling dialog box pretty much as you use the Spell Check bar in Word Pro. (See Chapters 1 and 6, respectively, for more information on using the SmartSuite Spell Check feature in general and for Word Pro.) Spell Check finds a misspelled word and offers suggested replacements. Then you click buttons to skip the word, skip all occurrences of the word, replace the word, replace all misspelled words automatically, or add the word to your user dictionary.

You may want to keep the following things in mind while spell-checking 1-2-3 worksheets:

- ✔ If you know you want to spell-check just a certain range, select that range before you open the Check Spelling dialog box. Then select Selected Range in the Look In drop-down list box.

- ✔ As discussed in Chapter 1, all the major SmartSuite programs share the same main and supplemental dictionaries. If you add words to the spelling dictionary in Word Pro, you don't need to add the same words again in 1-2-3. Check out Chapter 1 for more details on spell-checking.

Lots more stuff is available in 1-2-3 than we can possibly cover in this book. We hope that this part of the book provides enough information to get you started in the program. If you want to know more, however, check out *Lotus 1-2-3 Millennium Edition For Dummies,* by John Walkenbach (published by IDG Books Worldwide, Inc.).

Part IV

Caution — Database Approaching

The 5th Wave   By Rich Tennant

"I think the cursor's not moving, Mr. Dunt, because you've got your hand on the chalk board eraser and not the mouse."

In this part . . .

This truly is the information age. Trying to manage and keep up with the tons of information that companies — and even individuals — constantly accumulate is a Herculean task. Good news. By using Approach, you don't need to be Hercules to wrestle mountains of data into submission. If you possess just enough strength to tickle your computer keyboard's ivories (and, of course, the smarts to read this part), you can get your data under control in no time.

Chapter 12

Boot Camp for Approach

. . . .

In This Chapter

▶ What's a database (and why should I care)?

▶ The need for planning

▶ Getting started with Approach

▶ Putting data in

▶ Printing data out

▶ Custom-tailoring your own database

. . . .

*A*s part of your wonderful SmartSuite Millennium package, Lotus includes a database called Approach. Although Word Pro is great for writing letters to people you may not want to call and 1-2-3 is great for calculating future profits you may never see, Approach is handy for storing information you don't want to lose, such as a catalog of your used toothpick collection, an inventory of video tapes of people you're blackmailing, or profiles of corrupt politicians who owe you a favor.

Lotus Organizer (included in your SmartSuite Millennium package and discussed in Chapters 19 through 21) is also technically a database. Organizer is specifically designed for storing certain kinds of information, such as appointments, records of calls, and names and addresses. Approach, on the other hand, is better for creating custom databases to store more esoteric information. For example, Approach can store the names of all the wines stored in your wine cellar, credit card numbers of customers ordering products from you, financial values of all your business assets, or serial numbers of all the counterfeit money you've created by using your desktop publishing program.

Because you can design your own databases in Approach, it's a far more flexible, powerful, and (unfortunately) confusing program than Organizer.

Setting Up a Base Camp — Databases Defined

Telling you that Approach is a *database* is useless if you don't have the slightest clue what a database is. Even if you're not familiar with the idea of a computer database, you've probably used a paper database at one time or another. A telephone book, a restaurant menu, and a library card catalog are all examples of paper databases because they contain information that's useful to keep.

Approach is nothing more than a program to help you store information in your computer so that you can get it back out again. To give the illusion of organization, every Approach database consists of the following three parts (see Figure 12-1):

- ✔ Files
- ✔ Records
- ✔ Fields

Fields organize your information into categories, such as name, address, and telephone number. Records consist of one or more related fields. In a telephone book, each person's name, address, and telephone number together make up one record. Database files consist of one or more records. From a computer's point of view, a telephone book is considered a file.

Database file

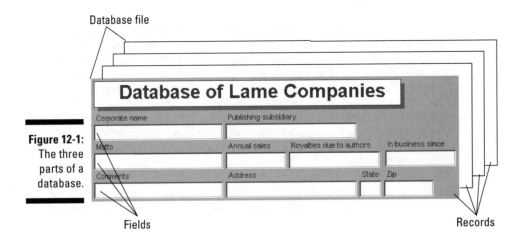

Figure 12-1:
The three parts of a database.

Fields

Records

Planning Your Database

You can just take information and dump the data into your database. Unfortunately, this approach is much like dumping your laundry on the floor and then wondering why finding a matching pair of socks takes so long. Before you can store any information in an Approach database, you must decide what type of information you want to store. Do you want to store names and addresses, telephone numbers and dates, or serial numbers and salaries?

No matter what you want to save, a database enables you to store a variety of information. For example, the Internal Revenue Service stores names and addresses of potential tax cheats (unless they're prominent politicians, of course); the Central Intelligence Agency stores personality profiles of suspected terrorists; and the National Security Agency stores signatures (specific noises) of Russian submarines.

To help you plan your database, try designing that database on paper first. If you want to create a database to track business contacts, for example, write down all the information you want to save, such as the person's name, company name, telephone number, e-mail address, and fax number. By first designing your database on paper, you can see how useful your completed database is going to be.

Starting Approach

Before you can store any information in an Approach database, you must start the program. Depending on how you like to use your computer, you can start Approach in any of the following ways:

- ✔ The simplest way to start Approach is to click its SuiteStart icon in the taskbar's system tray. The Approach icon has a blue diamond background behind what looks like an upright paper clip with a paper airplane glued to the front, giving the thing an A-shape. (If you put the cursor over this icon, you see a pop-up Help label that reads: *Lotus Approach*.)

- ✔ If SmartCenter is running, you can click the SmartSuite drawer to open the drawer, click the Lotus Applications folder, and then double-click the Lotus Approach icon. (If you need a refresher on working with SmartCenter, refer to Chapter 2.)

- ✔ The other (just slightly more complicated) way to start Approach is through the Windows Start menu. Just click the Start button, point to Programs, point to Lotus SmartSuite, and finally choose Lotus Approach from the cascading menus.

The moment you start Approach, the program displays a Welcome to Lotus Approach dialog box (see Figure 12-2). At this point, Approach is asking you: "Hey, do you want to use an existing database or create a new one of your own?" You can build a database from scratch, as explained in the section "Designing Your Own Database," later in this chapter. Approach, however, has a couple of ways to get you up and running in a database quickly: by loading an existing database or by creating a new database using a SmartMaster.

Figure 12-2:
The Welcome to Lotus Approach dialog box.

Loading an existing database

If you know you want to load an existing database rather than create a new database from scratch, you can perform the following steps:

1. **Click the Open An Existing Approach File tab in the Welcome to Lotus Approach dialog box.**

   A list of existing files appears on the left side of the dialog box. Of course, if this is the first time you are using Approach, the list will be empty unless someone has set up an existing database for you. After you create some databases of your own, they will be listed here.

2. **If the file you want to use appears in the list box, select the file and click OK.**

   If you want to use a different existing database file, click the Browse For More Files button to open the Open dialog box. Choose the database file you want to open from the list box, and click Open.

Creating a new database with a SmartMaster

If you don't have an existing database with which to work, Approach enables you to create a new database quite easily. Approach contains more than 50 different database templates — called SmartMasters — that you can use as the basis of a new database. The SmartMasters are predesigned databases, complete with all the fields and forms you need. All you need to do is enter your data. You can create a new database using a SmartMaster directly from the Welcome to Lotus Approach dialog box by following these steps:

1. **Click the Create A New File Using A SmartMaster tab.**

2. **Select from the list the SmartMaster that you want to use and click OK.**

   Approach provides both database templates and applications from which you can choose. (You can choose to list Applications or Templates in the SmartMaster Types drop-down list box.) Select either Applications or Templates and then select a SmartMaster. (Try the Customer Contacts SmartMaster if you're just exploring.) If you really insist on creating your own database from scratch, select Blank Database. A New dialog box appears.

3. **Type the name of your new database in the File Name text box and click Create.**

   Stick with the default setting in the Create Type drop-down list box unless you have a specific reason to change it. (The Create Type option is explained later in this chapter in the "Designing Your Own Database" section.) When you click Create, Approach creates the database and a data entry form for that database appears in the Approach window.

Getting to know Approach is easier if you start out working with an existing database or one based on a SmartMaster template. The Customers or Customer Contacts templates are good choices for your initial explorations, because these templates contain a variety of fields that nearly everyone can relate to.

Approach includes more than 50 SmartMaster templates and more than a dozen SmartMaster applications. Both templates and applications are predesigned databases that you use as the basis for new database files into which you add your own data. The difference between templates and applications is that applications have a slick point-and-click interface that guides you through your work with the database.

Entering Data

After you create a database file, Approach gives you two ways to enter data into a database file:

- ✔ In the Form view
- ✔ In the Worksheet view

Form view and *Worksheet view* are both generic terms. The specific forms and worksheets in your database might be labeled differently. For example, in a database based on the Customer SmartMaster, the default Form view is labeled Customers.

As you may expect, Form view mimics the appearance of an actual paper form. Form view enables you to see all the fields on the form at the same time (see Figure 12-3). The advantage of Form view is that this view enables you to see the field contents (the categories of information) for one record at a time.

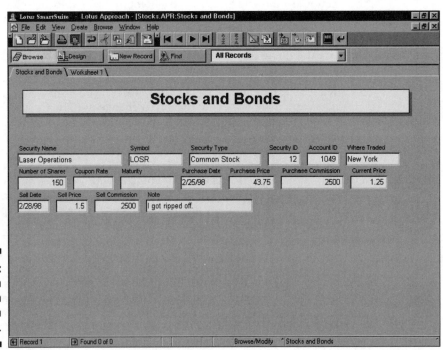

Figure 12-3:
The Form view of an Approach database.

Worksheet view, on the other hand, displays your fields as headings in a spreadsheet (see Figure 12-4). The Worksheet view arranges fields in columns, and each record appears on a separate row. The advantage of Worksheet view is that this view enables you to see a good chunk of the information stored in your entire database (although seeing the information that individual records contain is difficult).

To switch between Form and Worksheet views, just click the tab that appears in the upper-left corner of the screen. (Because you can create multiple views and give them different names, the trick is to remember what name you give each form and worksheet view so that you click the correct tab.)

To choose a field to enter data, Approach gives you the following two choices:

✔ Click the field in which you want to enter data.

✔ Press Tab or Shift+Tab until the cursor moves to the field in which you want to enter data.

Fields   Worksheet tab   Blank row

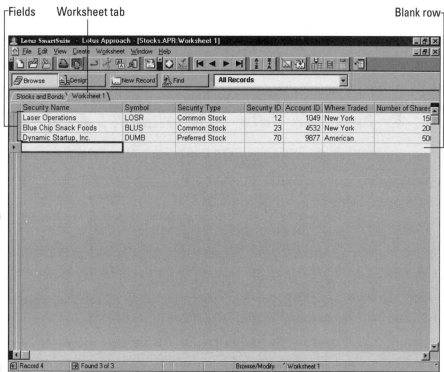

Figure 12-4:
A Worksheet view showing fields displayed as columns and records as rows.

Entering data in Form view

Form view is most convenient if you're entering data for the first time. To enter data in Form view, follow these steps:

1. **Click the Form tab of your worksheet (displayed in the upper-left corner) to switch to Form view.**

   Remember that the tab may be labeled with the name of the form instead of the word Form. For example, in Figures 12-3 and 12-4, the form tab is labeled Stocks and Bonds.

2. **Choose Browse⇨New Record from the menu bar, click the New Record button, or press Ctrl+N.**

   Approach creates an empty record.

3. **Click a field in the empty record and type the information you want to store.**

   Repeat this step as needed to fill in the form.

   If you prefer to keep your hands on the keyboard, you can move to the next field by pressing Tab instead of clicking the field with the mouse pointer.

4. **After you get to the last field on the form, press Tab.**

   Approach creates another empty record for you to fill.

Entering data in Worksheet view

Worksheet view is most convenient if you are editing data. To enter data in Worksheet view, follow these steps:

1. **Click the Worksheet tab to switch to Worksheet view.**

2. **Choose Worksheet⇨Records⇨New, click the New Record button, or press Ctrl+N.**

   Approach creates an empty record at the bottom of the worksheet. (If you have lots of data, you may need to scroll down to the bottom of the worksheet to see this empty record.)

3. **Click a field in the empty record and type the information you want to store.**

   Repeat this step as needed to fill in the record. You can move to the next field by clicking it with the mouse or by pressing Tab.

4. **After you get to the last field on the row, press Tab.**

   Approach creates another empty record.

Because Approach automatically creates a new, blank record after you complete data entry into the preceding row, you always have a blank row at the end of your database. That's normal. You don't need to worry about that empty record in your database.

Printing Your Database

After storing vital information in a database, you may want to print it so that you can view the entire database contents on paper. Approach enables you to print in either Form view or Worksheet view. (You can also create and print reports, but that's the topic of another chapter — Chapter 15 to be exact.) Before you print your database, you can save paper by using the Print Preview feature. If the preview looks good, you can print your database.

To see a preview of what your document is going to look like after you print the file, follow these steps:

1. **Click the Form tab to see what your forms are going to look like, or click the Worksheet tab to see what your worksheets are going to look like.**

 2. **Click the Print Preview SmartIcon (which looks like a piece of paper in a computer monitor), choose File⇨Print Preview, or press Ctrl+Shift+B.**

   Approach displays the preview screen of your form or worksheet (see Figure 12-5).

3. **Browse through your database to see what different records look like before printing.**

4. **To exit Print Preview, click the Print Preview SmartIcon, choose File⇨Print Preview, or just press Ctrl+Shift+B.**

To print a database, follow these steps:

1. **Click the Form tab (to print the Form view) or click the Worksheet tab (to print the Worksheet view).**

 2. **Click the Print SmartIcon (which looks like a printer), choose File⇨Print, or just press Ctrl+P.**

   A Print dialog box appears.

3. **Click Print to print.**

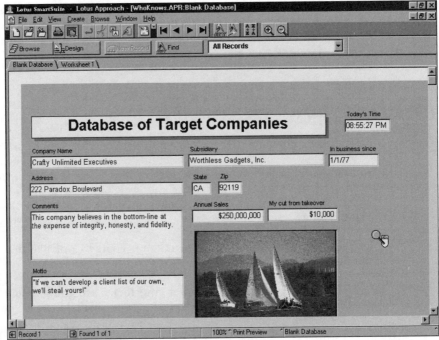

Figure 12-5:
A typical
print
preview of
a Form
view.

If you want, you can adjust settings in the dialog box to print different records from your database instead of the default current record (for forms) or all records (for Worksheet view) before you click Print.

Designing Your Own Database

The section "Starting Approach," earlier in this chapter, teaches you the two easy ways to begin using an Approach database — loading an existing database and creating a new database by using one of Approach's samples. But what if you don't find what you're really looking for among the sample templates? No problem. You can create your own database from scratch. Creating your own database is slower and clumsier than using one of the sample templates but enables you to create custom databases to store exactly the type of information you want.

To create your own database, you need to define two parts:

✔ The file format for your database

✔ The fields in which to store the actual information in your database

Choosing a database file format is like choosing whether to store your clothes in the closet or in a dresser. What you choose doesn't really matter as long as you're happy with your decision. Usually, you're better off sticking with Approach's default setting (the dBASE IV.DBF format) unless you have a specific need for another file format.

After you decide which database file format to use, the next step is to make fields that actually store your data. A *field* divides your information into categories such as names, addresses, and phone numbers. In defining the fields that make up your database, you can exercise real control over what kind of information your database contains and how that information is organized. Approach gives you lots of options. You can create database fields, define what kind of data each field contains, determine the lengths of the fields, and much more.

How do you want to save your data?

Whenever you create a database file, Approach gives you a choice about whether you want to store your data in one of a long list of file formats. For example, the formats you're most likely to use are Paradox (with a file extension of DB), Access (MDB), dBASE (DBF), or FoxPro (DBF) file formats. Although Approach couldn't care less which file format you choose, you may want to store your data in a certain file format so that other people using a different program can access the file.

Why does Approach offer so many different database file formats from which to choose? If you need to share data with people who use dBASE, save your database files in a dBASE (DBF) file format. If you need to share data with people who use Paradox, save your database files in Paradox (DB) format. By giving you so many choices for storing data, Approach tries to make sure that you can share your data with practically anyone.

Unless you specify otherwise, Approach stores your data in the dBASE IV (DBF) file format.

After you choose a file format, you can't change it, but you can make a copy of your data in another format if you need to share it with someone else. Choose File⇨Export Data to open the Export Data dialog box, where you can select the file format and what portion of the database you want to export. Give your file a name and click Export to create the file.

Making sure that you get the right data

Database fields can hold any type of information such as names, addresses, phone numbers, ages, or marital status. Inevitably someone thinks he's being clever by typing in nonsensical information in a database field, such as typing **Yes** in the following database field:

Sex: _____

Besides revealing a lack of imagination and creativity, typing the wrong data in a database field can mess up the integrity of your database. After all, if you create a database to hold names and addresses, but some jerk types in phone numbers and ages, your database is next to worthless.

To ensure that fields actually contain the type of information they're designed to hold, Approach enables you to define the name of a field and the type of data that a field is supposed to store. Fields can store the following different types of data:

- *Text fields* typically contain information such as names, addresses, and phone numbers.

- *Numeric fields* typically contain information such as ages, salaries, and quantities.

- *Memo fields* typically contain supplementary information such as brief notes or comments that you want to add. In a personnel database, a memo field may contain information such as "Unreliable worker" or "Groom him for a management position because he owes me money."

- *Boolean fields* contain information such as Yes, No, Y, N, 1, or 0. Boolean fields can be used for storing information such as "Yes! I want a free trial subscription to *The Weekly World News.*"

- *Date fields* contain (surprise!) dates in a variety of formats, such as July 4, 2006; 7-4-06; or 7/4/06.

- *Time fields* contain (another surprise) time in a variety of formats, such as 5:34 p.m. or 17:34.

- *PicturePlus fields* contain pictures, graphics, charts, and the like. For example, in a personnel database, a picture field may contain actual digitized photographs of each employee.

- *Calculated fields* contain formulas that calculate a result. A calculated field may be used to add up the number of vacation days someone has, based on the number of years they've been employed.

- *Variable fields* store a value in memory while the Approach file is open. The same value applies to all records in the database. Variable fields are an advanced feature that you won't need unless you develop and use macros.

See Figure 12-6 for examples of different types of database fields.

Okay, now that you've got an idea of the kinds of database fields you can define in Approach, the next section shows how you can use that information to create fields in a database.

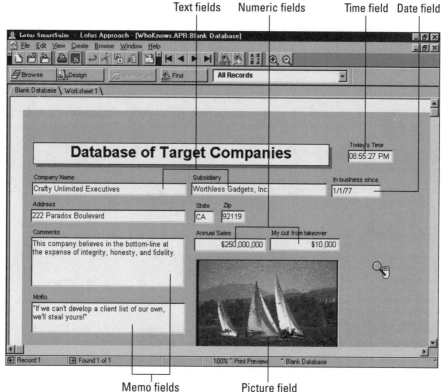

Text fields   Numeric fields   Time field   Date field

Figure 12-6:
Examples of
different
types of
fields in a
database.

Memo fields   Picture field

Making your own fields of dreams

Assuming that none of the Approach SmartMasters exactly meets your
needs for a new database, you can define your own database structure by
creating the fields that you do need to meet your particular needs. In the
name of freedom, Approach provides two ways to define the fields of a
database:

- Create them yourself.

- Modify a predefined database template that Approach has already
  created.

If, for example, you raise show dogs and want a database to store their
names, medical records, and ancestry, you aren't going to find a
SmartMaster with the correct fields predefined for you. So you have two
choices: You can use a predefined database template and modify that
template, or you can just create your own database from scratch. The
method you choose depends on how easily you can modify a predefined
database template to do what you want.

Creating fields from a template

Just as in high school, the easiest way to do anything is to copy from somebody else and pass the work off as your own. Because Approach has predefined more than 50 database templates already, using one of these templates is a lot easier than creating your own. To create fields by using one of Approach's predefined templates, follow these steps:

1. **Choose File⇨New Database (or click the Create a New Database File SmartIcon).**

   A New dialog box appears, as shown in Figure 12-7.

Figure 12-7: A list of available templates on which to base your database.

2. **Choose Templates from the SmartMaster Types drop-down list and then select from the list the SmartMaster template you want to use.**

   Do not choose the Blank Database SmartMaster. If you insist on starting from scratch, read the next section, "Creating fields from scratch."

3. **Click OK.**

   A different New dialog box appears. This one is similar to the Save Approach File As dialog box.

4. **In the Create Type drop-down list, select the file format you want Approach to use for your database.**

5. **Type a name for your database file (such as ShowDogs) in the File Name text box, and click OK.**

Creating fields from scratch

Creating database fields from scratch isn't necessarily hard, just a bit more time-consuming and troublesome than using one of Approach's templates — kind of like buying ingredients at a supermarket and then cooking yourself a gourmet meal instead of going to a restaurant and ordering from the regular menu.

To create database fields from scratch, perform the following steps:

1. **Choose File➪New Database (or click the Create a New Database File SmartIcon).**

   A New dialog box appears. (Refer to Figure 12-7.)

2. **Choose Blank Database from the SmartMaster list.**

3. **Click OK.**

   A different New dialog box appears. This one is similar to the Save Approach File As dialog box.

4. **In the Create Type drop-down list, select the file format you want Approach to use for your database.**

5. **Type the name you want for your new database in the File Name text box, and then click Create.**

   A Creating New Database dialog box appears, as shown in Figure 12-8.

Figure 12-8:
The
Creating
New
Database
dialog box.

You're not too late — you can still choose to use a template instead of creating fields from scratch. Just select a template from the Template drop-down list and click OK to fill the Creating New Database dialog box with fields from the template.

6. **Type the name of your field under the Field Name category and press Tab.**

   The names of your fields can be as logical or irrational as you like. You can name your field *NAME* and store people's names in the field, for example, or you can name your field *SDIOEK* and store addresses. Approach doesn't care what you name your field, so use any name you want. Just pick a name that makes clear what kind of information the data field contains; otherwise, you (and anyone who uses your database) may have a hard time entering and looking up stuff later.

7. **Click the Data Type list box and choose a data type (such as Text, Numeric, and so on) and press Tab.**

8. **Type a size for your field in the Size text box and press Tab.**

   Make sure that the size you choose for your field is large enough to hold the longest block of data for that field. If you know that somebody has a last name of 10 letters, for example, make sure that you specify a Last Name field that can contain 10 or more characters. (*Note:* Some fields, such as Date, Time, and Boolean, don't enable you to choose a size.)

9. **Repeat Steps 6 through 8 for each field that you want to create, and then click OK after you're done.**

Your new database is complete and ready for you to begin entering data!

Chapter 13

Designing Database Forms That Work

• •

• •

*F*orms are nothing more than windows that enable you to look at one record stored in your database. (If you need to look at two or more records simultaneously, you must switch to the Worksheet view.) As you create a database, Approach creates one form for you automatically. Because Approach is just a dumb computer program, however, the forms that Approach creates are functional but visually dull.

Fortunately, you can modify forms or create new forms altogether. By creating or modifying forms, you can create your own unique views of your database records that look pretty or display only certain information. You may, for example, have a personnel database that lists your coworkers' names, addresses, ages, and salaries. You probably don't want to give your coworkers access to everyone's salaries, so you can create a form that displays everything except the salaries.

Creating a New Form

Every time you create a database, Approach creates one form with all your database fields on it. You can create as many forms as you like, however, to give you different views of the data stored in your database. To create a form, follow these steps:

1. Choose **C**reate➪**F**orm.

A Form Assistant dialog box appears with its Layout tab open, as shown in Figure 13-1.

Figure 13-1:
The Form
Assistant
dialog box.

2. Click the **V**iew Name & Title text box, and type a name for your form.

If you don't choose a name, Approach gives your form a boring name such as Form 2 or Form 3. (Nothing exciting, such as "Fred" or "Zon.")

3. Click the **S**tyle drop-down list box, and select from the list the style that you want to use.

The style you choose simply affects the appearance of your form for aesthetic purposes. The Sample Form on the right side of the dialog box shows a preview of the style.

4. Select the layout that you want to use from the **L**ayout list box.

Blank creates a form without any database fields on it. *Standard* creates a form with all database fields arranged in rows. *Columnar* creates a form with all database fields arranged in columns.

5. Click the **N**ext button.

The Form Assistant dialog box displays Step 2 of your available options, the Fields tab, as shown in Figure 13-2.

Figure 13-2:
The Form
Assistant
dialog box,
displaying
Step 2 of
your
options.

6. Click each field displayed in the Fields list that you want to add to your new form and click Add.

As a shortcut, you can double-click a field name to add it. You can also select two or more fields by holding down the Ctrl key and clicking each field that you want to add. After you click Add, the field names appear in the Fields To Place On View list.

7. After you finish selecting fields to add to the form, click Done.

Approach displays your newly created form.

In case you're wondering, you can also delete a form, thereby destroying all your hard work of creating the form in the first place. To delete a form, you must switch to Design view by pressing Ctrl+D and then choose Form⇨ Delete Form from the menu bar.

Editing a Form's Design

After you create a form, you can use the form right away or pretty the form up a bit so that the poor thing looks less like an eyesore. Any design changes that you make to a form affect only its appearance and not its function (much like bad sports teams that get new uniforms).

Approach offers two views for displaying your form: the *Browse view* and the *Design view.* The Browse view enables you to see what your form looks like and to add data if you want. The Design view enables you to change the appearance of your form. In Design view, Approach enables you to change the form's name, the form's border, and the form's background color.

You can switch between Browse view and Design view by choosing a menu command, pressing a shortcut key, or clicking a button in the Action bar. (The Action bar is located just below the SmartIcons. If the Action bar isn't showing, choose <u>V</u>iew⇨Show <u>A</u>ction Bar.) To switch views, use one of the following methods:

- ✔ Choose <u>V</u>iew⇨<u>D</u>esign or <u>V</u>iew⇨<u>B</u>rowse & Data Entry.
- ✔ Press Ctrl+D (for Design view) or Ctrl+B (for Browse view).
- ✔ Click the Design or Browse buttons on the Action bar.
- ✔ Click the status bar button that shows the current view and choose a new view from the pop-up menu that appears.

Changing the form's name

The form's name normally appears in three places, as shown in Figure 13-3: on the *form* itself, as a *tab* at the top of the form, and on the *status bar*.

Form name appears as a tab   Form name appears on form itself

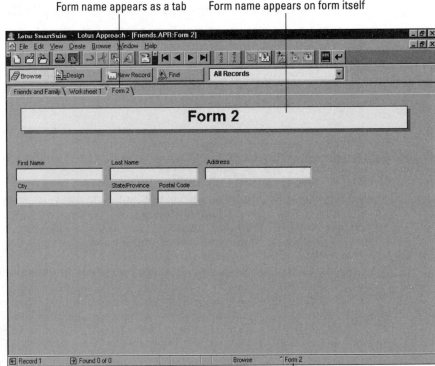

Figure 13-3: The three places where a form's name appears.

Form name appears on status bar

You can name a form anything you want (including four-letter words, if you're so inclined), but you should choose a name that identifies the main purpose of the form. If a form displays only telephone numbers, for example, you may want to name the form PHONES.

To change the form name that appears on the form, follow these steps:

1. **Click the Design button on the Action bar to switch to Design view.**

   Approach displays your form on a grid.

2. **Click the form name text object that appears on the form.**

   Small black handles appear around the corners of the form name text object (that's the big Form 2 in Figure 13-3), and the pointer turns into a hand.

3. **Move the pointer hand over the form name text object and click.**

   The pointer turns to an I-beam, and a text-editing cursor (a blinking vertical line) appears.

4. **Press Backspace or Delete to erase the current form name, and then type a new name.**

5. **Click anywhere on the form outside the form name you just typed.**

The form's name is changed on the form itself. To change the form name that appears as a tab and in the status bar, follow these steps:

1. **Click the Design button on the Action bar to switch to Design view (if you're not already there).**

   Approach displays your form on a grid.

2. **Choose Form⇨Form Properties from the menu bar; or press Alt+Enter; or click the Show InfoBox SmartIcon; or right-click anywhere on the form and choose Form Properties from the pop-up menu.**

   A Form Properties InfoBox appears, as shown in Figure 13-4.

┌Color, Border, and Line Style tab

Basics tab

Figure 13-4:
A Form
Properties
InfoBox.

3. **Click the Form Name text box in the Basics tab and type a new name for your form.**

   As soon as you move the insertion point to another InfoBox option, Approach changes the name of the form.

4. **Click the InfoBox's Close (X) button to remove the box from sight.**

You can also edit the form name by double-clicking the form tab when you are in Design view. The tab enlarges and becomes a text box. Edit the form name and press Enter.

Changing the border and background color

Approach also enables you to modify the following properties of your form's border: the border *width*, the border *color*, the border *frame*, and the border *location*.

To change the form's border and background color, follow these steps:

1. **Click the Design button in the Action bar.**

   Approach displays your form on a grid.

2. **Open the form's InfoBox by clicking the Show InfoBox SmartIcon, choosing Form⇨Form Properties, pressing Alt+Enter, or right-clicking the form and choosing Form Properties from the pop-up menu.**

   A Form Properties InfoBox appears.

3. **Click the Color, Border, and Line Style tab.**

   The Color, Border, and Line Style options appear in the InfoBox, as shown in Figure 13-5.

Figure 13-5:
The Color, Border, and Line Style options in the Form Properties InfoBox.

4. **Click the Width drop-down list box in the Border area and select a width from the list.**

5. **Click the Color drop-down list box and select a color.**

   If you choose a width that's too small, you may barely be able to see your border. If you choose a width that's too wide, your border may look obnoxious. You may need to experiment with different widths and colors to get the right look.

6. **Click the Fill Color drop-down list box in the Effects area and select a background color for your form.**

7. **Click the Style drop-down list box and select a border style.**

8. **Make sure that a check appears in each Border area check box (Left, Right, Top, or Bottom) where you want a border to appear on the form.**

   As you make changes in the InfoBox settings, Approach updates the form to show the results of your selections. You can continue to refine your selections to achieve the effect you desire.

9. **After you're through adjusting the form's border and background color, click the InfoBox's Close (X) button to close the InfoBox.**

Changing the Form Layout

As you create a form, Approach throws your database fields on the form into neat, organized rows or columns. To further customize your form, you can move database fields around, change their sizes, or change the color, font, or border of the database field.

Moving and resizing a database field

Changing the position of your database fields on a form doesn't affect your data. The whole purpose of changing the layout of your fields is to keep yourself amused and your users happy by creating pretty forms that make your database more interesting to use.

To move a database field, follow these steps:

1. **Click the Design button in the Action bar.**

   Approach displays your form on a grid.

2. **Click the database field that you want to move.**

   Black handles appear around your chosen database field, and the pointer turns into a hand.

3. **Press and hold the mouse button and drag the mouse.**

   As you drag the mouse, a box appears and shows you the new location of your database field, as shown in Figure 13-6.

4. **Release the mouse button after the database field is where you want it.**

To resize a database field, follow these steps:

1. **Click the Design button in the Action bar.**

   Approach displays your form on a grid.

2. **Click the database field that you want to resize.**

   Black handles again appear around your chosen database field, and the pointer turns into a hand.

3. **Move the pointer over one of the handles at the corner of the database field until the pointer turns into a double arrow.**

4. **Press and hold the mouse button and drag the mouse.**

   As you drag the mouse, a gray box appears and shows you the new size of your database field.

5. **Release the mouse button after the database field is the size you want.**

Figure 13-6:
Moving a
database
field.

Changing the font, color, and border of a database field

Approach gives you a wide variety of options for modifying the appearance of your database fields. The more bizarre your database fields are, however, the more confusing the form may appear to the user. Generally, you're better off not getting too wild with fluorescent colors and unusual fonts, or your database fields may look more like graffiti than a useful database that normal people want to use.

Modifying the appearance of a database field changes only the way the field looks; the modifications don't change the actual data stored in your database.

To modify a database field, follow these steps:

1. **Click the Design button in the Action bar.**

   Approach displays your form on a grid.

2. **Click the database field that you want to modify.**

3. **To open the field's InfoBox, click the Show InfoBox SmartIcon; or choose Field Object⇨Object Properties; or press Alt+Enter; or right-click the field and choose Field Properties from the pop-up menu.**

   A Field Properties InfoBox appears.

4. **Click the Color, Border, and Line Style tab.**

   The Color, Border, and Line Style options appear.

5. **Click the Style drop-down list box and select a frame or border to use for your field.**

6. **Click the Width drop-down list box and select a width.**

7. **Click the Color drop-down list box and select a color.**

   Gaudy colors may look nice if your border is narrow, but the same colors can look disastrous if your border is too wide.

8. **Click the Fill Color drop-down list box and select a background color for your database field.**

9. **Click the Shadow Color drop-down list box and choose a color.**

10. **Make sure that a check appears in each check box of the Borders area (Left, Right, Top, or Bottom) where you want a border to appear on a field.**

11. **Click the Font, Attributes, and Color tab and then select the Label radio button to access the options shown in Figure 13-7.**

12. **Select a font from the Font Name list box.**

Figure 13-7:
The Label
options in a
Field
Properties
InfoBox.

13. **Select the type size for your label from the Size list box.**

14. **Click the desired font styles (Bold, Italic, or Underline) in the Attributes list box.**

15. **Click the Alignment buttons to choose Left, Center, or Right alignment for the label text.**

16. **Click the Label Text text box and type a new label name.**

17. **Click the Label Position drop-down list box and select a position (such as Above, Below, and so on) for your label.**

    The label position is in relationship to the field itself, not the form as a whole.

18. **Click the Text Color drop-down list box and select a color for the label.**

    Remember that colors make your database field easier or harder to see. If you're color-blind, you may want to skip this step altogether.

19. **Click the Text Relief drop-down list box and choose a text relief style.**

    You can use the text relief option to make your text appear normal, appear as raised letters, or appear as if someone chiseled the text into your form. Try the different options and see what you like.

20. **Click the InfoBox's Close (X) button to close the InfoBox.**

Hey! Just look at those snazzy fields on that attractive database form. But do you have enough fields? Too many? Read the next section, "Adding and Removing Fields."

Adding and Removing Fields

As you create a new form, Approach enables you to choose which fields to display on your form. But people, being the forgetful, imperfect creatures that we are, may later decide to add a new database field or delete an existing database field.

To add an existing database field to a form, follow these steps:

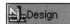

1. **Click the Design button in the Action bar.**

   Approach displays your form on a grid.

2. **Choose Form⇨Add field; or right-click anywhere on the form and choose Add Field from the pop-up menu.**

   The Add Field dialog box appears.

3. **In the Add Field dialog box, click the database field that you want to add to your form and then press and hold the mouse button.**

4. **Drag the mouse pointer from the Add Field dialog box onto the form.**

   The pointer now appears as a fist holding the name of your database field, as shown in Figure 13-8.

5. **Release the mouse button after you've positioned the database field where you want that field to appear on the form and then click the Close (X) button to close the Add Field dialog box.**

Now that's great if the field you want is one that already exists. But to add an entirely new database field to a form, follow these steps:

1. **Open the Add Field dialog box, as described in the preceding steps.**

2. **Click the Field Definition button in the Add Field dialog box.**

   The Field Definition dialog box appears, as shown in Figure 13-9.

Figure 13-8: Dragging a database field from the Add Field dialog box to a form.

Figure 13-9:
The Field
Definition
dialog box.

3. **Click the Insert button to create an empty row in the fields list at the center of the dialog box.**

4. **Type the name for your new field in the Field Name column and press Tab.**

   The cursor moves to the Data Type column, and the Data Type cell on this row becomes a drop-down list box.

5. **Click the Data Type drop-down list box, choose a data type (such as Text or Numeric), and then press Tab.**

6. **Type a size for your database field in the Size column and click OK.**

   The size of your database field is measured by the number of letters or numbers that the field can hold. So a Size 4 field can hold a maximum of four letters.

7. **Click Close (X) to close the Field Definition dialog box.**

   The Add Field dialog box displays your newly created field.

8. **Follow Steps 3 through 5 of the preceding set of steps to place your newly created field on your form and close the Add Field dialog box.**

You may also want to delete a field from your form if you discover that you no longer have a need for that field.

If you delete a database field from a form, Approach does not delete the actual data stored in your database. Deleting a database field simply keeps you from seeing certain data on your form, much like pulling a curtain over a window keeps you from seeing the parking lot outside but does not physically destroy the parking lot.

To delete a database field from a form, follow these steps:

1. **Click the Design button in the Action bar.**

   Approach displays your form on a grid.

2. Click the database field that you want to delete.

Black handles appear around the database field.

3. Press Delete.

If you discover that you made a mistake and deleted the wrong field, choose Edit⇨Undo to save the day (and your database field). But you must choose the Undo command immediately — *before* you do something else — for the command to undo the delete.

Using the Tools Palette

As a shortcut to using menus all the time, Approach displays a Tools palette that you can move around the screen, as shown in Figure 13-10. The Tools palette enables you to quickly choose commands to perform the following tasks:

- Draw text boxes and type text in those boxes.
- Draw squares and rectangles.
- Draw circles and ellipses.
- Draw rectangles with rounded corners.
- Draw lines.
- Draw a field.
- Draw a check box.
- Draw a radio button.
- Draw a macro button (which runs a series of recorded commands).
- Draw a PicturePlus field to hold a picture or OLE object. (OLE objects typically contain text or graphics created by another program and stored in another file.)
- Display or Hide the Add Field dialog box.

Figure 13-10: The Tools palette.

Select objects — Draw text blocks
Draw squares and rectangles — Draw circles and ellipses
Draw rounded rectangles — Draw lines
Draw fields — Draw check boxes
Draw radio buttons — Draw buttons
Draw PicturePlus fields — Show the Add Field dialog box

To display or remove the Tools palette from sight, choose View⇨Show Tools Palette or press Ctrl+L.

To move the Tools palette around, move the mouse pointer over the Tools palette title bar, press and hold the mouse button, and move the mouse. Then release the mouse button after you've positioned the Tools palette where you want the palette on-screen.

Typing text and drawing circles, lines, and squares

For purely decorative purposes, Approach enables you to create text boxes and draw geometric shapes such as lines, circles, and squares on a form. Text that you type on a form and geometric shapes that you draw on a form have no effect on your actual data. To draw a text box on a form, follow these steps:

1. **Click the Draw text blocks button in the Tools palette.**

   The pointer turns into a crosshair accompanied by the letters abc.

2. **Move the pointer to where you want to create a text box, press and hold the mouse button, and drag to draw a rectangular text box.**

3. **Release the mouse button.**

   Approach draws a text box on the form. A flashing text-editing cursor appears in the upper-left corner of the text box.

4. **Type any text that you want, such as instructions explaining what the form does, decorative labels, or nasty words to your boss.**

   While you're creating and editing text, you can use the usual SmartIcons — such as bold, italic, and center alignment — for formatting your text.

5. **Click outside your text box.**

To draw a geometric shape on a form, follow these steps:

1. **Click the Draw squares and rectangles, Draw circles and ellipses, Draw rounded rectangles, or Draw lines button on the Tools palette.**

   The pointer turns into a crosshair.

2. **Move the pointer onto the form (where you want the shape), press and hold the mouse button, and drag to draw your geometric shape.**

3. **Release the mouse button.**

Adding radio buttons and check boxes

Radio buttons and check boxes can display your data in more visually appealing ways than can an ordinary database field. A database field may be called Marital Status, for example, and may contain Single, Married, or Divorced as its data. Rather than display a dull database field labeled Marital Status, however, you could use a radio button or check box to make the marital status data easier to see. A check box or radio button also has the advantage of restricting the user's input to predefined choices. And that avoids the problem of what to do with inappropriate responses such as "winner" in a Race field. A set of radio buttons is used to present mutually exclusive options. A check box presents a yes/no choice; the check box has one value if checked and another if unchecked.

To draw radio buttons (or check boxes) on your form, follow these steps:

1. **Click the Draw radio buttons (or Draw check boxes) button in the Tools palette.**

   The pointer turns into a crosshair.

2. **Click in the location where you want your radio buttons (or check boxes) to appear.**

   A Define Radio Buttons dialog box appears. (A similar Define Check Box dialog box appears if you're creating a check box instead of a radio button. By the way, don't worry right now about the exact size of your radio buttons or check boxes; Approach automatically resizes them in Step 5.)

3. **Click in the Field list and select the name of the database field that you want to display as a set of radio buttons (or check boxes).**

4. **Click the Create Radio Buttons From Field Data button (or its counterpart, the Create Check Box From Field Data button, if you're doing check boxes).**

   Approach automatically fills in values for the Clicked Value and Button Label columns based on information in that field in your database. (If you haven't stored any data in the database field you selected in Step 3, nothing happens at this step and you must manually enter something appropriate in the Clicked Value and Button Label columns.)

5. **Click OK.**

   Approach creates the radio buttons (or check boxes) that you defined on your form.

Adding a field from the Tools palette

Although you can add database fields to your form by using menu commands, this task can be accomplished much more easily by using the Tools palette instead. The Tools palette provides two buttons for adding database fields to your form: the Draw Fields button or the Show The Add Field Dialog Box button (to display the Add Field dialog box).

To add a field by using the Draw Fields button, follow these steps:

1. **Click the Draw fields button in the Tools palette.**

   The pointer turns into a crosshair.

2. **Move the mouse to the form, press and hold the mouse button, drag the mouse down and to the right until the field is just the size that you want, and then release the mouse button.**

   The Field Properties InfoBox appears.

3. **Click the Basics tab and then click the database field that you want to add in the Field drop-down list box.**

4. **Click the Close (X) button to close the InfoBox.**

To add a field by using the Show The Add Field Dialog Box button, just click the button to open the Add Field dialog box and follow the steps listed in the section "Adding and Removing Fields," earlier in this chapter.

Saving Your Forms

While changing the appearance of your forms, make sure that you save your work periodically by choosing File⇨Save Approach File or pressing Ctrl+S.

Approach automatically saves any data you type into your database fields. But the data and the forms in which the data is displayed are saved in two different files, and Approach does not automatically save any changes you make to your forms. To prevent a power blackout from destroying all your hard work in creating a form, save your form frequently. Doing so may seem inconvenient at first, but it is a lot more convenient than trying to re-create an entire lost form from scratch. Really. Trust us.

Chapter 14

Finding Needles in Database Haystacks

. . . .

In This Chapter

▶ Setting up a database Find

▶ Sending the Assistant to find records

▶ Sorting your database

▶ Saving a Find or Sort for later use

. . . .

*S*toring information in a database and viewing that information in different ways may be all well and good, but information is useless if you can never find it or organize it into a useful order. If you have a database listing potential customers for a new product, you can use a database find to help you select those people most likely to buy your product at full retail price. Then you can sort those records into groups by zip code so that you can prepare a mailing list.

You may, for example, demand of your database: "Hey, give me the name of everyone who works in Washington, D.C., makes more than $2,500,000 a year, and owns more than one home." Then your database may list those people most likely to buy carbonated beverages for their dogs, donate money to the Save the Dandelion Foundation, and visit ski resorts located in the Himalayas.

By selectively displaying certain information stored in a database, Approach helps you uncover hidden information that you may not otherwise discover. For those single people out there, this procedure is how computer dating services match people up. ("Find me all the single people interested in scuba diving, tennis, and iguana raising.")

Creating a Find

In the technical, confusing, and totally unnecessary jargon of computers, searching and finding information in a database is usually called a query. In an Approach database, however, the same process is called a *Find*.

Until you create a Find, however, Approach hasn't the slightest clue what information you want found. So, like the dumb brute of a program that it is, Approach displays a blank copy of your database form or worksheet on-screen and says, "Okay, fill in the blanks with all the data you want me to find, and then I'll go find that data for you."

To create a Find, follow these steps:

1. **Choose Browse⇨Find⇨Find Using Form.**

   If you're currently in the Worksheet view, choose Worksheet⇨Find⇨ Find Using Worksheet. Or better yet, in any view, press Ctrl+F or click the Find button on the Action bar (the row of buttons that usually appears between the SmartIcon palette and the view tabs).

   Approach displays a blank form (or worksheet), along with five buttons in the Action bar: OK, Cancel, New Condition, Clear All, and Find Assistant, as shown in Figure 14-1.

Figure 14-1:
A typical blank form for a Find.

2. Click a database field and type the information that you want to find.

If, for example, you want to find all people of French nationality in the database of lonely single people, click the Nationality database field and type **French**. (Finds aren't case sensitive, so you could type **french**, or even **fRENch**.)

3. Click OK.

Approach displays the first record containing the information that matches your Find. (If you are in Worksheet view, all matched records appear.) Approach also displays the total number of records found at the bottom of the screen in the status bar, as shown in Figure 14-2. If Approach can't find any record matching your Find, the program displays an error message.

4. Click the Go to Next Record or Go to Previous Record button in the status bar, or press PageDown or PageUp, to view the next or previous record that matches your Find.

If another match isn't found, nothing happens.

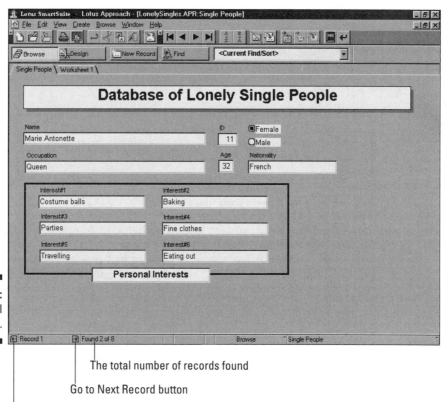

Figure 14-2:
A typical
Find result.

The total number of records found

Go to Next Record button

Go to Previous Record button

After you find the information you seek, guess what? Approach refuses to show you the rest of your database until you specifically tell the program, "Okay, I'm done with my Find. (What a stupid term!) Now show me the contents of my entire database again."

5. **Choose <u>B</u>rowse⇨<u>F</u>ind⇨Find <u>A</u>ll; or press Ctrl+A; or select All Records from the drop-down list in the Action bar.**

To prove that it is now displaying all the records in your database, Approach displays a message listing the total number of records in your database at the bottom of the screen, such as Found 8 of 8.

Finding records that match a single criterion

Approach enables you to search for anything stored in a database, such as text, numbers, data displayed as a radio button or check box, or even empty database fields. Approach not only gives you plenty of freedom in searching a database but also provides employment for authors to write explanations for using all these confusing possibilities.

Finding text

Approach enables you to search for text in a database the following three ways:

- ✔ You can search for a *text string* (whether as part of a longer text string or not). Text strings are simply words or phrases such as *German, Napoleon Bonaparte,* and *Going Camping.* Text strings can even be parts of words, such as *Ger.*

- ✔ You can search for the *exact* text string.

- ✔ You can search for *part* of a text string.

Normally, if you ask Approach to find text, you just need to type the text into the database field that requires that Find information. If you want to search for *Sam* in a database, for example, you can just type **Sam** into the First Name database field. Approach then finds not only all records containing *Sam* but also all records containing *Sam*antha, *Sam*uel, or Hus*sam*. If this sort of return is what you want, fine. Just go ahead and type **Sam** in the First Name database field. (See if we care.)

If you want Approach to find only an exact text string (*Sam* instead of *Sam*antha), on the other hand, you must type an *equal sign* (=) in front of the text string, as follows: **=Sam**.

If you want to find all records that do *not* contain a specific text string, use the *not equal sign* (<>) in front of a text string. To find all records that do not have *George* in the First Name field, for example, you type: **<>George**.

Sometimes you may know part of a word that you want to find, but you don't know the exact word. Rather than throw your arms up in despair, you can use wildcards. *Wildcards* enable you to tell Approach, "Okay, I know part of what I want to find, so I'll just type that part and let you find the rest."

Approach provides two different wildcards: the *asterisk* (*) and the *question mark* (?). The asterisk represents multiple characters, and the question mark represents a single character.

Suppose, for example, that you type the following into a City database field: **De***. Approach finds all records beginning with *De,* such as *De*troit, *De*s Moines, or *De*Paul. (Actually, if you type **De** without the asterisk, Approach finds the same records because the program finds partial matches to Find entries by default. But this example gives you the idea of how the wildcard thing works.)

Here's where the asterisk earns its keep. Suppose that you type the following into a Last Name database field: ***ck**. Approach finds all records that end with the letters *ck,* no matter how long the word, such as Bla*ck,* Lu*ck,* or Smartale*ck.*

Now, say that you type the following into a First Name database field: **B???**. Approach finds all records that are four characters long and begin with *B,* such as *B*lue, *B*orr, or *B*uck — and only those records. The program doesn't match longer words, such as *B*aker.

You can combine both the asterisk and question mark wildcards. Suppose, for example, that you type the following: **L?t***. Approach finds all matching records, such as *Lo*tus, *La*therton, or *Li*tton.

Strangely, you can't combine equals (=) and not equals (<>) search specifications with wildcards. So, a search for *<>Smith* will find all records that don't contain *Smith,* but a search for *<>Sm** generates an error message saying that no matching records were found.

Finding numbers

Approach also enables you to find the following types of numbers:

- ✓ Exact numbers ("Show me all the people who make $35,000 a year.")

- ✓ Numbers that are greater than or less than a certain value ("Show me all the people who make less than $35,000 a year.")

- ✓ Numbers that fall within a specified range ("Show me all the people who make more than $35,000 a year but less than $50,000 a year.")

To find an exact number, just type the number you want to find in a database field. If you want to find all records containing a value of 35,000 in a Salary database field, type **35000** in the Salary database field. Don't bother typing commas or dollar signs ($) because Approach gets confused and doesn't recognize a dollar sign or a comma as part of a number.

To find a number greater than or less than a certain value, type one of the following in the Salary database field:

> **> 35000** (finds all records containing values greater than 35,000)

> **>= 35000** (finds all records containing values greater than or equal to 35,000)

> **< 35000** (finds all records containing values less than 35,000)

> **<= 35000** (finds all records containing values less than or equal to 35,000)

Whether or not you put a space between the symbol (=, >, <, >=, <=, and so on) and the Find string (either words or numbers) doesn't really matter. The program works equally well with or without the space.

To find all records that do *not* contain a certain value, use the not equal sign (<>): **<> 35000** (finds all records that do *not* contain 35,000).

To find a value that falls within a certain range, use the ellipsis (. . .): **35000 . . . 50000** (finds all records containing values that are equal to or greater than 35,000 but less than or equal to 50,000).

Finding data in radio buttons and check boxes

If a form displays data as a radio button or check box, just click the radio button or check box containing the value you want to find. For example, a form may display a person's sex as radio buttons labeled Male and Female. To search for all males, just click the Male radio button.

Finding blank (or nonblank) fields

How good data is depends on how accurately it was typed in. Just think of the last time you made a hotel reservation, but the hotel had no record of your reservation. All your information may have been typed into the computer database correctly, but someone may have forgotten to type your last name into the Last Name database field. So when the hotel clerk tries to find your reservation by typing your last name, the database never finds your last name because the name was never typed in its field. As far as the computer is concerned, your hotel reservation doesn't exist, and you must sleep in the lobby instead.

To help you find blank fields in your database, just type an equal sign (=) all by itself in a database field. If you want to find nonblank fields in your database, just type a not equal sign (<>) all by itself in a database field.

Finding records that match multiple criteria

Searching a database by using only one field can be too general. For example, searching a database for single people isn't enough; perhaps you're interested in finding only names belonging to people of the opposite sex. Just as you can use a dating database to match desired characteristics, you can use Approach to search a database by using multiple criteria. You can, for example, ask Approach: "Look in my high school database and show me all the people who live in this zip code and earn less than $50,000 a year." Then Approach may display the names of your high school prom queen, class president, and the poor guy voted Most Likely to Succeed (what a joke *that* turned out to be).

By using multiple criteria to search through a database, Approach enables you to narrow your search so that you find exactly what you're looking for. To use multiple criteria to search a database, just type the information you want to find in two or more database fields. To find all males in a database who are younger than 30 years old, for example, you may enter the information shown in Figure 14-3.

Age database field   Male and Female radio buttons

Figure 14-3:
An example
of a search
that uses
multiple
criteria.

If you search for data in two or more database fields, you're telling Approach: "Find me all records containing information A *and* information B."

Sometimes you may want to search for all records containing information A *or* information B. You may, for example, want to find all people in a database whose nationality is American or British. In this case, you type the following in the Nationality database field:

American, British

The comma tells Approach: "Find all records that contain either 'American' or 'British' in the Nationality database field."

Hooked on phonics — finding sound-alike data

In spite of the insistence of our public school systems, not everyone knows how to spell correctly. Of course, in conversation, that doesn't really matter as long as you know what you're trying to say. If you search a database, however, you find that Approach is usually pretty picky about the commands it accepts.

If you tell Approach to find all names beginning with *C,* Approach may find names such as *Caryn, Crystal,* or *Carol.* But what if you don't have the slightest idea how something is spelled but remember how it sounds? If this were high school, you'd get a failing grade (or maybe not, considering the quality of too many of today's schools). Fortunately, Approach accommodates such problems by enabling you to search database fields phonetically (or, to use phonics, *fonetikalee*).

To tell Approach to search the database phonetically instead of just searching a database for, say, all names beginning with *C,* type the name the way it sounds and put a tilde symbol (~) in front of it. To search for *Carol Johnson,* for example, you could type the following in the Name database field:

~Karol Jonson

Approach does its best to figure out what you're trying to spell and digs up the names that most closely match what you write phonetically. Oddly, a phonetic search doesn't find a name that actually matches the phonetic spelling. But that's seldom an issue because you normally use a phonetic search only after a regular search has failed.

If you spell something phonetically but Approach says that it can't find anything, that could mean that no data matches your phonetic Find — or that Approach simply can't understand what you tried to phonetically write out. Try again with a different spelling.

Sending the Find Assistant on a Search

If entering all those symbols (=, <, ~, *, <>, . . .) into the database form seems confusing, you may want to try Approach's other way of defining Finds — the *Find Assistant*. Basically, the Find Assistant does the same things we describe on these last few pages. You just define the Find in a dialog box instead of a database form or worksheet. The difference is that you can choose the *operator* (equals, does not equal, and so on) from a list of descriptive words instead of typing arcane symbols.

To create a Find with the Find Assistant, follow these steps:

1. Choose Browse⇨Find⇨Find Assistant from the menu bar; or click the Find button and then the Find Assistant button on the Action bar; or press Ctrl+I.

The Find Assistant button appears on the Action bar after you enter the Find Definition mode by clicking the Find button.

Approach displays the Find/Sort Assistant dialog box, as shown in Figure 14-4.

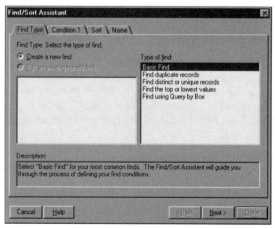

Figure 14-4: The Find/Sort Assistant dialog box offers some predefined Finds as well as the capability to define your own Finds.

2. On the Find Type tab, click the Create A New Find radio button and then select Basic Find from the Type Of Find list.

The Type Of Find list also gives you the option of some partially pre-defined Finds. For example, you can find duplicate records or the top ten records in some category.

3. Click the Next button to access the Condition 1 tab, as shown in Figure 14-5.

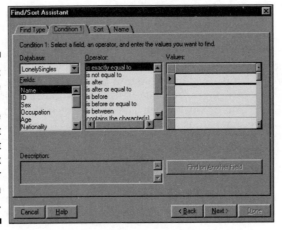

Figure 14-5:
Using the
Condition 1
tab of the
Find/Sort
Assistant
dialog box
to further
define a
Find.

4. **Select a database field from the Fields list box.**

5. **Select the kind of match you want from the Operator list box.**

   This list is where you can choose search criteria such as is exactly equal to or contains the characters (instead of those confusing symbols) to control the kind of match between the database records and the value you seek.

6. **Enter the text or number you want to find in the Values box.**

   Approach assembles a description of your Find in the Description text box at the bottom of the dialog box. Surprise! The description reads like a semi-intelligible sentence. After a Find criteria is defined, the Done button becomes available. You can click Find On Another Field to define additional Find criteria or tell Approach to start searching for matching records now.

7. **(Optional) Click Find On Another Field to open another dialog box tab where you can define additional search criteria.**

   You can define searches on additional fields by choosing Find Fewer Records (AND), or you can define searches on additional criteria by choosing Find More Records (OR). After choosing AND or OR, select the fields, operator, and values for the search criteria just as you did in Steps 4, 5, and 6.

8. **Click the Done button to start the Find.**

   Approach displays the matching records just as the program does after you find records from a form or worksheet.

Sorting Explained

Each time you type data into an Approach database, Approach cheerfully stacks the data in exactly the order you type that information. Because most people enter data in a way that's personally convenient — without concern for how the data's organized — most data isn't organized in a way that's useful.

Fortunately, you can tell Approach: "Hey, stupid, sort all my information." Approach then asks: "Okay, boss, but how do you want to sort your information?" After smacking Approach upside the head, you can tell the pesky program: "Sort the information alphabetically by last name." In the blink of an eye, Approach obeys your commands and sorts your data alphabetically.

Whenever you want to sort a database, you must tell Approach these two things:

✔ Which database field to use for sorting

✔ How to sort the data (the only choices being in *ascending* or *descending* order)

To sort a database alphabetically by last name, tell Approach to sort by using the Last Name database field. To sort by state, tell Approach to sort by using the State database field. And to sort by age, tell Approach to sort by using (what else?) the Age database field. Then, after you decide which database field to use for sorting, you must tell Approach whether you want to sort in ascending or descending order.

Ascending order sorts data from lowest to highest, such as from A to Z or 0 to 9. *Descending order* sorts data from highest to lowest (surprise!), such as from Z to A or 9 to 0.

Changing the sort order by using one field

The easiest way to sort a database is to use one database field, such as the Last Name field or the Zip Code field. You can sort your database while in Worksheet view or Form view. For more on Worksheet view and Form view, see Chapter 12.

Because Worksheet view shows multiple records of your database at the same time, you can see your data more easily if the data is sorted in Worksheet view rather than in Form view.

If you used a Find to display a portion of your database records, press Ctrl+A before sorting your database. Otherwise, Approach sorts only the limited number of records that your Find displays. The remaining records remain in the order in which they were originally entered.

To sort a database in Worksheet view, follow these steps:

1. **Choose View⇨Browse & Data Entry; or click the Browse button on the Action bar; or press Ctrl+B.**

2. **Click the Worksheet tab to view your data in the worksheet grid.**

3. **Click any field in the database field (the column) that you want to use for sorting.**

   To sort by last name, for example, click the Last Name database field. Approach highlights the entire column. (See Figure 14-6.)

4. **Choose Worksheet⇨Sort to display a cascading menu of sorting options.**

5. **Choose either Ascending or Descending from this menu.**

   Approach magically sorts your database.

To sort a database in Form view, follow these steps:

1. **Choose View⇨Browse & Data Entry; or click the Browse button on the Action bar; or press Ctrl+B.**

2. **Click the Form tab to view your data in Form view.**

3. **Click the database field you want to use for sorting.**

   To sort by last name, for example, click the Last Name database field.

4. **Choose Browse⇨Sort to open the Sort cascading menu.**

5. **Choose either Ascending or Descending from this menu.**

   Approach sorts your database, although in Form view, you can't easily tell that the program really does any sorting.

As a shortcut to sorting, just click the database field that you want to sort by and then click either the Ascending or Descending Sort SmartIcon. (Refer to Figure 14-6.)

Multifield sorting

Sorting by a single database field is nice, but for more power, Approach enables you to sort by using two or more database fields simultaneously. If you're using multiple database fields for sorting, you must tell Approach the order in which to sort your data. If you sort a database alphabetically by

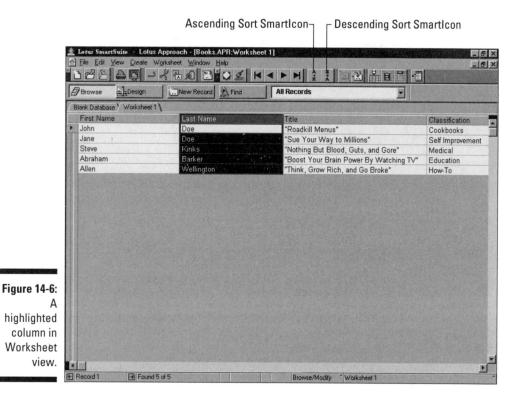

Ascending Sort SmartIcon — ┌ Descending Sort SmartIcon

Figure 14-6:
A highlighted column in Worksheet view.

last name, for example, what happens if you have two Smiths or three Johnsons in your database? To avoid this dilemma, tell Approach: "Okay, sort my data by last name. And if you have any duplicate last names, sort the duplicates alphabetically by first name."

In this case, the Last Name field first tells Approach how to sort data. If any duplicates exist, the next database field tells Approach how to sort the duplicates, and so on.

To sort a database by using multiple fields in Worksheet view, follow these steps:

1. **Choose View⇨Browse & Data Entry; or click the Browse button on the Action bar; or press Ctrl+B.**

2. **Click the Worksheet tab to view your data in the worksheet grid or the Form tab to view your data in Form view.**

3. **Choose Worksheet⇨Sort⇨Define in the Worksheet view; or choose Browse⇨Sort⇨Define in the Form view; or press Ctrl+T in either view.**

   The Sort dialog box appears. (See Figure 14-7.)

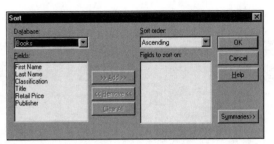

Figure 14-7:
The Sort
dialog box.

4. **In the Fields list box, click the first database field that you want Approach to use for sorting.**

5. **Click the Add button.**

6. **Click the database field in the Fields To Sort On list and then select either Ascending or Descending from the Sort Order drop-down list.**

7. **In the Fields list box, click the next database field that you want Approach to use for sorting and click Add again.**

   Repeat Steps 6 and 7 for each database field that you want to use for sorting.

8. **Click OK.**

   Approach sorts your database in the order that you added fields. (Isn't it nice to boss your computer around for a change?)

Get back — returning the database to its original sort order

After sorting, rearranging, and reshuffling your data in a myriad of multiple combinations, you may want to return your database to its original Sort order. To return a database to its original order, Approach gives you the following two choices:

✔ If you're in Form view, choose Browse➪Find➪Find All. (If you're in Worksheet view, choose Worksheet➪Find➪Find All.)

✔ Press Ctrl+A.

Your original Sort order? It's baaaaaack!

Saving a Find or Sort

Creating a Find can be simple or complicated. The simple ones are easy to do, but a complicated Find can take a few minutes to set up. Likewise, performing a simple Sort takes just a few mouse clicks, but setting up a useful multifield Sort requires at least a modest time investment.

If you create a complicated Find or Sort that you may need to use again in the future, you can tell Approach to save that Find or Sort. Then, the next time you need to search your database for the same information, you just tell Approach: "Remember the last time I asked you to find everyone who lives in Oregon, Washington, or Idaho, makes more than $30,000 a year, owns a home, and subscribes to *Soldier of Fortune* magazine? Well, find that information for me again and sort it for use as a mailing list."

Saving your Finds and Sorts enables you to store often-used searches so that you don't need to specify the search criteria and sorting order all over again.

Saving the Find saves the criteria, not the results of the Find. When you reuse the Find, Approach performs a new search of the database by using the saved criteria and displays the results — including all the latest updates to the database that match the find criteria.

One strange thing about saving a search is that you can define a Find alone, but to save a Sort you must define a Find as well as a Sort. But that requirement is not really as strange as the idea may seem, because you often want to combine a Find and a Sort anyway. And if you really need to save only the Sort, just define a Find that finds all the records in the database.

To save a Find or Sort, follow these steps:

1. **Choose Browse⇨Find⇨Find Assistant; or choose Worksheet⇨Find⇨ Find Assistant; or press Ctrl+I.**

   This action opens the Find/Sort Assistant dialog box.

2. **Define a Find.**

   Refer back to the "Sending the Find Assistant on a Search" section earlier in this chapter if you need a refresher on defining a Find.

   If you want to sort all the records in the database, define a Find that finds all the records. For example, you can choose a Basic Find on the Find Type tab and then, on the Condition 1 tab, select any field and choose Is Not Blank from the Operator list. Click Find On Another Field to display the Condition 2 tab; then click the Find More Records (OR) radio button. Select the same field again and choose Is Blank from the Operator list. This procedure absolutely guarantees that the Find selects the entire database.

3. **Click the Sort tab to display the options shown in Figure 14-8.**

Figure 14-8:
The Sort tab of the Find/Sort Assistant dialog box.

4. **In the Fields list box, click the first database field that you want Approach to use for sorting.**

5. **Click the Add button.**

6. **Click the database field in the Fields To Sort On list and then select either Ascending or Descending from the Sort Order drop-down list.**

7. **Click the next database field that you want Approach to use for sorting and click Add.**

   Repeat Steps 6 and 7 for each database field that you want to use for sorting.

8. **Click the Name tab to display the options shown in Figure 14-9.**

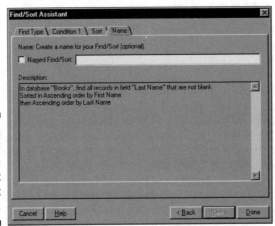

Figure 14-9:
The Name tab of the Find/Sort Assistant dialog box.

9. **Click the Named Find/Sort check box and type a name in the text box.**

   You can click the Back or Next buttons or click the dialog box tabs to move from tab to tab and refine the find and sort criteria until you achieve the effect you want.

10. **Click Done.**

    Approach applies the find and sort specifications to your database and also saves them for future use.

To run a stored Find or Sort, follow these steps:

1. **Choose Create➪Named Find/Sort.**

   The Named Find/Sort dialog box appears, listing the available Finds in the Name list box.

2. **In the list, click the name of the Find that you want to run.**

3. **Click the Run button.**

   Approach finds the matching records for you according to the instructions in the saved Find.

You can also apply named Finds by selecting the name from the drop-down list box in the Action bar of your form. Approach applies the Find immediately. Now *that's* slick!

Chapter 15

Putting Your Database on Report

• •

• •

*F*orm view is great for displaying one record at a time and giving you the capability to customize its appearance. Worksheet view is great for displaying multiple records at once, but you're stuck viewing your data through a boring grid.

If a form or worksheet isn't sufficient, you can use a report. As do forms, reports enable you to customize their appearance. As with worksheets, reports enable you to view multiple records at once. But the main difference that makes reports so valuable is that they can also display calculations based on your data. If your database contains all the names of your salespeople, for example, a report may show you which salesperson is making the most sales and which salesperson has the highest expenses (and needs to be fired).

Standard versus Columnar — Choosing a Report Type

Approach offers the following two basic report types:

✔ *Columnar* reports

✔ *Standard* reports

A *Columnar report* displays your data in columns and rows, much like the Worksheet view. Columnar reports are best for cramming as much information as possible on a single sheet of paper. A *Standard report*, on the other hand, displays your data as a complete record, much like Form view does. Standard reports take more space to display but make studying individual records stored in your database easier. To see the difference, look at Figure 15-1.

Figure 15-1:
Comparison between a Columnar (left) and a Standard (right) report in the Report Assistant dialog box.

Columnar report   Standard report

To create a Columnar or Standard report, follow these steps:

1. Choose Create⇨Report.

The Step 1: Layout tab of the Report Assistant dialog box appears (see Figure 15-2).

Figure 15-2:
The Report Assistant dialog box displays the Step 1: Layout tab.

2. **Type a name for your report in the <u>V</u>iew Name & Title text box.**

3. **Click either Columnar or Standard in the <u>L</u>ayout list.**

4. **Click the <u>S</u>tyle drop-down list box and choose a style that appeals to you from the list.**

   Approach displays a preview of your report layout and style in the Sample Report box.

5. **Click the <u>N</u>ext button.**

   The Step 2: Fields tab of the Report Assistant dialog box appears (see Figure 15-3).

6. **In the <u>F</u>ields list, click each database field that you want to appear on your report and click the <u>A</u>dd button.**

   Each database field that you choose appears in the Fields To Place On View list box.

7. **Click <u>D</u>one.**

   Approach displays your report. Initially, the report appears in Design view. Click the Browse button on the Action bar to see the report without the distracting design grid. Then your report should appear much like the one shown in Figure 15-4, depending on the style and layout you choose.

Figure 15-3:
The Report
Assistant
dialog box
displays the
Step 2:
Fields tab.

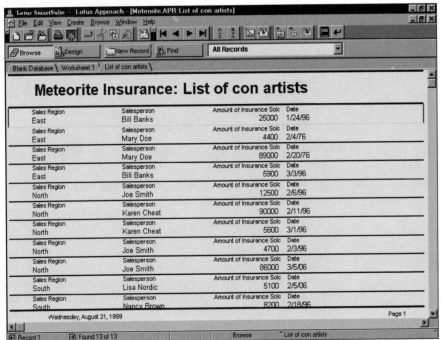

Figure 15-4:
A typical
Standard
report.

Adding Totals

Standard and Columnar reports simply display your data in a neat format.
To help you better understand your data, however, reports can display three
different types of summaries (groups and totals), as shown in Figure 15-5.
These report layouts offer the following options:

- ✔ *Columnar With Grand Totals* adds calculated totals to each column of a
  columnar report.

- ✔ *Columnar With Groups & Totals* enables you to group your information
  and calculate subtotals for each grouping in addition to the grand totals
  for the report.

- ✔ *Summary Only* enables you to dispense with all the details and look at
  the calculated totals only.

Summaries serve two purposes: to group database fields together and to
calculate a total result. Figure 15-6, for example, shows a typical report using
the Columnar with Groups and Totals layout. A summary can group data
together according to Sales region or Salesperson. By reorganizing your data

Figure 15-5:
The three
types of
summary
reports.

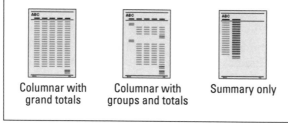

according to sales region, you can more easily see which salespeople are
working in which sales region. By reorganizing your data according to
salesperson, you can see which salesperson is selling a lot and which
salesperson is doing practically nothing.

Summaries can also calculate a total result. You may, for example, want to
know the total sales for each sales region. Instead of calculating this value
yourself, have Approach do the job for you automatically. The following
steps show how to group data and calculate a total result in a report:

1. **Choose Create⇨Report to access the Step 1: Layout tab of the Report
   Assistant dialog box (refer to Figure 15-2).**

2. **Type a name for your report in the View Name & Title text box.**

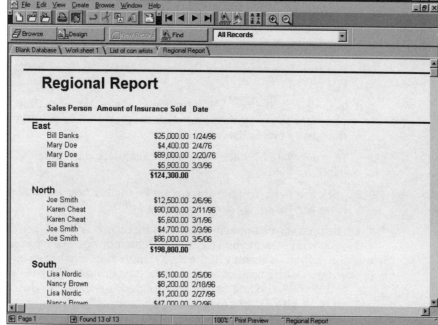

Figure 15-6:
An example
of a
summary
grouping
data
according
to Sales
region.

3. Click the <u>S</u>tyle drop-down list box and choose your favorite style.

4. In the <u>L</u>ayout list, click Columnar With Groups & Totals.

At this point, you could choose any of the report layouts that offer summaries: Columnar With Grand Totals, Columnar With Groups & Totals, or Summary Only. After you choose a layout, Approach adjusts the tabs (Steps) in the dialog box to present the options and settings pertaining to that layout. We're going through the steps here for creating a report by using the Columnar With Groups & Totals layout because this type of layout demonstrates all the available options. The following list describes how the other layouts differ from the one used in this example:

- *Columnar With Groups & Totals* includes tabs for Layout, Fields, Groups, and Totals.

- *Columnar With Grand Totals* includes tabs for Layout, Fields, and Grand Totals (which includes the same options as on the Totals tab of the preceding layout type), but omits the Groups tab because those settings don't apply to this layout type.

- *Summary Only* includes tabs for Layout, Groups, and Summary (which is the same as Totals) but skips the Fields tab.

5. Click the <u>N</u>ext button to access the Step 2: Fields tab of the Report Assistant dialog box (refer to Figure 15-3).

6. Click each database field that you want to appear on your report and click the <u>A</u>dd button; or simply double-click each field.

Each database field that you choose appears in the Fields To Place On View list box.

7. Click the <u>N</u>ext button.

The Step 3: Groups tab of the Report Assistant dialog box appears (see Figure 15-7).

8. In the <u>F</u>ields list box, click the name of the database field by which you want to group data and click the <u>A</u>dd button to add that field to the <u>G</u>roup Fields list box.

To group data by sales region, for example, click the Sales Region database field.

9. Click the field name in the <u>G</u>roup Fields list box and make a selection from the Gr<u>o</u>up By drop-down list.

The options available in the Group By drop-down list vary depending on what kind of field you select. The Default option always creates a group for each unique entry in the field (Smith and Smyth are separate groups). Other grouping options include grouping by the first letter of a text field (Smith and Smyth are grouped together with the other entries starting with S); grouping dates by month or year; or grouping numbers into groups of 10 or 10,000.

Figure 15-7:
Step 3 of
the Report
Assistant
dialog box:
the Groups
tab.

10. Click the <u>N</u>ext button to move to the Step 4: Totals tab of the Report Assistant dialog box, shown in Figure 15-8.

11. To have Approach calculate the sum of the data in a certain field, click the field name in the <u>F</u>ields list box and click <u>A</u>dd; or just double-click the field name.

12. Select the field in the <u>S</u>ummary Fields list and select a calculation from the <u>C</u>alculate The drop-down list.

    In addition to the obvious selection that sums a column of numbers, Approach can calculate the average, the maximum, the minimum, the count (that is, the number of entries), and several other useful values. Repeat Steps 11 and 12 for each column that you want to calculate.

13. Click <u>D</u>one.

    Approach displays your report in Design view (see Figure 15-9).

14. Choose <u>F</u>ile⇨<u>P</u>rint Preview.

    Approach now displays your report as it would look if you printed out the report.

Figure 15-8:
Step 4 of
the Report
Assistant
dialog
box: the
Totals tab.

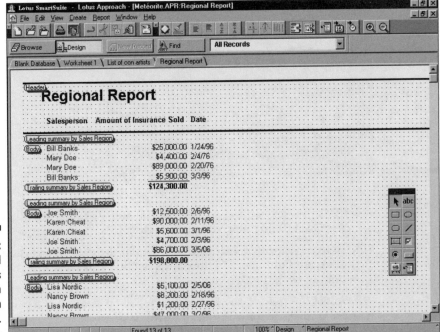

Figure 15-9:
A typical
report as
seen in
Design
view.

When viewing a report in Print Preview, you can zoom in for a closer look by clicking on the preview to make the image larger. Conversely, you can zoom out (make the image smaller) by right-clicking the preview image.

Making Your Reports Look Great

Approach automatically creates reports for you, but you may still want to modify the appearance of your reports for the sheer joy of it (which probably means that you have waaay too much time on your hands). Approach enables you to add or modify the following parts of your report:

- ✔ A title page
- ✔ Headers and footers
- ✔ Line and color settings of database fields
- ✔ Position and size of database fields

Before you can modify your reports, you must first display your reports in Design view. Choose View➪Design, click the Design button on the Action bar, or press Ctrl+D.

Adding and modifying headers and footers

Headers appear on the top of every page and can be useful for listing the database field as column headings. *Footers* appear at the bottom of every page and are more useful for listing mundane information such as page numbers, the date that the report was created, and the person to blame in case the report data is wrong.

To add or modify a header or footer, follow these steps:

1. Choose Report⇨Add Header (or Add Footer).

Approach displays the header (or footer) on your report.

2. Add any text, lines, or other geometric shapes to the header or footer by using the Tools palette, as described in Chapter 13.

Often you find that having Approach insert certain values, such as a page number, into your report for you is useful — especially in headers and footers. To insert a value into the body of your report, click the report body, choose Report⇨Insert to open a cascading menu, and then choose Today's Date, Current Time, Page Number, or Field Value from this menu. To insert a value into the header or footer, click the header or footer and choose Panel⇨Insert to open the same cascading menu.

To hide your header or footer from view, choose Report┤Add Header (or Add Footer).

Changing line settings and colors of database fields

To make your database fields look pretty, Approach enables you to draw frames around the fields and change the background color. Of course, if you get carried away, your database fields can appear in eye-popping fluorescent green against a brilliant orange background. (Psychedelic, man!) Unless you're an artist, keeping frames and colors to a minimum is a good idea.

Using multiple colors can make your reports easier to read, but your reports still print out in black and white — unless, of course, you have a color printer.

To add frames or background colors to your fields, follow these steps:

1. Click the database field that you want to modify on your report.

Approach highlights the entire column of database fields (see Figure 15-10).

Figure 15-10:
A report
with
columnar
database
fields
highlighted.

   2. Choose Column⇨Column Properties; or press Alt+Enter; or click the
Show Info SmartIcon. The Column Properties InfoBox opens.

3. Click the Font, Attribute, and Color tab; the Color, Border, and Line
Style tab; the Number Format tab; or the Basics tab to change the
settings of the highlighted database fields.

4. Make any changes that you want in the different tabs of the InfoBox
to modify the appearance of your database fields.

Chapters 1 and 13 give you some additional guidelines on working with
InfoBoxes.

5. Click the Close (X) button after you're done making changes in the
InfoBox.

Moving and resizing database fields

As Approach creates a report, the program tries to cram in as many database fields as will possibly fit on a single page. Most of the time this approach works, but sometimes Approach squeezes your database fields so
narrowly that the data inside is partially hidden. Other times, Approach may

display two separate database fields so close together that determining where one field ends and the next one begins is difficult. To touch up a report and make the thing readable, Approach enables you to move database fields around and resize them.

To move a database field, follow these steps:

1. Click the database field that you want to move on your report.

Approach highlights your selected database field and turns the pointer into a hand.

2. Press and hold the mouse button and drag the mouse.

Approach displays a box to show you the new position of your database fields (see Figure 15-11).

3. Release the mouse button.

Approach moves your database field, along with its corresponding header, to the new location.

To resize a database field, follow these steps:

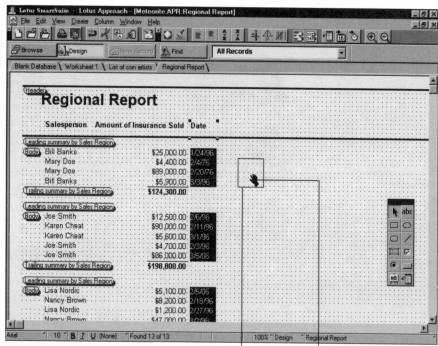

Figure 15-11:
Moving a
database
field.

Box showing the new position of the database field   Hand pointer

1. **Click the database field that you want to resize on your report.**

   Approach highlights your selected database field.

2. **Move the pointer to the right edge of the highlighted database field.**

   Approach turns the pointer into a double arrow.

3. **Press and hold the mouse button and drag the mouse.**

   Approach shows the new size of your database field as a box, as shown in Figure 15-12.

4. **Release the mouse button after the database field is the size you want.**

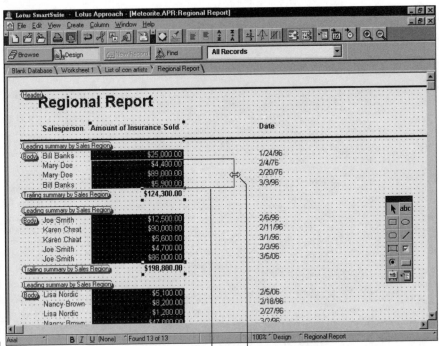

Figure 15-12: Resizing a database field.

Box showing the new size of the database field   Double-arrow pointer

Finishing up — Adding Summaries

Normally the best time to create a report with a summary is as you're creating the report in the first place. That way, Approach does most of the hard work in creating the summaries for you. Those of us who don't have the patience to plan ahead, however, can always add summaries to an existing Columnar or Standard report at a later time.

Make sure that you switch to Design view by choosing View⇨Design, clicking the Design button on the Action bar, or pressing Ctrl+D.

To display grouped data records on an existing Columnar or Standard report, follow these steps:

1. **Click the database field of the report that you want to use to group records together.**

   For example, click the Sales Region database field to group records according to sales region. Approach highlights your database field (see Figure 15-13).

2. **Click the Leading Summary or Trailing Summary SmartIcon.**

   Approach groups your records according to the database field you selected.

To add calculations to a report, follow these steps:

1. **Click a database field containing numbers that you want Approach to use to calculate a total result.**

   If you want Approach to calculate the total sales of insurance sold, for example, click the Amount of Insurance Sold database field. Approach highlights your database field.

2. **Click the Sum icon.**

   Approach displays the total you requested.

You can also click the Average icon to calculate average sales or the Count icon . . . well, you get the idea.

Printing Reports

After you spend countless hours (or minutes) making your reports look pretty, printing the reports so that you can share your masterpieces with others only makes sense. Before wasting paper (and contributing to global deforestation), however, view your report on-screen first. That way, if

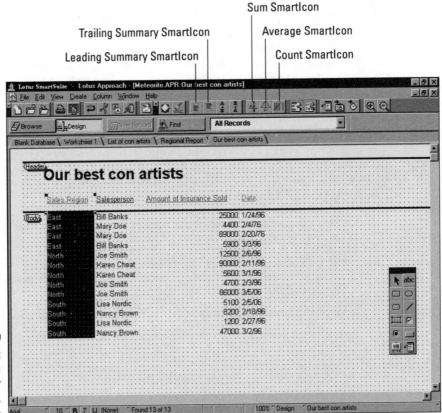

Sum SmartIcon

Trailing Summary SmartIcon

Average SmartIcon

Leading Summary SmartIcon

Count SmartIcon

Figure 15-13:
Modifying a
Columnar
report.

something is totally out of whack, you can fix the problem before wasting
time and printing out a report that you may have to throw away after all. To
preview your report on-screen, follow these steps:

1. **Choose File➪Print Preview or click the Print Preview SmartIcon.**

2. **Click the left mouse button to see your report in greater detail (or the
   right mouse button for lesser detail), or choose View➪Zoom In (or
   Zoom Out) from the menu bar.**

3. **Choose View➪Zoom To➪100%, or press Ctrl+1 to return your report
   to its actual size.**

4. **Choose File➪Print Preview or click the Print Preview SmartIcon
   again to stop viewing your report on-screen in Preview mode.**

When you're ready to print your report, choose File➪Print, click the Print
SmartIcon, or press Ctrl+P to open the Print dialog box (and then click the
Print button in the dialog box). Now just stand back and watch that sucker
print!

Part V

Freelance's Presentation Power

The 5th Wave   **By Rich Tennant**

@RICHTENNANT

"Of course graphics are important to your project, Eddy, but I think it would've been better to scan a _picture_ of your worm collection."

In this part . . .

Don't fret and sweat over your upcoming presentation at the shareholders' meeting. Freelance Graphics gives you the tools you need to get prepared and organized. This part shows you how to put together all the materials you may need for a professional presentation. If you don't need to worry about your presentation materials and organization, maybe you can actually get some sleep the night before so that you really look like you know what you're doing. (You do, don't you . . .?)

Chapter 16

Boot Camp for Freelance Graphics

· ·

· ·

*J*ust the thought of public speaking causes many a mere mortal to break into a cold sweat. Worrying yourself sick about a presentation that you must make probably doesn't make your talk go any smoother. But fear not — Freelance Graphics can! Freelance makes putting together all the materials that you need for a truly stunning presentation easy — well, relatively easy. With the presentation materials under control, you can safely concentrate on the more important issues — such as remembering to show up on time so that the show can go on.

Presenting Freelance Graphics

If you ever must present information to an audience — or create snappy presentation materials for someone else to use — you should be pleased to know that using Freelance Graphics makes the entire experience practically painless. By using the power of Freelance Graphics (henceforth referred to just as *Freelance* to emphasize its user-friendly nature), you can delight and amaze audiences — and persuade them to your point of view every time. If you're wondering exactly what a presentation graphics program such as Freelance can do for you, check out some of the following nifty features:

✔ Creating presentations with a uniform look is a piece of cake with more than a hundred professionally designed SmartMaster sets.

✔ Create title pages, bulleted lists, charts, tables — you name it — by using Freelance's preformatted page layouts.

✔ Create speaker notes to help you get through your presentation without freezing.

✔ Create astonishing on-screen slide presentations with big-time special effects and transitions but with small-time effort.

Getting the Show on the Road

You start Freelance the same way you start any of the other SmartSuite Millennium Edition programs; just follow these steps:

1. **If SuiteStart is running, click the Lotus Freelance Graphics icon in the taskbar's system tray; or you can open the SmartSuite drawer in SmartCenter, click the Lotus Applications folder, and then double-click the Lotus Freelance icon. Otherwise, click the Start button in the taskbar, point to Programs, point to Lotus SmartSuite, and then choose Lotus Freelance Graphics.**

   The Welcome to Lotus Freelance Graphics dialog box appears, as shown in Figure 16-1.

2. **Make sure that you have the Create A New Presentation Using A SmartMaster tab selected.**

Figure 16-1: The Welcome to Lotus Freelance Graphics dialog box enables you to start from scratch or edit an existing presentation.

To work on an existing presentation instead of creating a new one, select the Open An Existing Presentation tab and select a presentation file you worked on recently from the list of presentations. If you don't see the presentation listed, click the Browse button to open a dialog box that enables you to locate the file on your system. Click Open to open the presentation.

3. **Choose the SmartMaster design that you want to use as the basis of your presentation.**

Normally, to choose a design, first you choose a content topic (which includes a set of preformatted presentation pages you can use), and then you choose a look (color scheme and background graphics) for your presentation. However, for your first explorations of Freelance, you may want to choose (No content topic) to keep things simpler.

4. **After you make your choices from the lists in this dialog box, click OK to open the New Page dialog box.**

5. **Choose a page layout from the list on the Page Layout tab of this dialog box and click OK.**

6. **Enter your text in the page layout template that appears.**

Congratulations, you've created the first page of your presentation.

That's the overall procedure of creating a presentation, offered in a bare-bones nutshell (mixing of metaphors intended). But, of course, each of the preceding steps involves much more effort than described in this section's overview, and the following sections go into the gory details.

You've got the look

The first step on the road to creating a stunning Freelance presentation is to pick a *look* from the more than 125 professionally designed SmartMaster sets that come with the program. You pick a look for your presentation from the lists in the New Presentation dialog box as part of the process of creating a new presentation file. Because these SmartMaster looks are designed by professionals, you don't need to worry about things such as artistic balance, color, fonts, type size, and so on. Of course, you *can* make all these decisions yourself, but why bother if the work's been done for you?

Don't feel pressured to make a final choice for your presentation's look right now. You can change your mind at any time during the process of creating your presentation. After you create some presentation pages, you can choose Presentation⇨Choose a Different SmartMaster Look to open the Choose a Look for Your Presentation dialog box. Then you can select a different look from the list and click OK to apply that look to all the pages in your presentation.

Okay, but how do you decide which SmartMaster look to use? Freelance thoughtfully provides you with a preview of any SmartMaster look that you highlight in the lists in the New Presentation or Choose a Look for Your Presentation dialog boxes. An easy way to browse through the list of SmartMaster sets is to use the scroll bar or the down-arrow key. As you scroll down the Select A Look list, a thumbnail-sized preview of each highlighted SmartMaster appears on the right side of the dialog box. If you're a do-it-yourself kind of guy or gal, choose Blank Background in the lists of looks in either the New Presentation or Choose a Look for Your Presentation dialog boxes to make all the creative decisions yourself. Unless, however, you possess no small measure of graphic design talent, don't try this one at home.

Getting a head start with a Content Topic

Freelance SmartMasters can affect more than the look of your presentation. SmartMasters can provide templates for the content as well. A SmartMaster Content Topic serves as the skeleton for your presentation with an assortment of predesigned pages, arranged in a suggested order, complete with text placeholders. You just fill in the blanks with your own text and data to produce a professional-quality presentation in a hurry.

Picking a layout

After you choose the look that you want for your presentation, you need to pick the kind of page layout that you want to create. Whichever SmartMaster set you choose, Freelance provides 13 page layouts with the appropriate elements included. In fact, as soon as you choose your SmartMaster set, the New Page dialog box appears, as shown in Figure 16-2. (This is the dialog box that you see if you chose (No content topic) when you started the presentation.) Just as when you choose a SmartMaster set, you see a preview of the various page layouts in the right side of the New Page dialog box. You can click a layout name or use the up- or down-arrow keys to highlight a layout in the list in the dialog box.

If you chose to use a content topic when you started the presentation, the New Page dialog box has two tabs. The Page Layouts tab offers the same choices as the standard New Page dialog box. The Content Pages tab offers a selection of predesigned pages, as shown in Figure 16-3. Again, you highlight a topic in the list to see a preview of the page in the right side of the dialog box.

Figure 16-2:
The New Page dialog box lists the page layouts at your disposal.

Figure 16-3:
The Content Pages tab enables you to choose one of the predesigned pages that are part of the Content Topic you chose for this presentation.

To choose the page layout that you want, click an item name in the list on either the Page Layouts or Content Pages tabs of the New Page dialog box and then click OK. A page layout template appears — complete with dummy elements, called *Click here blocks,* ready for you to replace with whatever you want on the page — as shown in Figure 16-4. If you chose a content page, some of the text may already be filled in for you.

In choosing a page layout, keep the following points in mind:

✔ You don't need to choose a layout that *exactly* matches what you have in mind for the page. You can add, rearrange, or even delete elements in any of the layouts. Picking a layout that is at least *close* to what you want, however, is a good idea.

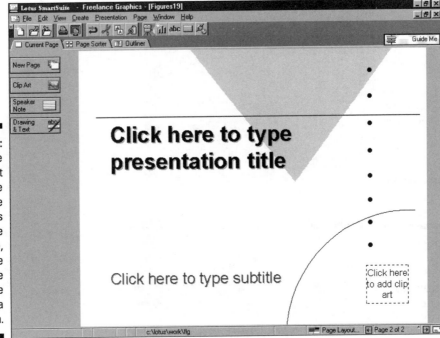

Figure 16-4:
A page layout template with the elements for a title page, usually the first page you create for a presentation.

✔ If you're creating a title page — something almost every presentation has — choosing the Title layout usually makes a great deal of sense.

✔ If none of the layouts come close to what you want, choose the Basic Layout, which gives you only the graphic elements of the SmartMaster set and a title for the page. If even the Basic Layout has more stuff than you want, choose [Blank Page] to get just the background color with no graphic or text elements at all.

✔ If you realize that you chose the wrong page layout, don't panic. Just choose Page⇨Switch Page Layout and select a different layout from the Switch Page Layout dialog box.

Add text (and stir)

With your chosen page layout on-screen, replacing text elements with your own text is as simple as clicking and typing. As you can see from the example in Figure 16-4, each element in the Title layout tells you to click the element to add your own data or graphics. To type the text for the presentation title on the presentation's title page, for example, follow these steps:

1. **Click the page layout element that reads** `Click here to type presentation title.`

   A text box appears in place of the instructions for you to type your title.

2. **Type the text that you want for the presentation title.**

3. **Click OK or just click anywhere on the page outside the title element's frame to accept the title.**

   The text box window and its buttons disappear, leaving the text you typed.

All the elements in all the page layouts work the same way. Click the element and add the data. Some elements require additional or different steps. Adding a chart or symbol, for example, requires more than just typing, but all the instructions are right there for you. If, for example, you're working on a title page and you click where the text reads `Click here to add clip art`, Freelance takes you right into a dialog box where you can choose clip art to add. If you want more details on a lot of this stuff, check out *Freelance Graphics 96 For Windows 95 For Dummies,* by William Harrel and Roger C. Parker (published by IDG Books Worldwide, Inc.) for the full scoop. In the meantime, keep the following in mind as you add elements to your page layout:

✔ You can't get too lost adding elements in a page layout. Notice the Tips button in the title text box. Every element of every page layout has a Tips button or a Help button. Click the Tips or Help button to access a dialog box explaining how to create the particular element you're working with.

As you enter text, you can use the Bold, Italic, and Underline SmartIcons. You can also change fonts and sizes by using the Font and Size buttons on the status bar, just as you can in the other SmartSuite programs. You can also change font size by using the size icons (the ones with the pairs of big and little *A*s) found on the bar at the top of the text entry box. (You may not want to change the font and size, however, because that affects the consistency provided by the SmartMaster.)

✔ You can edit text as you create it by using the Backspace and Delete keys. If you need to edit text after accepting a text entry, double-click the text element to select that block of text and reopen the text box with the insertion point so that you can make your changes.

Adding clip art

Because adding clip art is part of creating a normal title page, this section is a good place to sneak in a bit about this nifty feature.

Clip art in Freelance is just a little graphic — a picture — stored in a Freelance symbol library. Freelance includes zillions of clip art images for every occasion. Assuming that you select the Title layout, as described in the preceding steps, you can add clip art by following these steps:

1. **Click the page layout element that says** `Click here to add clip art.`

   The Add Clip Art or Diagram to the Page dialog box appears, as shown in Figure 16-5.

Figure 16-5: The Add Clip Art or Diagram to the Page dialog box, displaying six symbols from the Arrows category.

2. **If necessary, choose Clip Art in the View area in the lower-right corner of the dialog box.**

3. **Select a category from the Category drop-down list.**

   After you click a category name, the first six clip art images appear at the bottom of the dialog box. (Some categories have fewer than six images.)

4. **Choose a clip art image by scrolling through the images (using the arrow buttons below the images) in the chosen category and double-clicking the one that you want to insert. Click outside the clip art image when you're finished.**

   The clip art image appears on the page.

Inserting a New Page

After you know how to create a title page, you already know just about everything you need to know to add new pages. To add a new page, simply choose Create⇨Page (or press F7) to display the New Page dialog box.

Surprise, this dialog box is the same one you use to create the first page of your presentation. So you already know how to use the thing. (Check out the section "Picking a layout," earlier in this chapter, if you need a refresher on using the New Page dialog box.)

Here are a couple of points to remember as you add pages to your presentation:

✔ Clicking the New Page button is an even quicker way to open the New Page dialog box. (You find the New Page button located in the upper-left corner of the Freelance window in Current Page view — the only view you've used so far.)

✔ After you click OK, Freelance inserts the new page in your presentation following the page that you were on when you opened the New Page dialog box. The new page appears in the Current Page view editing window, and the creation process goes on. Don't worry too much about keeping the pages in your presentation in order as you create them. Freelance's Page Sorter view enables you to rearrange the pages easily after you create them. See Chapter 18 for details on moving among presentation pages, rearranging presentation pages, and changing views.

Saving Your Presentation

Saving a Freelance presentation is just the same as saving a document in any other SmartSuite Millennium program. Choose File➪Save, enter a name in the File Name text box of the Save As dialog box, and then click Save. Freelance saves all your presentation pages in one file.

Chapter 17

Presenting (Ta Daaah!) Tables and Charts

• •

• •

*1*f you really want your presentation to persuade your audience that you know what you're talking about, you probably need to throw in more than just some fancy titles. Good news. Freelance enables you to add just about any element of persuasion, including tables and charts. And, just like text and symbols in title pages, charts and tables are just a click away.

Adding Tables

One good presentation device is putting data in a table — rows and columns — to give your data an air of organization and authority. Okay, of course your data *is* authoritative, but you must persuade your audience of that fact.

Although you can create a table on any of the page layouts, typically you create a table by inserting a new page using the Table layout. To insert a new page containing a table, follow these steps:

1. **Choose Create⇨Page, press F7, or click the New Page button (located just below the Current Page tab) to display the New Page dialog box.**

2. **Select the Page Layouts tab (if you're using content topics) and double-click Table in the list of available layouts.**

   The new page, with the elements for the Table layout, appears, as shown in Figure 17-1. The two standard elements on a Table page layout are a page title and, of course, a table.

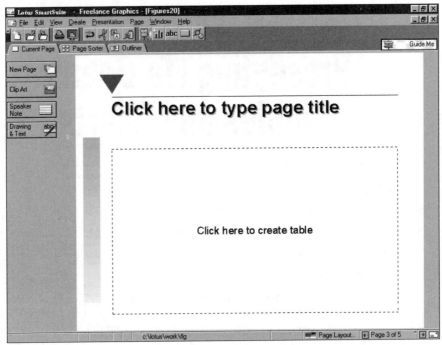

Figure 17-1:
A new page
created by
using the
Table page
layout.

3. **Click the text that reads** `Click here to type page title` **to open the text box for the title.**

4. **Type the title of the page and click OK in the text box.**

5. **Click inside the box containing the text** `Click here to create table`.

The Table Gallery dialog box appears, as shown in Figure 17-2, giving you four available styles.

Figure 17-2:
The Table
Gallery
dialog box
provides a
choice of
basic table
styles.

6. **Click the box displaying the table style that you want to use.**

7. **Click the up- or down-arrow buttons next to the Rows or Columns box to change the number of rows or columns in your table.**

   The default is four rows and four columns, but you can specify the numbers you need to present your data. If you are unsure of the number of rows or columns needed, don't worry. You can add or delete rows and columns at any time while you're creating or editing your table.

8. **Click OK.**

   The empty table with the specified attributes appears on the page. Figure 17-3 shows a table created by using the default settings and after you enter some text.

When the empty table first appears on the page, selection handles surround the table. These handles enable you to size or move the table. You can size a table by positioning the mouse pointer over one of the selection handles so that the pointer turns into a double-headed arrow; then just press and hold the left mouse button and drag the handle until the table is the size you want in that direction. You can move a table by positioning the mouse pointer inside the selected table, pressing and holding the left mouse button, and dragging the table to a new location.

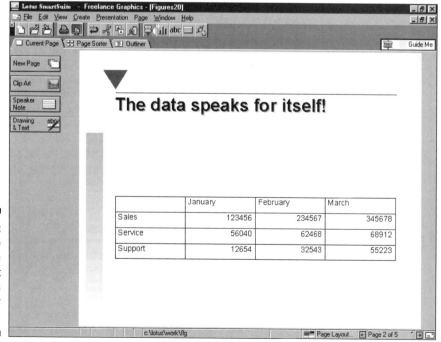

Figure 17-3:
This table
uses the
default
four rows
and four
columns.

Entering table text

To enter text in your new table, click the *cell* (one of the rectangles in the table) in which you want to enter text. A thick gray border appears around the table, and a text insertion point appears in the cell you clicked. (If you haven't selected the table yet, just double-click the cell where you want to begin editing.) Type the text you want to enter and then click the next cell in which you want to enter text — or press the Tab key to move to the next cell or Shift+Tab to move to the previous cell. You can use the arrow keys to move the insertion point within the text in the table.

If you enter more text in a cell than can fit, the words automatically wrap to the next line, just as in Word Pro tables, and the row height expands to accommodate the extra lines. (See the section on tables in Chapter 6, for more on working with Word Pro tables.)

After you enter all the text, click outside the table to accept the entries.

Editing table attributes

These tables are not created in stone. You can change any attributes — table style, number of columns and rows, drop shadows, fonts, and so on — during the creation process.

You can apply certain attributes, such as text formatting, colors, and borders, to just the current cell (the one that the insertion point is in as you make the change) or to all selected cells. For changes that apply to more than one cell, you must select the cells that you want to change by pressing and holding the left mouse button and dragging the insertion point over the cells you want to modify. You don't need to worry about including the entire contents of a cell in the selection, because you select the entire cell as you drag the insertion point to the next cell.

To make any changes to a table's attributes, choose Table⇨Table Properties while the table (or any cell in the table) is selected. The Table Properties InfoBox appears, as shown in Figure 17-4.

You can choose which aspect of the table you want to change by clicking the appropriate tab in the InfoBox. If, for example, you click the Font, Attribute, and Color tab (the default option), you can change the text attributes for the entire table. To change the attributes of the selected cell instead of the entire table, choose Selected Cell in the Properties For drop-down list in the InfoBox's title bar.

You can also open the InfoBox by right-clicking the table and choosing either Cell Properties or Table Properties from the pop-up menu.

Font, Attribute, and Color tab
Alignment tab
Color, Pattern, and Line Style tab
Columns and Rows tab
Table Layout tab

Figure 17-4:
The Table
Properties
InfoBox.

You can modify the following attributes in the InfoBox:

✔ You can change the fonts, size, alignment, and so on of the table's text. In fact, you can make just about all the changes to your table's text that you can in Word Pro or any of the other SmartSuite Millennium programs. Just choose the attributes that you want to change from the appropriate drop-down lists, check boxes, and buttons.

You can also change selected table text to bold, italic, or underlined by selecting the text and clicking the SmartIcons for those attributes or the corresponding buttons on the status bar.

✔ You can use the Color, Pattern, and Line Style tab in the InfoBox to assign borders, drop shadows, and background colors to table cells.

✔ The Table Properties InfoBox also enables you to change the size of a column or row and change the table style from one of the four table styles to another.

If you make a change that you didn't mean to make, remember that you can almost always undo that change by choosing Edit⇨Undo Set Attributes (or by pressing Ctrl+Z). Figure 17-5 shows the table after making a few minor modifications.

To add or remove columns or rows, use the Table⇨Insert or Table⇨Delete commands. For example, you can select a cell in the row where you want to add another row and then choose Table⇨Insert⇨Row. Freelance adds a new row to your table below the row where the cursor is located.

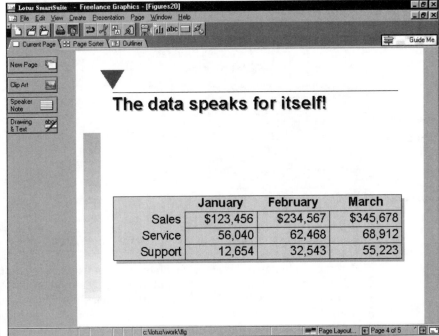

Figure 17-5:
A table
with new
fonts, text
alignment,
and style.

Adding Charts

What would a presentation be without charts? If we learned nothing else from the 1992 presidential race — at least on *Larry King Live* — we learned that charts are required accoutrements for effective presentations. Wait a minute — that guy with all the charts *lost!* Oh well, charts are still important. (And he probably wasn't using *Freelance* charts anyway.)

You usually add charts, as you do tables, by inserting a new page, using one of the page layout options that include one or more charts. Of course, you can add a chart to any page layout.

The concepts for creating charts in Freelance are the same as for creating charts in 1-2-3. If this information all seems like foreign territory to you, take a look at Chapter 10 of this book before diving in — or at least before you get confused and frustrated.

To create a page containing a single chart, follow these steps:

1. **Choose <u>C</u>reate⇨<u>P</u>age or click the New Page button (located just below the Current Page tab) to open the New Page dialog box.**

2. **Click 1 Chart in the list on the Page Layouts tab of the New Page dialog box, and then click OK.**

   A new page with two Click Here Blocks (one title element and one chart element) appears. Initially, this page looks very similar to the blank table page shown back in Figure 17-1.

3. **Click the text that reads Click here to type page title and then type a title for the page.**

4. **Click inside the box containing the text Click here to create chart.**

   The Create Chart dialog box appears, as shown in Figure 17-6.

Figure 17-6:
The Create Chart dialog box features more chart types than you can shake a pointer at.

5. **Click the chart type that you want to use in the Select A Chart Type list at the left side of the dialog box.**

6. **Click one of the buttons in the middle of the dialog box to select a variation of the basic chart type.**

   The buttons change to reflect the available variations for the chart type that you chose in Step 5.

7. **Select the style you want in the Select A Chart Style area.**

   The style selection controls chart formatting details, such as color scheme and the appearance of grid lines and such. The box just to the right of the Select A Chart Style area shows a preview of the chart that you are about to create, including chart type, variation, and style.

8. Click OK to display the Edit Data dialog box, opened to the Data tab.

If this dialog box looks somewhat familiar to you, it should (provided, of course, you have already read Part III of this book). Its grid of numbered rows and lettered columns looks much like a 1-2-3 worksheet. You enter text for Legend and Labels and numbers to chart in the cells, just as you do in a 1-2-3 worksheet. The options and grid in the Edit Data dialog box vary depending on the chart type you choose. If you choose a pie chart, for example, only one column for a data series is available, because a pie chart can have only one data series.

9. Enter the labels for each data series in the Labels column, the labels for the legend in the Legend rows, and the numbers for the data series in the appropriate cells.

The *Labels* identify the different divisions in a chart. If your chart shows the earnings for each quarter, for example, you may have axis labels for 1st quarter, 2nd quarter, 3rd quarter, and 4th quarter. You can also add an axis title that labels the entire set of entries. In this case, the axis title may be "Quarters." We tell you how to add axis titles in just a bit.

You may need to experiment a little to discover how to enter the data so that it produces the chart you expect. But the procedure is not too difficult to figure out — and viewing your data charted in different ways may generate some insights and pleasant surprises. Don't be afraid to experiment!

You can see a preview of what the chart looks like in the Edit Data dialog box. But remember that this representation *is* just a preview — not an exact representation of what the chart looks like on your page. This preview is helpful, nonetheless.

Figure 17-7 shows a filled-in Edit Data dialog box for a bar chart.

Figure 17-7:
The Edit Data dialog box displaying filled-in data for a bar chart with three data series.

10. After you have the chart data filled in, click OK to see the chart on the new page, as shown in Figure 17-8.

As you're creating and modifying charts in Freelance, keep the following points in mind:

- Notice that, if you select the chart, the menu choices in the menu bar change. To explore all the options for creating and modifying Freelance charts, take a look at what's available under the Chart menu.

- Just as you can for 1-2-3 charts, you can add headings, notes, and axis titles to your Freelance charts. You can add them while you're creating the chart by clicking the Titles tab in the Edit Data dialog box. The tab displays a group of text boxes, as shown in Figure 17-9. By the way, the Text Labels tab of the Edit Data dialog box looks just like the Data tab where you enter the plotting data for the chart, but the Text Labels tab allows you to enter numbers or text labels that appear on or beside the bars (or lines, or whatever) in the chart.

- When you edit an existing chart, you can choose a different chart type by double-clicking the chart to open the Chart Properties InfoBox, selecting the Type tab, and then choosing a different chart type. (If the Plot Properties InfoBox appears, just click the chart *outside* the plotting area.)

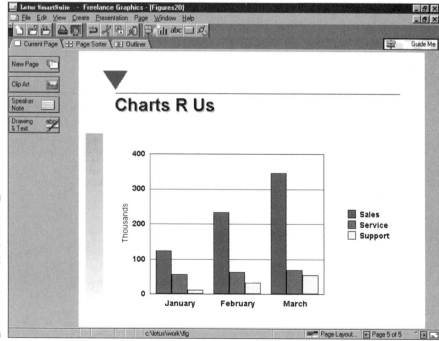

Figure 17-8:
A simple bar chart— but one that sure adds pizzazz to the presentation.

Figure 17-9:
The Titles
tab of the
Edit Data
dialog box.

✔ Another quick way to change chart types is simply to select the chart and then click the SmartIcon for the chart type that you want to use.

✔ Don't forget to save your work (by clicking the Save the Current Presentation SmartIcon) before making too many changes to your chart. That way, you can retrieve the original if you mess up too badly.

✔ To edit a chart that you already created, right-click the chart and choose Edit Data from the pop-up menu to display the Edit Data dialog box.

✔ Just as in 1-2-3 charts, you can modify each element of a Freelance chart independently. The x-axis is a chart element, for example, so you can double-click the x-axis to open a dialog box for editing the chart legend.

Because 1-2-3 is a full-featured spreadsheet program, 1-2-3 enables you to do a lot more with numbers and charts than Freelance does. If you already have a perfectly good chart created in 1-2-3 — or even just the data for a perfectly good chart entered in some other program — you needn't re-enter all the data into Freelance. You can copy charts from 1-2-3 or import data from 1-2-3 and a variety of other programs. The same principle applies to tables. Sometimes it's easier to copy an existing table from Word Pro or 1-2-3 than it is to re-create the table in Freelance.

Chapter 18

Final Touches and Shortcuts
à la Freelance

- -

In This Chapter
▶ Choosing from the three page views
▶ Using the Freelance drawing tools
▶ Creating a screen show

- -

*O*kay, so you've created a bunch of spiffy pages for your presentation —
an eye-catching title page, an informative table, a compelling chart or
two, and maybe some pages with other elements, such as bulleted lists and
organizational charts — now what? Time to add some final flourishes and
get this presentation put together.

Changing Views

Freelance gives you several ways to look at your presentation's pages on-
screen: *Current Page* view, *Page Sorter* view, and *Outliner* view. So far, you've
seen pages only in the Current Page view, which is the view you're in as you
create a new page. Current Page view is also the view that you use to edit
pages. You can change views by choosing the view you want from the View
menu, but the easiest way to change views is by clicking one of the view
tabs just below the menu bar and SmartIcon palette.

Sorting presentation pages

To change to the Page Sorter view, click the Page Sorter tab. Page Sorter
view displays all the pages in your presentation as thumbnails (small
versions) so that you can see a bunch of them on a single screen. You can
choose View⇨Zoom⇨Out or View⇨Zoom⇨In to make the thumbnails

smaller or larger so that more or fewer thumbnails fit on the screen. You can use the scroll bar to see any of the thumbnails that don't fit on one screen.

Figure 18-1 shows a presentation in Page Sorter view.

Figure 18-1:
Page Sorter view gives you a bird's-eye view of your presentation.

In Page Sorter view, you can remove, duplicate, add, and sort pages, as follows:

✔ To remove a page from your presentation while in Page Sorter view, click the page you want to zap and then press Delete.

✔ If you change your mind after pressing Delete, you can bring the zapped page back by choosing Edit⇨Undo Delete Page(s).

✔ To duplicate a page, click the page that you want to copy and then choose Page⇨Duplicate Page (or press Alt+F7). Freelance places an exact copy of the page right after the original.

You rarely want an *exact* duplicate of a page. Usually, you need to modify the new page in some way, which you must do in Current Page view. You can change to Current Page view to edit your copy by double-clicking the page or by selecting the page and clicking the Current Page tab.

✔ To add a new page, click the page that is just before the location where you want to insert your new page and then choose Page⇨New Page. The New Page dialog box appears so that you can choose the layout for the new page. Unless you make another choice in the dialog box, the new page uses the same layout as the page you're on when you add the new one. Click the layout you want in the dialog box and then click OK to insert the new page.

✔ Just as when you duplicate a page, you must edit a new page in the Current Page view. Double-click the new page to see that page in Current Page view.

✔ To change the order of the pages in the presentation, just click the page you want to move in Page Sorter view and then press and hold the mouse button as you drag the page to its new location. A gray vertical bar and an outline of the page show you where the moved page is going to land, as shown in Figure 18-2.

✔ You can select several pages and move them all at once. To select multiple pages, just press and hold the Shift key as you click the pages you want to select. Then perform the move normally by dragging the selected pages to their new location.

✔ If you change the position of a page in the Page Sorter view, the page number that appears below the page changes to reflect its new location.

Figure 18-2:
Page 5
of this
presentation
is about to
be dropped
between
Pages 2
and 3.

Outliner view

Although graphic elements often seem to be the most important parts of your presentation, the words also need to be right — or the whole thing can fall apart. In Current Page view, you can see only the text on the current page. In Page Sorter view — unless you have a large, expensive, high-resolution computer screen — any text, other than large titles, is difficult to see. The Outliner view enables you to view just the text in all the pages of your presentation, including titles, subtitles, and bulleted lists.

To switch to Outliner view, click the Outliner tab. Your presentation appears in Outliner view, as shown in Figure 18-3. Notice the row of buttons across the top of the page just below the view tabs. These buttons come in handy for manipulating your presentation pages and text.

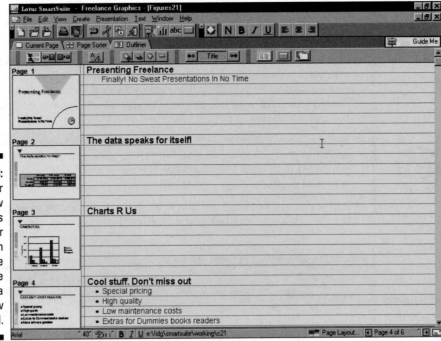

Figure 18-3:
Outliner
view
displays
your
presentation
as if the
text were
written on a
yellow
notepad.

Outliner view enables you to work with your text in the following ways:

✔ The thumbnail representations of your presentation pages on the left side of the outline give you some clues about what graphical elements are in the page. These thumbnails are small but are adequate for distinguishing bar charts from organization charts from title pages.

✔ You can hide the thumbnails by clicking the Hide/Display Thumbnails button (at the far left of the row of buttons, just below the Current Page view tab). You can make the thumbnails larger or smaller by clicking the buttons to the right of the Hide/Display Thumbnails button.

✔ You can *promote* (change to a higher outline level) or *demote* (change to a lower outline level) the headings in titles or bulleted lists by clicking the line containing the title that you want to change and then clicking the Promote button (the one displaying a left arrow, located in the row of buttons just below the view tabs) or the Demote button (the one displaying a right arrow, on the same line). You can also demote an item by pressing Tab or promote an item by pressing Shift+Tab. While you're working in Outliner view, Freelance indents the different levels of headings in traditional outline form. You need to remember, however, that the indents you see in Outliner view don't all carry over to your finished presentation pages.

If you promote a Level-1 heading, that head becomes the page title for a new page. If you find that you've inadvertently promoted a heading, you need to choose Edit➪Undo Change Level.

✔ To enable you to more easily see the important stuff — and conceal unnecessary details — you can *collapse* (that is, *hide*) all the text of any level below that of the page title, either for the entire presentation or just for selected pages. To collapse all the text except the title for a particular page, click any of the text on the page and then click the minus sign (–) button in the row of buttons below the view tabs. To collapse the text for the entire presentation, as shown in Figure 18-4, click the Collapse All button (the one with stacked minus signs).

Any pages with hidden text levels display a plus sign next to the page number at the left of the screen.

✔ To expand the collapsed text for one page in Outliner view, click any of the visible text on that page and then click the plus sign (+) button in the row of buttons below the view tabs. To expand the text for the entire presentation, click the Expand All button (the stacked plus signs).

✔ While in Outliner view, you can double-click one of the thumbnails to switch to Current Page view with that page displayed.

✔ You can also add or edit text while in Outliner view, which can be very handy.

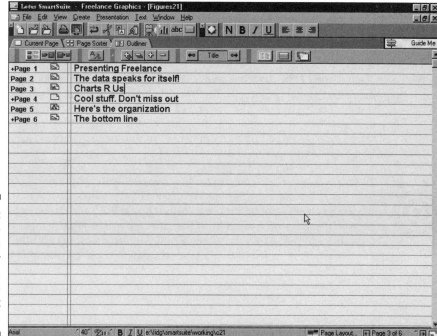

Figure 18-4:
A presentation in Outliner view, collapsed to show just the titles.

Freelance Drawing

Just as in the other SmartSuite programs, you can spruce up your Freelance pages by using a variety of drawing elements. The drawing tools are available in a Tools palette that appears on the left side of the Current Page view window after you click the Drawing And Text button. The Tools palette (shown in Figure 18-5) includes tools for creating polygons, rectangles, lines, arrows, open curves, polylines, circles, arcs, text boxes, and freehand drawing.

Figure 18-5:
The
Drawing
And Text
Tools
palette.

In addition to these drawing tools, you can create various shapes with text inside. The Tools palette even enables you to draw special connectors between shapes. The Shapes With Text tools and Connectors tools, however, are mostly used for drawing diagrams from scratch. If you're the adventurous type who enjoys creating complex drawings, see *Freelance Graphics 96 For Windows 95 For Dummies,* by William Harrel and Roger C. Parker (published by IDG Books Worldwide, Inc.) for more information.

To use one of the drawing tools, click that tool in the Tools palette and then move the mouse pointer to the part of the page on which you want to place the element. Then simply press and hold the mouse button and drag the mouse to create the drawing element. Chapter 11 gives you a bit more detailed instruction on using the more common drawing tools (as used in 1-2-3).

To help you place drawing objects more precisely, you can display the *drawing ruler* along the top and left sides of the window. You display the drawing ruler by choosing View⇨Show Ruler. With the drawing ruler displayed, *guide markers* appear in the ruler as you move the mouse pointer (which is shaped like a crosshair when you are drawing) so that you know exactly where you are drawing your shapes. A finished object is shown in Figure 18-6.

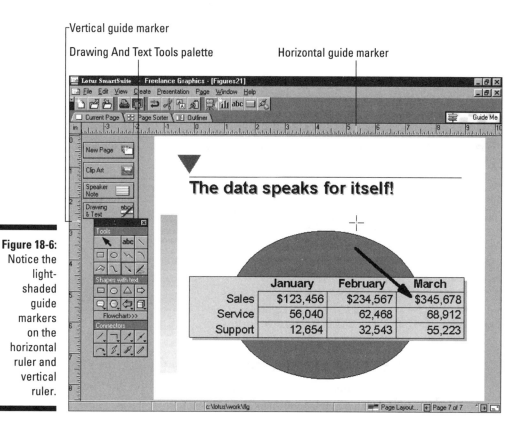

Figure 18-6:
Notice the light-shaded guide markers on the horizontal ruler and vertical ruler.

Roll Camera: Creating a Screen Show

Ways to actually give your presentations abound. You can, of course, simply print your presentation pages to use as handouts or as overhead transparencies. You can save your presentation files so that they can be transformed into 35mm slides. You can even publish your presentation on the Web.

To create slides, you usually send your file to an imaging center for processing. You can find information on these procedures by choosing Help⇨ Help Topics and then clicking the Index tab and typing **slides** in the text box at the top of the tab. Choose Slides from the list and click the Display button.

In addition to all those presentation methods, you can create your own on-screen presentation — called a *screen show.* You can even choose your effects for the transitions from one page to the next.

You can set up screen show effects in any view, but you can more easily work with the flow from page to page in Page Sorter view.

To create a screen show, follow these steps:

1. **Select a page and choose Page⇨Screen Show Effects.**

   The Page Properties InfoBox appears with the Screen Show tab (the one displaying a picture of a movie camera) displayed, as shown in Figure 18-7.

   You don't need to select a page in Current Page view. The screen show effects affect the current page. (Gee, I bet you'd never have guessed that.)

Figure 18-7:
The Screen
Show tab of
the Page
Properties
InfoBox.

2. **Scroll through the Transition list box and choose the effect you want.**

   Determining exactly what the effects do just from their names isn't always easy, so you need to experiment to see which ones provide the desired effect.

3. **(Optional) If you want a sound to play after the page appears in the screen show, choose a sound from the Sound drop-down list or click the Browse button to locate a sound file elsewhere on your system.**

4. **If you want the screen show to run automatically, you can choose the Trigger Automatically, After *X* Seconds option and type in the text box the number of seconds that you want the page to remain on-screen before the next page appears.**

   The default display time is three seconds.

   You can omit a page from a screen show without deleting that page from your presentation file by clicking the Do Not Display This Page During Screen Show option.

5. **Choose another page and repeat Steps 2 through 4 for the remaining pages in the presentation.**

The InfoBox stays open until you click the Close (X) button, so you can select another page and set its screen show properties. In Outliner or Page Sorter views, you can select another page by clicking the page. In Current Page view, you can use the arrow buttons in the status bar to go to another page.

6. Choose Presentation⇨Run Screen Show⇨From Beginning or press Alt+F10 to start the presentation.

Again, you can create and run a Freelance screen show starting from any view.

If you ever want to stop a running screen show before it reaches the end, press Esc to open the Screen Show Pages dialog box and then click Quit Screen Show. Freelance dutifully abandons the screen show and returns you to the previously scheduled Freelance presentation window.

Before you begin your presentation, you may want to consider the following points:

✔ By default, the screen show runs manually, which means that you must click the mouse (the left button) or press either PageDown or Enter to move to the next page. Press PageUp to move to the previous page.

✔ If you want the screen show to run automatically, you must set the timing for each page, as described in Step 5 of the preceding steps, or set all the pages to advance after a fixed time delay. To do that, start in Current Page or Page Sorter view, choose Presentation⇨Set Up Screen Show to open the Set Up Screen Show dialog box, click the Page Effects tab, choose After X Seconds, enter in the text box the number of seconds that you want each page to remain on-screen, and click OK.

✔ If you want the screen show to run continuously — for example, at a trade show for your products — open the Set Up Screen Show dialog box (by choosing Presentation⇨Set Up Screen Show), click the Options tab, choose Run Screen Show In A Continuous Loop, and click OK.

✔ Freelance saves the screen show settings with the presentation file.

Part VI
Organize Your Life

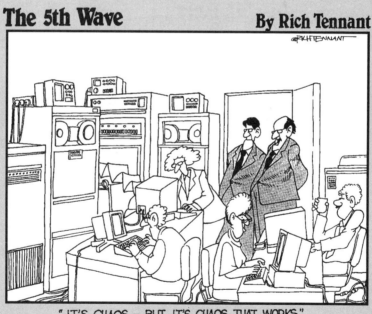

The 5th Wave   By Rich Tennant

" IT'S CHAOS – BUT IT'S CHAOS THAT WORKS."

In this part . . .

1 f you find that you constantly have trouble keeping up
with all those little scraps of paper on which you
scribble important notes, you need some organization in
your life. This part shows you how to use Organizer —
SmartSuite Millennium Edition's answer to the pocket day
planner — to keep track of every aspect of your day-to-
day activities. After reading this section, you may actually
have fun getting organized. (Yeah, right!)

Chapter 19

Organizer Boot Camp (And Beyond . . .)

. . . .

In This Chapter

▶ Investigating Organizer

▶ Exploring Calendar

▶ Making appointments

▶ Creating To Do lists

. . . .

*H*ave you ever wished you could take your appointment book and shove the thing into your (now, now, keep it clean!) . . . er, computer? Have you ever considered stuffing your entire desk, drawers and all, into your briefcase? Wouldn't you love, just once, to find your appointment book right where you left it instead of hunting for it under mounds of paperwork? Anyone who has missed an important appointment, searched in vain for an appointment book, or left vital information behind on a business trip can relate, right?

Well, good news, soldier! Now you can organize your entire life (well, most of it) and have it all at your fingertips. All your fingers need to do is enter the information from your elusive appointment book into Lotus Organizer. Then just sit back and have Organizer keep track of your appointments. Heck, the program can even remind you a few minutes (or hours or days) before your appointment is scheduled.

Organizer: The Big Picture

We don't want to overwhelm you with euphoria, but Organizer can also track your incoming and outgoing calls, dial up other computers and fax machines for you, remind you of important dates, enable you to schedule events, keep a notepad, and do much more. After you enter the stuff that you want Organizer to remind you about, the program can do its reminding thing even if you're working in another program! Is that awesome or what!?

You own a day planner, right? (If not, bear with us anyway.) Does the planner manage your time, jump into your briefcase or purse, beep you at the time for an appointment, remind you when a birthday or holiday comes up, and warn you if you book conflicting appointments? No?!? Then check out the following feats that Organizer can do:

- ✔ The *Calendar* feature enables you to keep track of your appointments and calls. You can set alarms to remind you of stuff, and you can set up repeating appointments (such as that lunch with Mom every Thursday) simply by clicking the mouse button a couple of times.

- ✔ The *To Do* section enables you to keep a list of things you need to do and when they need to be done. To Do lists can be sorted by priority, status, or date.

- ✔ The *Address* section is like a Rolodex on speed. Oh, and you can also use the feature to dial phone numbers for you.

- ✔ The *Notepad* is a wonderful tool for jotting down notes, reminders, lists, memos — anything that you could put on a piece of paper and then promptly misplace.

- ✔ The *Calls* section helps you keep track of incoming and outgoing calls, duration of phone conversations, and status of the calls — and this feature even has a place for taking notes. You can dial and receive telephone calls as well as send and receive messages.

- ✔ The *Planner* is great for scheduling meetings, projects, and similar stuff. If you're on a network, you can use the Planner to track Calendar entries for a bunch of people.

- ✔ The *Anniversary* section enables you to store all those important dates.

- ✔ If you work on a network, you can also schedule meetings and invite coworkers, accept or decline a meeting invitation, and share work with a group of people.

The first thing you see after you start Organizer is a cute little notebook with charming icons around it. Don't let the scene fool you. Organizer is no powder puff, so dive right in and get acquainted.

The Calendar — Up Close and Personal

All right, so get started already! Like most SmartSuite programs, you get a choice of ways to start Organizer. Here are your choices:

✔ If you have SuiteStart running, a row of small icons appears in the System Tray at the right end of the taskbar. You can start Organizer by clicking the icon that looks like a notebook on a table. (A similar icon with an arrow on the left page activates the Organizer EasyClip feature. More on that later.)

✔ To start Organizer from SmartCenter, open the SmartSuite drawer, click the Lotus Applications folder, and then double-click the Lotus Organizer icon.

✔ If you don't have SuiteStart or SmartCenter running, you can access Organizer from the Windows Start menu. Click the Start button, point to Programs, point to Lotus SmartSuite, and then choose Lotus Organizer.

After you start Organizer, an open notebook appears on-screen, with a bunch of icons, called the Toolbox, to the left as shown in Figure 19-1. The Toolbox icons are incredible one-step time-savers. For example, you can drag an entry to the Clipboard icon in the Toolbox and copy the entry to other sections as many times as you like. You can open any of the entry dialog boxes by clicking a Toolbox icon, schedule group meetings, send and receive mail, make or log phone calls, and more. Pretty slick, huh?

Directly beneath the Toolbox are four other icons — the View icons. In Calendar, these icons give you a choice of how you want to view your appointments. You can choose from among the following view options:

✔ **View Day Per Page** shows one day per page.

✔ **View Work Week** shows one week on two pages (the default view).

✔ **View Week per Page** shows one week per page.

✔ **View Month** shows one month on two pages.

Organizer is set up just like those day-planner binders, complete with section tabs. To move to a different section, all you need to do is click its tab.

If you don't know what a certain SmartIcon does, move the mouse pointer to that icon and wait for Bubble Help to appear. (That's the yellow balloon with the message on it — remember?) Bubble Help also works with the Toolbox icons.

Setting appointments

Setting an appointment in Organizer is easy and fun. A Create Appointment dialog box helps you select the criteria for your appointment, including what tune plays if you set an alarm as a reminder!

One day per page
Clipboard
Entry icon
Drag within the same page
One month on two pages
Move to another page
Backtrack SmartIcon
Current date icon

Figure 19-1:
Organizer's
opening
screen,
with the
Calendar
displayed.

One month per page
Turn to previous page
Turn to next page
Trash can icon
One week per page

To set an appointment, you need to open the Create Appointment dialog box; set the date, time, and length of the appointment; enter a description for the appointment; and then exit the dialog box. You can also perform some optional steps within the Create Appointment dialog box, such as setting a repeating appointment, setting an alarm, choosing a category, and selecting cost codes.

To set an appointment, follow these steps:

1. **Double-click the day for which you want to enter the appointment, or click the Entry icon on the Toolbox (the icon with the little clock on it).**

   The Create Appointment dialog box appears, as shown in Figure 19-2.

Figure 19-2:
The Create
Appointment
dialog box.

2. **Click the Date drop-down arrow and then choose a date for the appointment from the monthly calendar page.**

   Use the left and right triangles on either side of the month name to move forward or backward a month at a time.

3. **Click the Time drop-down arrow to set the time and length of the appointment.**

   The TimeTracker opens as part of the Time drop-down list, as shown in Figure 19-3. The clock thingy on the TimeTracker provides you with three important pieces of information: The clock and bar at the top in the TimeTracker show the appointment's starting time; the Duration bar in the middle shows the appointment's length; and the clock and bar at the bottom show the ending time. Along the left edge of the TimeTracker, any existing appointments appear as a blue bar, and the current appointment appears as a green bar. If the current appointment conflicts with an existing appointment, the bar appears in red.

Time Tracker starting time

Figure 19-3:
The Time
drop-down
list with the
TimeTracker
displayed.

Duration bar

Time Tracker ending time

Blue bar showing an existing appointment

4. **Click the top clock button in the TimeTracker, press and hold the mouse button, and drag the clock up or down the <u>T</u>ime list to set the appointment starting time.**

   Release the button as you reach the desired appointment time.

   You can't drag the starting clock down past the ending clock (or the ending clock up past the starting clock, for that matter). If you want the appointment to start later than the current ending time or end earlier than the current starting time, just point to the new time to which you want to move the appointment and click. This action moves the entire clock thingy to the new starting time.

5. **Click the bottom clock and drag it to set the ending time.**

   The time in the Duration bar changes to reflect your starting and ending times. You can move the entire appointment to a different time by clicking the duration bar and dragging it to the new time; the starting and ending times adjust automatically.

   You can also change the duration time by clicking the plus (+) or minus (–) sign next to the Duration text box in the Create Appointment dialog box. This method closes the Time drop-down list and TimeTracker, so if you use this approach, skip the next step.

6. **Click the <u>T</u>ime drop-down arrow again to close the Time list and TimeTracker.**

   Click the Find Time button if your day is nearly booked. Each time you click the Find Time button, the next available time appears in the Time text box.

7. **Click the <u>D</u>escription text box and type a description for your appointment, just as you want the description to appear on your Calendar.**

   You could, for example, type **Lunch with David at Lenny's Restaurant**.

8. **Click the <u>A</u>dd button to create more appointments, or click OK to exit the dialog box.**

You can also choose some of the other options before closing the dialog box. Those options are explained in the following sections.

In addition to entering appointments directly into the Calendar section of your Organizer file, you can display and enter appointments in the Calendar drawer in SmartCenter. For this to work, you must configure the SmartCenter Calendar drawer to use your Organizer file for its calendar data instead of a separate text file. See Chapter 2 for more details.

To save your new file, click the Save Current File SmartIcon or choose <u>F</u>ile⇨ <u>S</u>ave from the menu bar. If you are on a network, you may want to use an abbreviated version of your name as the filename so that others can access your planner. (Make sure that you select a filename that conforms to the file-naming rules of your network.) To open your file after you start Organizer, click the Open File SmartIcon or choose File⇨Open from the menu bar. Check with your network guru on how to open and save on the network, as well as how to handle group scheduling.

If you want Organizer to automatically open your file when you start the program instead of beginning with a blank file, you can use Organizer's simple preference settings to make your preference known. Choose File⇨ User Setup⇨Organizer Preferences to open the Organizer Preferences dialog box. On the Default File tab, click the Automatically Open radio button and enter the path and file name for your Organizer file in the adjacent text box. (You might want to explore some of the other preference settings while you are in the Organizer Preferences dialog box. Click OK to close the dialog box and record the new settings.) The next time you start Organizer, it will automatically load your file, ready for use.

Ladies and gentlemen, choose a category

One convenient Organizer feature is the capability to assign any Organizer entry to a *category.* Then you can use the categories to pull together information on related entries scattered across several Organizer sections and view the entries by category.

Categories are very helpful for tracking projects and different kinds of activities. (Maybe you don't really want to know how much time you spend in meetings. But if you do, Organizer can tell you.) Organizer comes with an assortment of predefined categories — mostly for kinds of activities, such as calls, meetings, and travel — and you can create new categories to fill your needs. A single Organizer entry can belong to several different categories. So you can assign a meeting to consult on the Smith project, for example, to the Meeting, Smith Project, and Consulting categories.

The simplest way to assign a category to an appointment is to start out in either the Create Appointments dialog box (which you access by clicking the Entry icon in the Toolbox) or the Edit Appointments dialog box (which is really the same thing and which you access by double-clicking an existing appointment). Click the drop-down arrow for the Categories text box and select the category you want from the drop-down list. You can choose more than one category by clicking all that apply. If none of the categories suits your needs, type your own category in the Categories text box. The new category you create this way will be available for use with other appointments as well as for categorizing the current appointment. After you're done, simply click outside the Categories text box and drop-down list and then continue with any other editing that you need to do in the dialog box. You can also assign categories to an appointment by selecting the appointment in the calendar and then choosing Appointment⇨Categorize to open the Categorize dialog box, in which you can select or enter categories for the appointment. After selecting the appropriate categories, click OK to close the dialog box.

Could you repeat that, please?

Appointments that repeat are fairly common. With a regular desktop planner or calendar, you must write every meeting or appointment in by hand, right? This task can become very tedious — and maybe even dangerous. (What if you forget to enter one appointment?) Organizer can set all your repeating appointments or meetings for you, whether they repeat every week, month, quarter, or whenever — and you need to enter the appointment only once!

To set a repeating appointment, click the Repeat button in the Create Appointment dialog box to open the Repeat dialog box. (See Figure 19-4.)

Figure 19-4:
The Repeat
dialog box.

If you are currently in the Calendar and not the Create Appointment dialog box, double-click the existing appointment to open the Edit Appointment dialog box, which is identical to the Create Appointment dialog box. Then click the Repeat button in this dialog box.

After the Repeat dialog box appears, click the drop-down arrow next to the first text box in the Repeats area to view your choices for how often to repeat the appointment. (The default choice in the drop-down list is Weekly.) Select the one that works best for you. Suppose, for example, that you attend quarterly financial planning meetings. These meetings always occur on the first day of the month, so you select the Monthly [Dates] choice from this drop-down list.

Then you move down to the second text box. Click the drop-down arrow to open the list of choices. Staying with the quarterly example, you choose the Every third month on the selection.

You next select the days or dates from the list box right below the two drop-down list boxes. In our example, you choose 1st from this list. You can use the scroll button for more choices than the list currently shows.

The Starting Date for the recurring appointment is already set in the Duration area of the dialog box, so all you need to do is add an ending date. You can set the ending date in one of two ways — by specifying a date on which you want the recurring appointment to stop or by specifying the time period for which the recurring appointment should run. To set an ending date for a series of appointments, click the Until radio button and choose a date from the drop-down list. If you want the appointment to repeat for a period of time, click the For radio button and select the appropriate length of time from the accompanying text boxes. Say, for example, that you want a monthly appointment to continue for the next eight months. You click the For radio button and then select 8 in the first text box and Months in the second. (Note that this creates a total of nine appointments — the original appointment plus eight additional monthly repetitions. Notice, also, that Organizer sets the Until date for you if you go this route.)

Now click the drop-down arrow next to the At Weekends text box and choose how to handle dates that fall on a weekend. In our example, you might select Move to Nearest Weekday.

You can also enter specific dates in the Repeat dialog box. To do so, first select Custom in the top list box in the Repeats area. Next, go to the Custom Dates area, just below the Repeats area. Click the Custom Dates drop-down arrow and select from the list all the dates you want to include, clicking the Add button each time. Your chosen dates appear in the list box above the Custom Dates area.

After you finish creating your repeat appointments, click OK to return to the Create Appointment dialog box. Then, after you click OK to close the Create Appointment dialog box, Organizer copies your appointment in your Calendar to the recurring dates just as you specified in the dialog box.

What's the secret code?

The capability to assign *customer* and *cost codes* is a valuable tool in Organizer, especially if you already use cost or customer codes in your business or in other software. *Customer codes* assign a number or alphanumeric code to each customer or company you deal with. These codes help you track that customer throughout the computer or network and provide a cross-referencing ability. *Cost codes* work in a similar manner, except that this type of code can help you track how and where you're spending money. Tracking costs is ideal for a project that's on a budget. Customer codes and cost codes work much like categories. You can use them to select and display appointments and other Organizer items so that you can view only the items pertaining to a specific customer or cost center.

To use cost or customer codes, click the Cost button in the Create Appointment dialog box. (If you've already returned to the Calendar, double-click the existing appointment to open the Edit Appointment box and click Cost there.) The Cost dialog box appears.

Enter a Customer Code and a Cost Code in the appropriate text boxes. If you have previously entered codes, you can click the drop-down arrows next to these text boxes to reveal your existing code choices. Click OK to return to the Create Appointment dialog box after you have your codes set.

An alarming situation!

One of our favorite options in Organizer is the Alarm option. You can have a message flash on-screen and choose a little ditty or other sound to remind you of your appointment. As long as Organizer is running in the background, the alarm and message work no matter what Windows program you're using at the time. You can also set the alarm to go off a day or more in advance or several hours in advance of your appointment — the choice is yours!

To set an alarm, follow these steps:

1. **In either the Create Appointment dialog box or the Edit Appointment dialog box, click the Alarm button.**

   You can access the Create Appointment dialog box by clicking the Entry icon on the Toolbox. Double-clicking an existing appointment opens up the Edit Appointment dialog box.

   After you click the Alarm button, the Alarm dialog box appears. (See Figure 19-5.) Notice that the Alarm dialog box is preset to the date and time of the appointment. If that's the day you want the alarm to go off, skip to Step 3. If not, continue to Step 2.

Figure 19-5:
The Alarm
dialog box.

2. **Click the Date text box's drop-down arrow and select a date from the monthly calendar page that appears if you want the alarm to sound on a day other than the date of the appointment.**

   Use the left and right triangles on either side of the month heading to move forward or backward a month at a time.

3. **If you want the alarm to sound at a time other than the time of the appointment, click the Time text box's drop-down arrow.**

   The TimeTracker opens. The clock shows the time of the alarm (which is the starting time of the appointment initially). You can simply drag the clock up the TimeTracker to the time you want the alarm to go off. (*Note:* Moving this clock has no effect on the starting time of the appointment.)

4. **Click the Before or After radio buttons to tell Organizer to run the alarm either before or after the time you select.**

   You can use the Before or After setting in combination with the Time setting to control the exact time the alarm sounds. For example, you may want to leave the Time set for the start of the appointment and set the alarm to sound 10 minutes before that time. Or you can set the Time and leave the Before/After setting at zero to sound the alarm exactly at the time you set. You can even combine the two settings if you want. The tools are there. You get your choice of how to use them.

5. **Click the plus (+) or minus (–) buttons in the accompanying Before/After text box to increase or decrease the number of minutes that you want the alarm to sound before or after the time that appears in the Time text box.**

Preferences, shmeferences — just play me a tune

Organizer enables you to choose from myriad alarm sounds to delight your ears and amaze your coworkers. With the Create Appointment dialog box or the Edit Appointment dialog box open, click the drop-down arrow next to the Alarm dialog box's Tune text box, and a list of alarm tunes appears.

1. **Scroll through the Tune list and click a selection to choose a tune.**

2. **To listen to the tune, click the Play button.**

   Some computers can't play all the tunes. If one doesn't play, try another.

3. **Click the Message text box to type in a reminder.**

   As the alarm goes off, Organizer not only plays your musical selection, but it also displays your reminder text in a different version of the Alarm dialog box, as shown in Figure 19-6.

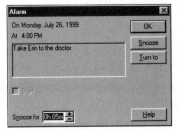

Figure 19-6:
This version
of the Alarm
dialog box
opens to
remind you
of an
appointment.

4. **Click OK to return to the Create Appointment or Edit Appointment dialog box.**

A Turn To button appears in the Alarm dialog box that pops up when the alarm goes off. If you are in another part of Organizer or in another program, you can click Turn To, and Organizer takes you to the page where the alarm originated. Suppose, for example, that you are working in Word Pro as the alarm goes off. You can't remember some specifics about the entry, so you click Turn To, and Organizer takes you to the page in the notebook where the entry is.

Launch time!

If you need to start another program at a specific time, you can set an alarm for a reminder and use the Start option on the Alarm dialog box to start that program automatically. (Refer to Figure 19-5.)

You're probably wondering: "Why would I need to take this action if I can start a new program simply by using the Start menu?" Well, you are absolutely right. You *can* start a program that way. But suppose that you have an appointment at 3 p.m. and you need to run a report to take with you. You know that whenever you work in 1-2-3 you lose all track of time. So you set an alarm by using the Start option, which not only reminds you in time to run the report but also takes you directly into the new program without any searching through the cascading Start menus. Neat!

While in the full Alarm dialog box, click the Start text box and type the full path name of the program you want to start or the file you want to open after the alarm goes off. (If you're like us and can't remember a full path name, you can click inside the Start text box and then click the Browse button. Select the program you want to launch by double-clicking the program folder to open the program and then scrolling through its files. After you find the file you want, double-click the file, or click the file once and click Open. The entire path is now visible in the Start text box.) Click OK.

After the alarm goes off, a message box appears to tell you that the program is launching. As soon as you click OK, the new program launches — even if you have the alarm set to go off a few minutes early as a warning. If you need time to finish up what you're currently working on, just click the Snooze button after the Alarm dialog box appears. You can adjust the amount of time set in the Snooze For text box so that it's enough to finish what you're doing before the new program starts.

Editing in the Calendar section

You can edit the description of an entry in the Calendar section two ways. You can double-click the appointment you want to edit, which opens the Edit Appointment dialog box, or you can edit directly on the page.

If all you need to do is change the appointment day, just drag the entry to a new day on the calendar. If you need to move your appointment to a day or month that's not displayed on the screen, click the grabbing hand icon in the Toolbox, click the appointment, and then find the appropriate date (either by using the Turn To Next Page area at the lower-right corner of the Organizer page or by clicking the Calendar tab and clicking the appropriate date on the yearly calendar that appears).

To edit on the page, follow these steps:

1. **Click the entry in the Calendar to highlight that entry.**

   A highlight box appears around the appointment. The mouse pointer now changes from a hand into an I-beam while over text inside the box.

2. **Click again at the place you want to edit within the highlight box.**

   A flashing cursor appears inside the highlight box, and the TimeTracker also appears. You can now edit the description of the entry and change the time, too.

   If the cursor isn't exactly where you want it inside the box, move the I-beam to the correct spot and click again or use the arrow keys and the Home and End keys to move the cursor.

3. **After you finish editing the appointment, close the highlight box by clicking any other open day or time in the Calendar page.**

After you click the appointment area of the page to close the highlight box, all the times for that day appear. To avoid having these times appear on-screen, you can click the date to close the highlight box without displaying the times. If the times are already visible and really bug you by being there, turn the page and then turn back again to get rid of them.

Moving around in the Calendar

After you start Organizer, the notebook is always open to the current week. You can move around in the calendar in the following two ways:

- ✔ To move a page at a time, click the turned-up corners at the bottom of the notebook pages. The mouse pointer turns into a pointing hand and the pages turn one at a time. The action is accompanied by the sound of turning pages, as long as you have a sound card and have enabled Organizer sounds (which is on the Environment tab of the Organizer Preferences dialog box, which you can reach by choosing File➪ User Setup➪Organizer Preferences).

- ✔ To move to another month, click the tab labeled Calendar at the top left-hand side of the notebook, and — lo and behold! — the notebook flips pages to display a calendar of the entire year. Double-click the desired date, and Organizer flips right to that week for you.

 If you are ready to return to the current date's page, you can flip back to the yearly calendar and double-click the date again, or you can click the Back-track SmartIcon (the one with the footprints traipsing across it). You may need to click the icon two or three times, depending on how many times you moved around. Better still, just click the current date icon below the Toolbox.

 Here's a nifty shortcut for moving around the Calendar: Just press the letter on your keyboard that corresponds to the first letter of the month you want to turn to, and Organizer flips to that month. Suppose, for example, that you want to go to June. You press J and — wait a minute! Organizer switched to January, not June! In the case of months with the same starting letter, you need to press the first *three* letters. So, for June or July, you need to press J-U-N or J-U-L. You can also type a number for a day of the month to display that day of the current month. (By the way, that's the real current month, not just the month you are currently viewing in organizer.)

 To move an appointment to another page or month, click the grabbing hand icon in the Toolbox. (Refer to Figure 19-1.) Then click the appointment entry in the Calendar that you want to move. Turn the pages or flip to another month. Click the new day for the appointment, and the appointment drops right in place.

 To simplify copying an entry, just click the entry and use the pointing hand icon to drag that entry to the Clipboard icon in the Toolbox. (Refer again to Figure 19-1.) Now you can drag the entry from the Clipboard to as many places in the Calendar as you like. You can also copy the entry to a To Do or Notepad page.

Delete and undelete

Deleting in Organizer couldn't be easier. Just click the item you want to delete, and drag that item to the Trash Can icon. The item even appears to burn up! Following are the basics on deleting and undeleting:

- To delete an appointment from the Calendar, click the appointment and drag the appointment to the Trash Can icon at the bottom left of the Calendar. (Refer — yes, *again* — to Figure 19-1.) If you're deleting a repeating appointment, a Delete Repeating Appointment dialog box appears. Radio buttons on the dialog box enable you to indicate whether you want to delete just this one appointment, the entire series, or just selected portions of the series. Choose which repeating appointments to delete and click OK.

- If you delete an appointment and then realize that you trashed the wrong one, you can retrieve the appointment — as long as that appointment is the most recent deletion. Choose Edit⇨Undo Appointment Delete from the menu bar.

The Undo command can't undo the deletion of repeating appointments.

Tie a String Around Your Finger — or Create a To Do List

To do or not to do? That is the question. Well, maybe yes and maybe no — because a To Do list in Organizer is a very effective way to help you manage your time. You can devote an entire page (or pages) to a single project, create lists, track any number of tasks for which you are responsible, and more. You can track your tasks by their status, start date, and priority.

Create a To Do list by clicking the To Do tab in your Organizer notebook. The notebook flips to a section divided by Overdue, Current, Future, and Completed tabs. (See Figure 19-7.) Double-click the empty page to open the Create Task dialog box. (See Figure 19-8.)

Notice in Figure 19-7 that the Entry icon in the Toolbox has changed from a clock to a checked box. Clicking this icon also opens the Create Task dialog box.

After the Create Task dialog box appears, the cursor is already in the Description box. Type a description of what you need to do. For example, you may write: **Follow up on new advertisers for restaurant promotion.**

Status view icon

Entry icon   Category view icon

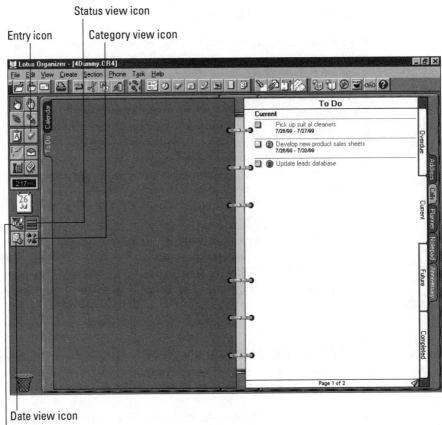

Figure 19-7:
A To Do
page at first
glance.

Date view icon

Priority view icon

Decide whether a date is necessary for this task. You can choose to have No Date, a Start date, a Due date, or both a Start and a Due date. Click the drop-down arrow for Start, and the nifty monthly calendar appears. Select the desired start date, and the monthly calendar closes by itself. Next, select a due date the same way (optional) by clicking the Due drop-down arrow.

Click the drop-down arrow next to the Categories text box and choose a category (or multiple categories if you like), or type in your own category name in the text box. Click the appropriate radio button for the Priority of the task; in other words, how important is this task in reference to other current projects? The Completed On text box marks the project or task as being finished and records the date the task was completed. And the Confidential check box is used in networking situations if you don't want others to read or write to your entry.

Figure 19-8:
The Create
Task dialog
box.

You can set an alarm and choose cost codes in the To Do section just as you can in the Calendar section. Just click the Alarm button in the Create Task dialog box and follow the instructions in the section "An alarming situation!" earlier in this chapter. As do the Create Appointment and Edit Appointment dialog boxes, the Create Task dialog box (and its companion Edit Task dialog box, discussed later in this chapter in "How To Do an edit — get it?") has a Repeat button. Refer to the section "Could you repeat that, please?" earlier in this chapter, for information on using this feature.

After you finish creating your task for the To Do list, click the Add button to continue creating tasks or click OK to return to the To Do list notebook.

View options

After you open the To Do section, you see four View icons, located below the Toolbox. (Refer to Figure 19-7.) These guys, explained in the following list, are great for helping organize the To Do lists. They can sort and separate your entries. Each time you click one, the To Do section sorts all entries by that view choice.

✔ *Priority* entries are sorted by the priority number. After you select the Priority view icon, the page tabs enable you to view all at once your priority 3 tasks, priority 2 tasks, priority 1 tasks, or tasks with no designated priority.

✔ *Status* entries are sorted by their status and separated into the following tabs: *Current, Future, Overdue,* and *Completed.* Click the appropriate tab to view the tasks in that status grouping.

If you want a future task to be located in the Future category, both the start date and the due date must fall sometime after the current date. Suppose, for example, that a proposal must be turned in one week after the task is assigned — say, on May 8. If you put the date that you were assigned the proposal in the Start Date text box of the Create Task dialog box and put the day that the proposal's due in the Due Date text box, Organizer files the proposal by its start date, which makes that task a Current project. By setting the start date a couple of days before the due date, however, you can have Organizer file the project or task in the Future category until the start date you specify. When the start date arrives, Organizer moves the task into the Current category.

✔ *Date* entries are sorted by their *start dates* only. The tabs along the right side of the page enable you to select a month and year. After you have the correct month, you can leaf through its pages by clicking the Turn To Next Page/Turn To Previous Page areas in the lower corners of the display.

✔ *Category* sorts entries by category. If you have an entry with more than one category, that entry appears on each category's page. Click the tab for the first letter of the category you wish to view.

You may notice that the description of each task appears in color on the To Do list (if you use a color monitor, of course). The color of the text signifies the status of each entry, no matter which view you are using, as described in the following table.

Color	*Status of entry*
Red	Overdue
Green	Current
Blue	Future
Black	Completed

How To Do an edit — get it?

You can edit any task by double-clicking its entry in the To Do list, which opens the Edit Task dialog box. The Edit Task dialog box looks and works just as the Create Task dialog box does. Use the Edit Task dialog box to change a date; change or add a priority, an alarm, or a cost code; or create a repeating task.

You don't need to open the Edit Task dialog box to edit the description of an entry or mark the task as completed. You can make those changes directly in the To Do section, as described in the following steps:

1. **Click the entry in the To Do list to highlight that entry.**

A highlight box appears around the task, and the mouse pointer changes from a hand to an I-beam if the pointer is over the description text.

2. Click again where you want to edit or insert text.

The text color changes to black on white, and a flashing cursor appears inside the highlight box.

3. Edit the description.

4. After you finish, click anywhere inside the highlight box (but outside the description text) to close Edit mode.

After you finish a task, you don't need to open the Edit Task dialog box to mark the Completed On text box. Simply click the gray box, called the Completed button, that appears to the left of the task on the To Do page. A check mark appears in the box, and the item moves to the Completed tab (when you view by status) or drops to the bottom of the list (in other views). If you go into the Edit Task dialog box, you find the Completed On text box filled in with the same date on which you marked the task's gray box on the To Do list. Pretty slick, huh?

You cannot use the Clipboard to copy a task to another page. If you try, the task simply reappears as a duplicate entry on the original page. You cannot use the pointing hand or grabbing hand icons to move or copy tasks either. The To Do tasks are very specific. These tasks are separated by their dates, priority, and status.

Copying To Do tasks

Organizer is big on sharing information, enabling you to copy appointments without having to retype all the information. Guess what? You can also copy tasks in the To Do section of Organizer in any of the following three ways:

- ✔ **Select more than one category for the task in the Create Task dialog box or the Edit Task dialog box.** Organizer includes the task in each category you select.

- ✔ **Use the Clipboard icon in the Toolbox.** Here's how: Drag the task to the Clipboard icon, copy the task back onto the page, and then double-click the copied task to open the Edit Task dialog box and change its information in the dialog box.

  This method also enables you to drag tasks to the Calendar. Simply drag the task to the Clipboard icon, click the Calendar tab near the Toolbox, click the appropriate date on the yearly calendar that appears, and drag the task to the appropriate date. You can then double-click the task to open the Edit Task dialog box and change the information.

✔ **Create a repeating task.** Click the Repeat button in either the Create Task or Edit Task dialog boxes, select Custom in the first drop-down list box of the Repeat dialog box, and then choose dates in the Custom Dates drop-down list box.

And what do you do after you're done with a To Do entry? If you don't want to keep a completed entry for your records, simply drag the entry to the Trash Can to delete that entry.

Chapter 20

Putting All the Little Black Books in One Place

. . . .

In This Chapter

▶ Using the address file

▶ Keeping a phone log

▶ Creating a planner

. . . .

*R*olodex cards, phone books, day planners, calendars — where do they all end? Why, with Organizer, of course! Keep these aids all in one place and within easy reach. After all, when was the last time you misplaced your computer?

If you use the Address section of Organizer as your new little black book, you get an organized, versatile address file. But the fun doesn't stop there! You can access information from the address file to help you fill in similar data in the Address section, as well as in the Calls section. Organizer brings the info to you — all you need to do is click the name, company, and so on to select the info. The Calls section of Organizer enables you to monitor the phone calls you make. By using categories and cost and customer codes, you can assign your calls to a group or project for tracking expenses. Using the Planner is a great way to plan blocks of time. What's really neat is that you can have all the engagements that are in your Planner show up in the Calendar, too, which keeps you from overbooking your appointments! What a deal!

Addressing the Issues of Organizer's Address Section

You can most readily compare the Address section with your old-fashioned Rolodex — but with a couple of twists (instead of spins). For one thing, you get two cards for each entry — a Business card and a Home card. The Home card is really neat. This card has a place for the spouse's and children's names and any personal info. The Business card includes extra fields, too.

To add new address information to the Address section, follow these steps:

1. **Click the Address tab on the right-hand side of Organizer's right page.**

   After you're in the Address section, the Toolbox's Entry icon changes into a cute little postcard. (Don't confuse this icon with the Toolbox button displaying an open envelope — that's your link to e-mail.)

2. **Click the Entry icon (or double-click the blank address page) to open the Create Address dialog box, shown in Figure 20-1.**

   The dialog box opens with the Business tab selected.

Figure 20-1: The Business tab of the Create Address dialog box.

3. **Fill in the text boxes with the new address information.**

   Start with the Title, First Name, and Last Name boxes. Then click the Job Title box or one of the other text boxes in the Business tab. Click each text box or press Tab to move forward through the boxes; press Shift+Tab to move back to the previous box.

4. **Type any notes or reminders in the Notes text box.**

   For example, you could type **Mr. Hall prefers to be called between the hours of 1 and 5 p.m.**

5. **Click the Home tab.**

   After filling in the Business card, you can fill in a card with more personal information by clicking the Home tab.

6. **Click the Categories drop-down list box and choose a category (if you want to put the address record in a category, that is).**

Organizer provides several preset categories, such as Calls, Clients, Follow up, Personal, and so on. You could keep all your friends in one category, for example, and all your business associates in another. You may also select a category to keep track of projects, companies, or clients. If you don't find one you like, type a new one in the Categories box.

7. Click the <u>A</u>dd button or OK button to record the information.

Click Add if you want to enter another address record. If you don't want to enter any more records right now, click OK or press Enter to enter the current record and close the dialog box.

The address entry appears on the appropriate letter-tabbed page of Organizer's Address section.

Because pressing Enter is just like clicking OK, pressing Enter closes the dialog box and takes you back to the Organizer page where you started. Don't worry if this happens — just double-click the address to open the identical Edit Address dialog box and finish entering your information.

If you have more than one contact within a company, you can have Organizer fill in the redundant data for you. After you fill in the company name, press Tab. A Similar Address Found dialog box appears, as shown in Figure 20-2. If the information listed in this dialog box is correct for the current record, click OK; Organizer adds the company information for you. Fill in any phone extension and any message in the Notes text box, and you're done.

Figure 20-2:
The Similar
Address
Found
dialog box.

You can also use the Clipboard icon in the Toolbox to copy similar information. From the Address book, drag a similar address card to the Clipboard and then drag that address back to the Address book. Double-click either address card to open the Edit Address dialog box.

Viewing a la mode

After you open the Address section of Organizer, you see four new View icons below the Toolbox, which offer four different ways to view the address files in the notebook. You can view by Address, Contact, Phone, and View All. In View All mode, each Address card is on its own page. (See Figure 20-3.)

Searching for Mr. Goodboy (or another address card)

Searching for an address card is simple as long as you have any piece of information from the card. If you want to find a new contact, knowing the contact's first name is enough information to conduct a search.

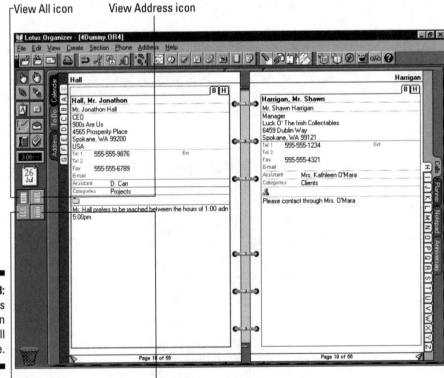

Figure 20-3:
Address
cards in
View All
mode.

To search for an address card, follow these steps:

1. **Click the Find Text SmartIcon (the one that looks like a flashlight); or choose Edit⇨Find; or press Ctrl+F.**

   The Find dialog box appears. (See Figure 20-4.)

2. **Type what you want to search for in the Find text box.**

3. **Click the Case Sensitive check box if you want the search to find only exact case matches.**

   If you want to find *McDonald* but not *MCDonald,* checking Case Sensitive ensures that Organizer finds only the addresses that match *McDonald.*

4. **Click the Whole Word check box if you want the search to find only the specified word and not the same letters occurring within another word.**

   With Whole Word checked, for example, you find instances of the word *the* but not the word *there.*

5. **Click the All Sections radio button or click the Section radio button and then the drop-down arrow for its text box, and select from the list what sections of Organizer to include in the search.**

   The Section list box deals with where you want your search to take place. Do you want to search only in one section of Organizer (the Address section, for example) or in All Sections?

6. **Click Find Next or Find All.**

   The Occurrences box displays all the data that matches your search request. If you search for only one occurrence or want to view occurrences one by one, click the Find Next button. If you want to view a list of occurrences, click the Find All button.

Use the Clear List and Append To List radio buttons if you're performing more than one search in the same Find dialog box. Clear List clears the Occurrences box for each search, while Append To List maintains all matches from previous searches in the Occurrences box. After you exit the Find dialog box, the Occurrences box clears automatically.

After you finish the search, highlight one of the matches in the Occurrences box and click the Turn To button to go to the page containing that entry. You can leave the Find dialog box open while you examine or edit the entry, and then return to the Find dialog box to select another occurrence and turn to that location or search for something else. When you are through with the Find dialog box, click Close.

Feeling out of sorts

You can use the Sort option to choose the order in which the address cards appear. Changing the sort order is useful if you need to access certain information more frequently than other information. Suppose that the normal view of the address cards is alphabetical by last name. You may deal with companies more than names; therefore, you may find that displaying the cards by company name is more logical for you. This is one of several preferences that you can set to control how Organizer presents addresses.

To change the sort order of your address cards and other preferences, make sure that you click the Address tab and then follow these steps:

1. **Choose View➪Address Preferences from the menu bar.**

   The Address Preferences dialog box appears, as shown in Figure 20-5.

Figure 20-5:
Sorting
address
cards in the
Address
Preferences
dialog box.

2. Click the radio button for the <u>V</u>iew that you want.

Actually, you can even leave these options alone. The View icons below the Toolbox govern these options; you can change views as often as you like by clicking those icons. You can, however, change the default View icon (the one that is in effect as you open the section) by choosing a new view here.

3. In the <u>S</u>ort By area, click the radio button for the field by which you want to sort the addresses.

If you want to view cards by company, for example, click Company (of course). This sort field is also the first field that appears on your address card. To select a field that is not offered, click the bottom radio button and select from the drop-down list a different kind of information by which to sort the cards (for example, zip code).

4. Click the <u>F</u>oreground Tab drop-down list box in the Options area and choose which tab you want your address cards to display: the Business tab (B) or the Home tab (H).

You can also choose Selected, which means that whichever tab you used last on each record is the one that appears. Choose Selected if you do not primarily use one tab over another.

5. Click the S<u>t</u>art Headings drop-down list box and choose how to display the pages.

Choose One after another in this list if you have blank pages. The other options keep the blank pages, while One after another displays only the filled-in pages.

6. Click the Show Address Tabs check box if you want the address tabs to show.

The Show Address Tabs check box enables you to decide whether you want the Business (B) and Home (H) tabs to show. The box is selected by default, which means that the tabs appear above the cards. (You use those tabs to switch between Business and Home address data for an address entry.)

7. Click Show Inde<u>x</u> Line if you want the index line to show.

The Show Index Line check box enables you to decide whether you want the title of your sort information to show. If you decide to use company names as your display and sort choice, the company name shows on the index line, above each card.

8. (Optional) Click the Sho<u>w</u> check box with the lock beside it to show whether you marked any information as confidential.

You generally use this option in a networking situation in which other people can access your files.

9. **Click the Turn To Entry After Create/Edit check box if you want Organizer to go to that entry after you close either the Create Address or Edit Address dialog boxes.**

   This entry is selected by default.

10. **Click OK after you finish.**

Your address list is now sorted by company name, and the other settings are adjusted to your preferences.

If all you want to do is change the sort order in the address book, the quickest way to do it is to right-click the yellow background of any address page and choose the sort option — By Last Name, By Company, By Zip, or Category — from the pop-up menu that appears.

Keeping Your Call Records On Call

The Calls section of Organizer helps you keep a record of your phone calls — incoming and outgoing. You can keep track of whom you spoke with, how long the call lasted, and the status of a follow-up call. You can assign a cost code to a call and set an alarm to remind you of a scheduled future call. The calls and address sections work well together because you can access address card information from the Create Calls dialog box.

Before you can use all the features in the Calls section of Organizer, your computer must have a modem linked to a phone line. You also need a telephone handset plugged into the modem. (If you need to know more about modems, contact your computer guru or read *Modems For Dummies*, 3rd Edition, by Tina Rathbone, published by IDG Books Worldwide, Inc.) Without a modem and a telephone handset, you can use the Calls features of Organizer only as a manual record of your calls.

To keep track of your phone calls, follow these steps:

1. **Click the Calls tab to move to the Calls section.**

   The Entry icon in the Toolbox now displays a phone receiver.

2. **Click the Entry icon (or double-click any blank area on a Calls page) to open the Create Call dialog box, shown in Figure 20-6.**

3. **Enter the contact information in the text boxes of the Contact tab.**

Type the first name of the person you are calling (or plan to call) in the First Name text box and proceed to fill in the other boxes as well. Or, if the names you are entering are in your Address section, you can let Organizer fill in the information for you. Just click the drop-down arrow in the Last Name box and select the name from the list. The box closes by itself, and like magic, Organizer automatically fills in the company name and phone number.

If you want to enter a different phone number, select `The phone number entered below` in the Phone At drop-down list and fill in the information in the Phone Number area.

Figure 20-6:
The Create
Call dialog
box.

Confirm the settings in the Dialing From and Dial Using drop-down list boxes. Normally, you don't need to change these settings, which control what modem to use and the dialing format for outgoing calls. Organizer picks up the information from your Windows telephony settings. The settings appear in this dialog box for convenience. The Dialing Properties and Configure buttons open the standard Windows dialog boxes for setting dialing properties and configuring your modem. (For more information on using the Windows telephony features, refer to *Windows 98 For Dummies,* by Andy Rathbone, published by IDG Books Worldwide, Inc.)

4. Click the Notes tab.

Organizer displays the options shown in Figure 20-7.

5. Select the appropriate information for the call in the Date, Time, and Duration list boxes.

What you enter here depends on what information you are filling in. Are you listing a call you already made or received? Are you scheduling a date to call someone or follow up on a call?

You can use the plus (+) and minus (–) signs next to the Duration text box to set or adjust the length of the call. You can also set the Duration of the call by using the TimeTracker, discussed in Chapter 19, or you can use the Stopwatch, which is explained in the following section of this chapter.

Figure 20-7:
The Notes
tab of the
Create Call
dialog box.

6. **Type any reminders for yourself in the Not<u>e</u>s text box.**

   For example, you may type **Have new proposal and layouts ready
   when calling.**

7. **In the <u>S</u>tatus box, select the setting to reflect the status of this call.**

   The Status drop-down list box tells you the result of the call or tells you
   that the call is a future call. If you intend to make the call at a future
   time, the text in the box should read `Planned`. If you are going to place
   the call right away, do not change the information in this box; Organizer
   automatically updates the information after you go into the Dialing
   dialog box, which is described in the following section. If you are
   logging an incoming call, click the drop-down arrow for the Status list
   box and select a status from the list that appears. (The list of Status
   choices may look short, but you can use the arrow buttons in the list
   box to scroll the list to display other options.)

8. **Click the <u>C</u>ategories drop-down list box and choose one or more
   categories.**

   You can use the same category that you assigned for this person
   elsewhere and/or a category pertaining to the call only.

9. **Click the Co<u>m</u>pleted check box if the call is finished and needs no
   follow-up.**

   The call remains in your Calls section even though you marked this call
   as completed.

10. **Set an alarm, assign cost codes, or configure repeating calls as
    needed.**

   As in setting appointments in the Calendar, you can set an alarm to
   remind you to make a call. Click the Alarm button in the Create Call
   dialog box and choose in the Alarm dialog box the date and time for the
   alarm, along with a tune, if you like. For details on using the Alarm dialog
   box, see Chapter 19. As for appointments, you can use the Repeat button

to set up calls that repeat. If you make a call regularly, click the Repeat button in the Create Call dialog box. Set up the repeating call in the Repeat dialog box, just as you would an appointment. For more information, refer to Chapter 19. Use the Cost button in the Create Call dialog box to assign a cost and customer code to the call. The codes assign the costs to a group, project, or client. See Chapter 19 for more info.

11. **If you plan to complete the call at a later time, click the OK button to close the dialog box and record the call record in Organizer; otherwise, proceed to the following section and follow the steps there.**

Calling with the click of a button

Now you're ready to make a call. (If you're on a network, however, check first with your network guru.) Follow these steps to make a call in Organizer:

1. **Click the Dial button in the Create Call dialog box to open the Dialing dialog box, shown in Figure 20-8.**

   Follow the steps in the preceding section to create a call if you haven't already done so.

   If you have a modem installed and configured, Organizer uses the modem to dial the number immediately, and the Call Status dialog box appears over the Dialing dialog box. After the phone starts ringing, pick up the telephone handset and click Talk in the Call Status dialog box to continue your conversation and return to the Dialing dialog box. Click Hang Up in the Call Status dialog box to break the connection (and close both dialog boxes).

2. **Click one of the buttons that describe how to log the call.**

   If you click the Answered button, the Stopwatch immediately begins to tick. Whichever button you click to log the call (Answered, Busy, No Answer, Left Message), the Status text box in the Create Call dialog box automatically updates with that information.

3. **After the call is over, click the Stopwatch icon to stop the timer.**

   The elapsed time appears in the Duration text box for you.

Figure 20-8: The Dialing dialog box.

The Hang Up and Redial buttons of the Dialing dialog box are for use with a modem. If you have a modem, the Calls section can perform a number of related options. Check with your network administrator or computer whiz for more help with these options.

Incoming calls and dialing shortcuts

If you receive a phone call that you want to track, start or switch to Organizer and choose Phone⇨Incoming Call from the Organizer menu bar. The Create Call dialog box appears. Click the Notes tab and then click the Stopwatch icon to start the timer running. You can fill in the rest of the information at your leisure.

The Telephone icon in the Toolbox is present in every section of Organizer. Use this icon as a shortcut to dialing a number. Click the icon, and the Dial dialog box appears, as shown in Figure 20-9. Or you can drag an address or call entry and drop it on the icon to open the Dial dialog box with the information from the entry already filled in.

Figure 20-9:
Open the
Dial dialog
box by
using the
Toolbox's
Telephone
icon.

Fill in the information as you would in the Create Call dialog box and then click Dial. The Dialing dialog box appears. As soon as you click your choice (Answered, Busy, No Answer, Left Message), the Create Call dialog box reappears, with all the information filled in. Again, if you choose Answered, the Stopwatch starts running.

Editing calls

You can edit any call by double-clicking the call listing in your notebook with the pointing hand pointer, which opens the Edit Call dialog box. This dialog box looks and works just like the Create Call dialog box. Use the Edit Call dialog box to add notes, add or change a category, or change the company or other name. The Edit Call dialog box also has a Follow Up button that you can click to create a follow-up call.

You can set a follow-up call for any date and time. The Create Follow Up Call dialog box, which appears after you click Follow Up, is identical to the Create Call dialog box. After you exit the dialog boxes and return to the Calls page, you see that the follow-up call is listed directly below the original call.

You can edit the description of an entry in the Calls section without using the Edit Call dialog box by following these steps:

1. **Click the entry once to highlight that listing.**

   The border around the call card changes to indicate that it's selected. The mouse pointer turns into an I-beam whenever the pointer touches any editable text inside the edit box.

2. **Click the text you want to edit again.**

   A flashing cursor appears in the text. You can edit the company, notes, and status.

3. **Edit the text.**

4. **Click the name above the highlight box after you finish your edits.**

   This action closes the Edit mode.

A call with a view

The Calls section also has four View icons below the Toolbox. You can choose to view your Calls section by Name, Date, Company, and Category. The Name, Company, and Category views have their respective titles indexed above each card, with alphabetical index tabs along the side. (See Figure 20-10.) The Date view has the date indexed above the cards and monthly index tabs along the side. In the Category view, if you have a call with more than one category assigned to that call, duplicate cards appear.

View by Name icon   View by Company icon

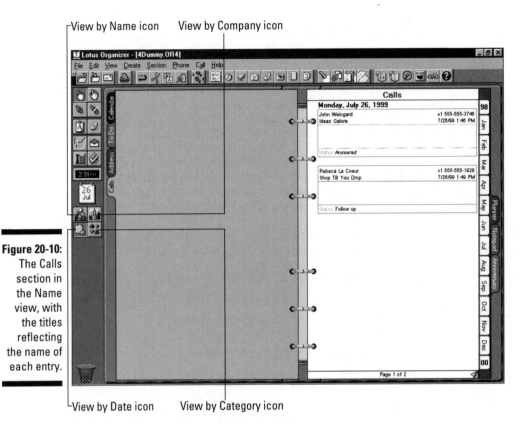

Figure 20-10:
The Calls
section in
the Name
view, with
the titles
reflecting
the name of
each entry.

View by Date icon   View by Category icon

Planning with a Purpose

The Planner is ideal for scheduling events that take one or more days, such as conferences, vacations, business trips, and so on. By marking events with color blocks or strips, the Planner makes seeing your scheduled events at a glance quite easy.

The following steps explain how to enter a Planner event:

1. Move to the Planner section by clicking the Planner tab.

After the Planner opens, the page takes up both sides of the notebook. You can "fold" the Planner page by clicking the little Planner icon (with the little red horizontal arrow) in the top right-hand corner of the page. You probably want to work with the Planner folded out and then fold it down to single-page size so that you can access other section tabs on the left side of the Organizer notebook. As you move the mouse over the page, the dates appear in a text box below the page.

2. **Click the Toolbox Entry icon, which now resembles (amazingly enough) a Planner page.**

   The Create Event dialog box appears, as shown in Figure 20-11. You can also open this dialog box by double-clicking the day you want an event to start on.

Figure 20-11:
The
Planner's
Create Event
dialog box.

3. **Click the drop-down arrow by the Event Type text box and select the desired event from the list that appears.**

   If the option you want is not visible, the list has a scroll button that you can use to view more options. If you have a week's vacation coming up on June 1, you can select Vacation from the drop-down list.

4. **Choose the Row in which you would like your event to appear in the Planner.**

   Although you can't see it until you assign an event, the Planner divides each day into four rows, from top to bottom. You may want to choose rows according to the importance of the event. For example, you may have an all-day meeting in row one and a lunch date in row two. Simply click the + or − keys to make your selection.

5. **In the Notes text box, write any messages or reminders.**

   For example, you may need to remind yourself to give all files for the Luck O' the Irish to a coworker before leaving for your vacation.

6. **Choose the dates for the event in the From and Until date boxes.**

   If your vacation starts on September 5 and ends on September 13, click September 5 from the drop-down calendar in the From list box and September 13 from the Until list box. Notice that Organizer then fills in the Days box for you. You can also select the beginning date in the From date box and then select the number of days in the Days box to have Organizer fill in the Until box for you.

7. **Click the Categories box and choose a category for this event from the drop-down list.**

   Remember that categories help you track people, events, and expenses.

The Book Free Time check box, if checked, books the events into your calendar for you. Use this option to keep from double-booking an appointment or event. Use this option in conjunction with the Show Through feature, explained later in this chapter.

The Repeat button enables you to schedule a recurring event or meeting in advance as many times as you like. See Chapter 19 for details. Likewise, the Cost button enables you to assign cost and customer codes to your planner events, just as you can assign codes to calendar appointments and other Organizer items. See Chapter 19 for more info.

Planning to alarm you

As you may remember if you've read the earlier sections, the Alarm button enables you to set an alarm as a reminder. You can set the alarm from either the Create Event or the Edit Event dialog box. Setting an alarm in the Planner is the same as setting one for appointments. For details, see Chapter 19.

Entering events directly

Two View icons appear below the Toolbox in the Planner. One (the icon on the right) is for viewing the Planner by the year, and the other (the icon on the left) is for viewing the Planner by the quarter. Using the Quarterly view has an advantage. Remember that, in the Create Event dialog box, you can assign events to up to four rows for each day, rows that otherwise don't appear. The Quarterly view shows all four rows of the Planner clearly, while the Yearly view shows only two rows without overlapping. For the following example, click the icon that switches to the Quarterly view. Notice that the side tabs change from yearly to quarterly indexing.

The Planner displays colored key codes at the bottom of the page. (See Figure 20-12.) After you select one of these with the mouse, the mouse pointer turns into a highlighting marker. Now you can choose where to mark the Planner. Just above the key codes is a text box that shows you the date that the mouse pointer is on or the dates covered by any box the mouse pointer is on. Move the mouse around the Planner, and you see how that box tracks your moves.

Click the key code you want and move to the Planner. Suppose, for example, that you have an all-day conference on May 5. You could click the Conference key and move the mouse pointer to May on the Planner. After the tracking box reads May 5, just click the mouse. May 5 now shows a conference. Wait a minute! What if you want an alarm set here? No problem —

Date box   Key codes

Figure 20-12:
Using the
mouse
pointer for
entering
events
directly into
the Planner
while in
Quarterly
view.

touch the event on the Planner page with the mouse pointer. After the pointer changes to a hand, click the right mouse button, and a pop-up menu appears displaying all the options available in the Create Event dialog box. See? You can do all your work right from the Planner page.

You can easily set aside several days for an event. Suppose that you want to attend a series of meetings in Seattle from October 12 through 16. You could set this event by clicking the Meeting key at the bottom of the Planner page. After you move the mouse to October 12 on the Planner page (so that the date appears in the tracking box), you click and hold the left mouse button and drag the Meeting color block that appears through October 16, as shown in Figure 20-13.

You can use the rows to set up more than one event on the same day. Suppose that you want to attend a training seminar in Seattle on October 15. Click the Training key, move the mouse up to October 15, and click right below the first event (not above the event block). Now you have two events for the same day.

Figure 20-13:
Marking
more than
one day at a
time on the
Planner.

The only significance to the rows is the significance you attach to them. You don't need to put a day's first event at the top; you can have your most important blocks at the bottom, if you so desire. And if you want to move blocks around, simply click the block you want to move and drag the block to the correct location. You can also change a block's length by moving the mouse to an end of the block (where the cursor changes into a two-headed arrow) and then clicking and dragging until the block is the desired length. To delete a block, simply click that block and press the Delete key. Poof — it's gone.

If you want all these bookings to appear in the Calendar, choose Section⇨ Show Through or click the Show Through SmartIcon to open the Show Through dialog box. (See Figure 20-14.) Select Calendar in the Show Into drop-down list and then highlight Planner in the From list box to enable the events to show through from the Planner to the Calendar; then click OK. After you return to the Calendar section of Organizer, all the Planner's events appear in your Appointment book. You can also use the Show Through dialog box to instruct Organizer to display Calendar (and other) entries in the Planner.

Figure 20-14:
The Show
Through
dialog box.

You may feel like looking at the Calendar section to make sure that the events are there, but you may notice a problem. You can't find the Calendar tab. This missing tab, however, is not really a problem. Click the Planner icon at the top-right corner of the Planner page (with a page and a red arrow), and the page folds up, revealing the rest of the notebook.

If you want to assign your own key codes in the unused keys of the Planner page, do so by choosing View⇨Planner Preferences. A Planner Preferences dialog box appears in which you can adjust the Planner to suit your needs. Click the Key button, and a master chart with the Planner keys appears. Click the key you want to change, drag over the existing name, and type in your own key name. Click OK to close the dialog boxes after you finish, and the new name(s) appear in the keys at the bottom.

Chapter 21

Organizer Final Touches and Shortcuts

- -

- -

*Y*ou've probably never been in the doghouse for forgetting an important date, right? You have? Then set up Organizer to remind you of those important times, and never be in trouble again (you hope).

You Say It's Your Birthday

The Anniversary section of Organizer is a simple, painless way to remember important recurring dates, holidays, birthdays, and so on. You can use the Show Through feature to transfer any events from Anniversary to Calendar so that you remember the dates. (For more information on the Show Through features, check out the section on entering events in Chapter 20.)

Click the Anniversary tab, and Organizer turns to the Anniversary section with the page open to the current month. Four View icons appear below the Toolbox that enable you to view your Anniversary calendar by Month, Year, Zodiac signs, or Category.

Remember that a category helps you track certain projects across all the Organizer sections. So why would you want to assign a category to an anniversary? Well, an anniversary is more than just birthdays and such, although you may want to add the birthdays of coworkers or friends and family. You can also enter other long-term planning dates — such as project milestones and the due dates for quarterly tax payments — and select an appropriate category for each entry. You can find more information on categories in the section on choosing categories in Chapter 19.

To use the Anniversary section to remember important dates, follow these steps:

1. **Double-click the month of your choice or click the Entry icon in the Toolbox (which now looks like a calendar page).**

   The Create Anniversary dialog box appears, as shown in Figure 21-1.

Figure 21-1:
The Create
Anniversary
dialog box.

2. **Type the name or description of the anniversary date in the Description text box.**

3. **Click the Date drop-down arrow and select the correct date from the list.**

   Suppose that you want to enter Mother's Day. This holiday always falls on the second Sunday in May, so for 2000 you select May 14.

4. **Click the Categories drop-down arrow and select a category, if desired.**

   You can assign new entries to categories if you want. For instance, Mother's Day may be assigned to the Personal category.

5. **Select the Occurs On Same Date Every Year check box, if appropriate.**

   The Occurs On Same Date Every Year option is selected by default. But in some cases, such as Mother's Day, the anniversary does not fall on the same date every year. Therefore, you must click the check box to deselect this option.

6. **If the anniversary doesn't occur on the same date each year, click the**
   Repeat button to open the Repeat dialog box so that you can enter
   this anniversary for following years; schedule the dates for recur-
   rences of this anniversary in the Repeat dialog box and then click OK
   to return to the Create Anniversary dialog box.

   If the anniversary doesn't fall on the same date each year, Organizer
   needs some help scheduling recurrences of the anniversary for following years. For dates such as Mother's Day, you can schedule future
   dates by selecting Monthly (Days), Every Twelfth Month On The, and
   2nd Sunday in the Repeats area of the Repeat dialog box. Then, in the
   Duration area, click For, enter a large number, and select Years to
   schedule the repetitions of this anniversary farther into the future than
   you will be using this program (or computers as we know them today).
   (For more information on setting recurring dates, refer to Chapter 19.)

   For example, to set the dates for Mother's Day, select Custom from the
   top list box in the Repeats area of the Repeat dialog box. Next, in the
   Custom Dates area, click the drop-down arrow button to display the
   calendar, click the right arrow to scroll to next May, and click the
   correct date (the second Sunday, remember?). Click Add to add this
   date to the list of dates in the Repeats area. Repeat this procedure for
   each year that you want to schedule the anniversary. In the Duration
   area, click the For radio button; then click the plus (+) button a few
   times to specify an appropriate number of years, and select Years from
   the drop-down list. After you finish scheduling recurrences of the
   anniversary, click OK to close the Repeat dialog box and return to the
   Create Anniversary dialog box.

7. **(Optional) Set an alarm as a reminder. (Refer to Chapter 19 for**
   information.)

8. **(Optional) Set any cost codes needed. (Refer to Chapter 19 for**
   information.)

9. **Click OK to return to the Anniversary section.**

If you want the dates that you are setting to appear in the Calendar, click the
Show Through SmartIcon to open the Show Through dialog box, as described in Chapter 20. Select Calendar in the Show Into drop-down list box
and then select Anniversary in the From list box before you click OK. After
you return to the Calendar tab, you see all your anniversaries displayed in
your Appointment book.

Keeping Notes — Plus a Whole Lot More

Organizer's Notepad is one of the most valuable tools for people who keep a notepad on their desk and can't find the thing half the time. You can keep notes, certainly, but you can also import spreadsheets, text files, pictures, graphs, maps, and so on onto a Notepad page and then link that page to another page as a reference.

Click the Notepad tab, and Organizer turns to a Notepad Contents page. Every time you enter a Notepad page, Organizer automatically updates the Notepad Contents page with the new page numbers and titles.

Another nice feature of Notepad is that you can have as many pages as you like for any entry. Notepad enables you to create chapters, too, to keep pages together. To enter a Notepad page, follow these steps:

1. **Click the Entry icon in the Toolbox (which now looks like a notepad); or double-click the Notepad Contents page; or click the Notepad Page SmartIcon to open the Create Page dialog box, shown in Figure 21-2.**

Figure 21-2:
The Create
Page dialog
box for
Notepad.

2. **Each entry has its own page, so give your page a title in the T̲itle text box.**
3. **Select the A̲utomatic radio button in the Page Number area if you want Organizer to add the new page to the end of your Notepad, or choose M̲anual if you want to assign the page number yourself.**

You need to place the page manually if you want to insert your new page between existing pages — perhaps to group the new page with other pages related to the same project.

4. **(Optional) In the Style area, you can check options to designate the page as the one to Start A Chapter, as a Links Page, or as a Folded page, and you can even define its Color if you want.**

   The Start A Chapter option makes your new page appear in bold on the Notepad Contents page. Having a page as a chapter heading can be handy if you're grouping Notepad pages on the same projects.

   The Links Page option creates a page of links to other Organizer items. We find that using the Link icon in the Toolbox is a better choice for linking pages, however, because this option enables you to combine text and links on the same page. (See the section "Linking Organizer Entries," later in this chapter.)

   The Folded option creates a double-width page to accommodate oversized items such as tables imported from a 1-2-3 worksheet.

   The Color option enables you to select the color of the page. Just click the drop-down arrow button to display a color palette and then click the color of your choice in the palette.

5. **Click the Categories drop-down list box and choose a category, if one applies.**

   A category can help you organize Notepad during a sort or if you're in the Category view, and it can help you track projects throughout Organizer.

6. **Click OK to create the page, close the Create Page dialog box, and go to the newly created page, or click the Add button to add the page to your Notepad section and begin defining another page.**

   Organizer displays the newly created page in the Notepad section. Click once anywhere on the blank page area (between the title at the top and the page number footer at the bottom) to put an edit box around the page. Click again to make an insertion point cursor appear, as shown in Figure 21-3. Now, just start typing your notes. If you reach the bottom of the page, just keep going; you can make the page as long as you like. Organizer adds a scroll bar to the right side of the page to enable you to scroll the page if all your notes can't fit on one screen.

View by Category

View by Date

View by Page Number

View by Title

Insertion point

Create a Notepad entry

I-beam pointer

Edit box

Figure 21-3:
A blank
Notepad
page ready
for you to
start typing
your notes.

Copying Information from Other Programs into Organizer

Sometimes, you have data in another program that you want to use in Organizer. You could always simply type the information into an entry in the appropriate Organizer section. But why do that when computers are so good at copying information?

Organizer gives you two different ways to copy existing information from another program and bring it into your Organizer file. You can copy documents and other files from another program and import them onto a Notepad page, or you can grab selected text from another program and insert into a new Calendar appointment, To Do task, Address card, or Notepad page.

Adding a file from another application

Importing a file from another application may seem technical, but the task is actually quite easy and the results are astonishing. By importing a file, map, graph, or spreadsheet onto a Notepad page, Notepad becomes a powerful tool to help you organize information, remember information from other programs, and keep pertinent facts with your notes. You may, for example, find that importing a spreadsheet about a client helps you remember important facts in designing a new proposal for the client's firm.

To import a file from another application, just follow these steps:

1. **Save your Organizer file by clicking the Save File SmartIcon.**

   Always save your work before opening other applications — the safe thing to do.

2. **Open the Windows program containing the file you want to import into Notepad.**

   If you're opening another SmartSuite program, you can click its SuiteStart icon or start the program by double-clicking its icon in the Lotus Applications folder in SmartCenter's SmartSuite drawer. For other Windows programs, such as WordPad, you probably need to select the program from the Start menu in the Windows taskbar.

3. **Open the file in the new Windows program, select the portion of that file (up to the entire contents of the file) that you want to see on the Notepad page, and copy the selection to the Windows Clipboard by choosing Edit⇨Copy.**

   If you need assistance with any of these procedures, you can refer to *Windows 98 For Dummies,* by Andy Rathbone (IDG Books Worldwide, Inc.).

   If you're copying from another SmartSuite program, you can use the Copy SmartIcon to copy the selected data to the Clipboard.

4. **Switch back to Organizer.**

   You can click the Organizer icon in SuiteStart, double-click the Organizer icon in SmartCenter, or press and hold the Alt key and press Tab until the Organizer title and icon are highlighted in the dialog box that appears.

5. **Click the Notepad section tab and create a page by clicking the Entry icon.**

6. **Title the page and click OK.**

7. **Click the new page to put an edit box around that page and click again with the I-beam pointer to get the blinking text insertion point cursor on the page; then click the Paste SmartIcon (or choose Edit⇨ Paste, or right-click the page and choose Paste from the pop-up menu).**

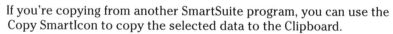

Organizer pastes the information from the Windows Clipboard onto the Notepad page. Figure 21-4, for example, shows a Lotus 1-2-3 spreadsheet that's been imported into Notepad. Notice that the columns at the top and bottom wrap to second lines because the page is not wide enough to hold all the information. Click the right mouse button and choose Page from the pop-up menu that appears (or choose Page⇨Page from the menu bar). Select the Folded check box in the Page dialog box that appears and then click OK. A Folded Page icon appears at the top of the Notepad page. Click the icon to view the entire spreadsheet across the page, as shown in Figure 21-5.

If you want to add text to an existing Notepad page, such as adding names to a list, go to the page you want to edit, click the page once to select that page, and then click the page again to place the insertion point where you want to edit. After you finish editing, click the page title to stop editing.

Using EasyClip

Lotus Organizer EasyClip is a new feature of SmartSuite Millennium Edition. It's a small utility program that serves as a companion to Lotus Organizer and allows you to quickly and easily select text from another program (another SmartSuite program or any other Windows program) and turn it into a Calendar appointment, a To Do task, an Address book card, or a Notepad page in Organizer.

For example, if you're writing a memo in Word Pro about an upcoming meeting, you can simply select some text from the memo and use EasyClip to transform the selected text into a Calendar appointment in organizer with just a few clicks of your mouse. You don't need to retype the information in Organizer. If Organizer is running, using EasyClip saves you a little bit of typing, which is nice but no big deal. The real advantage of EasyClip is that it works even if Organizer isn't running and your Organizer file isn't open. That means you don't have to launch Organizer and open your Organizer file every time you want to add a to-do task or appointment — and that is a real time-saver!

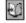 Because EasyClip is a separate program (and it must be in order to be available when Organizer isn't running), you must start it separately. However, there's a good chance that EasyClip is already running because the standard SmartSuite installation configures your system to launch EasyClip automatically when you start Windows. If EasyClip is running, it makes its presence known by displaying an icon in the system tray in the taskbar. (The EasyClip icon looks like the open notebook of the Organizer icon with a blue arrow added to the left page.) If EasyClip isn't running already, you

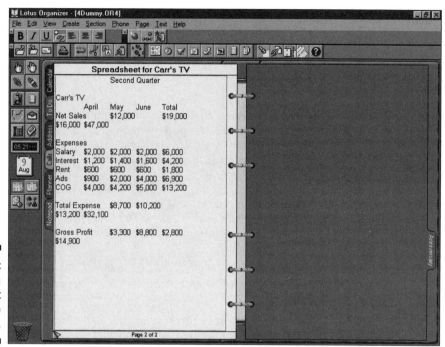

Figure 21-4:
Importing a
spreadsheet
into
Notepad.

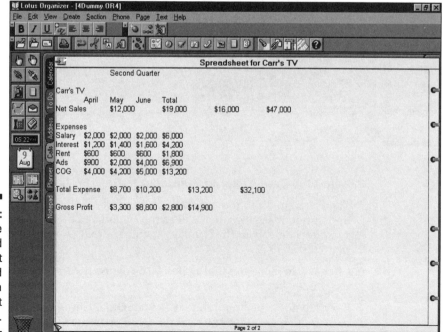

Figure 21-5:
The same
imported
spreadsheet
viewed
using a
fold-out
feature.

can start it by opening the Start menu and choosing Programs⇨Lotus SmartSuite⇨Lotus Accessories⇨Lotus Organizer EasyClip. Don't look for any logos or big windows to open when you start EasyClip. The only way you know that the program is running is by seeing its icon in the system tray.

Before you can use EasyClip to create entries in your Organizer file, you must tell the program where to find that file. Right-click the EasyClip icon and choose Preferences from the pop-up menu that appears in order to open a small Preferences dialog box. Type in the path and filename for your Organizer file (or click Browse and double-click the file in the Open dialog box that appears) and click OK.

After you configure EasyClip, using it is a snap — or, should I say, a *click,* because a few mouse clicks is all it takes. The following steps show you how to create an Organizer appointment using EasyClip:

1. **Start by selecting some text in another program.**

   Select the text that you want to transfer to the appointment entry in Organizer.

2. **Click the EasyClip icon in the system tray and choose Create Appointment from the pop-up menu.**

   EasyClip opens a small EasyClip Appointment dialog box (shown in Figure 21-6). EasyClip inserts the text that you selected in the Description box.

Figure 21-6:
The
EasyClip
Appointment
dialog box.

3. **Adjust the Date, Time, and Duration settings for the appointment.**

   The EasyClip Appointment dialog box enables you to define the basic appointment settings, but it does not include all the additional options that are available in the regular Organizer Create Appointment dialog box.

4. **Click OK to close the dialog box and record the appointment in your Organizer file.**

   EasyClip adds the appointment to your Organizer file, and the appointment will be available the next time you open the file in Organizer. After the appointment is entered in the Organizer file, you can edit and manipulate it just like any other appointment.

The preceding steps outline the procedure for creating an appointment using EasyClip. The procedures for creating a To Do task, an Address card, or a Notepad page are essentially the same as the steps for creating an appointment. The only differences are that you choose a different command from the pop-up menu that appears after you click the EasyClip icon and EasyClip presents a slightly different dialog box where you enter information appropriate for the kind of Organizer entry you are creating. The EasyClip Task and EasyClip Notepad Page dialog boxes are similar to the EasyClip Appointment dialog box. The EasyClip Address dialog box is larger and includes space to fill in more information such as name, address, telephone numbers, and so on. But the basic operation is still the same: EasyClip fills in some of the information in the dialog box using the text you selected; you fill in the remaining information and click OK to add the entry to your organizer file.

Tying Up the Loose Ends

This section describes some specialized topics that can make life with Organizer run more smoothly.

Filtering out the noise

A *filter* enables you to choose only particular data matching criteria that you specify. For example, you can use a filter to view all the entries in Calendar pertaining to a particular project — and only those entries. You can also filter information throughout several Notebook sections at the same time. If you need to locate all items pertaining to your client, Jonathon Hall, for example, you can create a filter to locate these items for you. Then you can view only those entries in Organizer, without all the distractions and clutter of other entries.

Using a filter is a two-step process. First, you must create a filter by defining what information you want to search for and what Organizer sections you want to search in. Then you apply the filter to view only the items that match the criteria you set up in the filter. After you define a filter, you can reuse that filter as many times as you like. The next time you want to use the same filter, all you need to do is apply the filter; you don't have to redefine the filter each time.

To create a filter, follow these steps:

1. **Choose Create⇨Filters from the menu bar.**

   The Filters dialog box appears, as shown in Figure 21-7. After you create any filters, those filters appear here in the Filters list for you to use again.

Figure 21-7:
The Filters
dialog box.

2. Click the New button.

The New Filter dialog box appears, as shown in Figure 21-8.

3. Type a name for your filter in the Name text box.

4. Click the empty box in the first row under the Section column; then click the drop-down arrow in the Section box and choose an Organizer section in which to search (Calendar, Notepad, Address, and so on).

5. Click the Field drop-down arrow and select a field in which to search.

For example, you may choose to search the Category field. (See, we told you those categories would be useful.)

6. Click the Test drop-down arrow and select the word(s) that best suit your search criteria (such as Begins With or Contains).

The selections available in the Test box vary depending on the kind of field you selected in the Field box. For example, the tests associated with a date field let you search for dates on, before, or after a given date, while the tests for a text field — such as a name — test for items that begin with a certain letter or contain a string of characters.

7. In the Value box, type the word or numbers you want to search for.

You can also create a filter that displays a dialog box and asks you to fill in the value every time you apply the filter. To do so, enter a question mark and then a value in the Value box. Suppose, for example, that you want a filter that enables you to search for a different last name in the Address section every time you apply the filter. You'd type **?** **Last name** in the Value box.

Figure 21-8:
The New
Filter dialog
box.

Section		Field		Test		Value	And/Or	

8. **Click the And/Or field and select And or Or if you want to add additional fields or sections.**

   Use the And selection if you want more than one field or section included in the application of the filter. For example, if you want a filter based on both the Start date and Category in the To Do section, choose And and define the second criterion on the next line. The filter selects only those items that meet both criteria. Click the Or selection if you want the filter to select items that meet either the criterion on the current line or the criterion on the following line. You can use this option to select items from more than one section, such as a filter based on a Start date in the To Do and Calendar sections. If you make an And/Or selection, you must fill in the next row in the dialog box to define a criterion for the And/Or choice to refer to.

9. **(Optional) Repeat Steps 4 through 8 to add other filter criteria as needed.**

   If, for example, you want to filter items in another Organizer section, you define additional criteria for each section. Each set of filter criteria takes up a separate row.

10. **(Optional) Select the Show in View — Apply Filter Menu check box if you want your new filter to be displayed in the View⇨Apply Filter menu.**

    This step places your newly defined filter on the menu that appears when you choose View⇨Apply Filter. Then, to use the filter in the future, all you need to do is choose it from the menu. However, if you don't plan to reuse the filter (or don't expect to use it often), you can leave the check box empty to keep the filter from appearing on the menu.

11. **Click OK after you finish defining the filter.**

    Organizer returns to the Filters dialog box.

12. **Select your new filter from the list and click Apply to apply it.**

    Organizer displays only those items matching the filter criteria in the sections to which the filter applies. All the other entries disappear.

After you define a filter, you can apply the filter by choosing Create⇨Filters to open the Filters dialog box, selecting the filter from the Filters list, and clicking Apply; you can also apply the filter by choosing View⇨Apply Filter⇨Filter Name (provided that you elected to include the filter in the Apply Filter menu, as described in Step 10 of the preceding steps).

To remove the filter and return your display to normal, choose View⇨ Clear Filter. Organizer again displays all the entries rather than only those matching your filter.

Linking Organizer entries

Cross-referencing entries in Organizer is called *linking*. Creating a link between data is very handy for quick retrieval of needed information. You may, for example, link an appointment in the Calendar section to the address card of the person or company in the Address section. Then, by clicking the Link icon in the Calendar entry, you can easily access information in this person's address card without having to turn to the Address section. You may also link an appointment for a meeting in Calendar to the Notepad page containing the agenda for the meeting. The Notepad page may have a link to the Freelance presentation file you're working on for that meeting. The possibilities are nearly endless.

To create a link, follow these steps:

1. **Open the Calendar section (or another section) and choose an appointment that you want to link.**

2. **Click the Link icon in the Toolbox and then click the appointment you want to link.**

   Suppose that you want to link Johnathon Hall's address card to the appointment with Hall listed in your Calendar. Start by clicking the Link icon and then click the appointment with Johnathon Hall. Notice that the pointing hand cursor now holds a chain. (See Figure 21-9.)

3. **Click the section tab and item you want to link to.**

   To continue our example, turn to the Address section by clicking the Address tab. Then click the H index tab and access the page containing Johnathon Hall's information. Click Hall's name on the page, and a link appears on the right-hand side of the card, as shown in Figure 21-10.

That's all you do! You've created a link between the appointment with Johnathon Hall and his address card. Now, to use the link, follow these steps:

1. **Click the Calendar tab and click the appointment you linked.**

2. **Click the Link icon next to the appointment.**

   A Link box appears with Mr. Hall's name and company displayed on a clickable button, as shown in Figure 21-11. If you had created more links from this appointment, you would see a separate button for each link.

3. **Click the button for the desired link in the Link box.**

   Organizer takes you to the linked information — in this case, Johnathon Hall's address card.

Link icon   Break link icon   Pointing hand cursor with chain

Figure 21-9:
Creating a
link from
calendar to
address
card.

You can create a link from any section of Organizer to any other section.

To disconnect a link, click the Break Link icon in the Toolbox, click the Link icon beside the linked appointment, and then click the link after the Link box appears. That's all you need to do!

Although the topic is beyond the scope of this book, we still think it is worth mentioning that Organizer is fully compatible with modems and Local Area Networks (LAN). With a LAN, as well as a modem, you can send and receive messages and mail through your computer by using Lotus Notes or cc:Mail. Organizer can coordinate with other Organizer users on the network to share appointment books and schedule meetings at mutually convenient times. Check with your network administrator for details on how to use these features.

The link

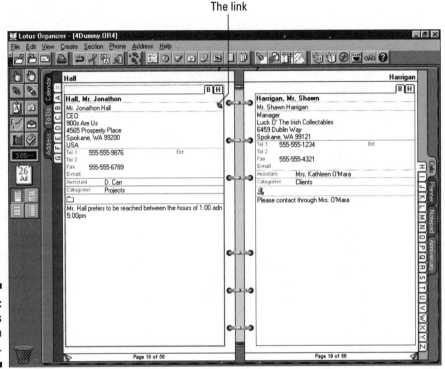

Figure 21-10:
An address
card with
link.

Figure 21-11:
A link box.

Link box

Part VII
Spinning a Web

The 5th Wave — By Rich Tennant

"IT HAPPENED AROUND THE TIME WE SUBSCRIBED TO AN ON-LINE SERVICE."

In this part . . .

The Internet and the Web are the happening places these days — you gotta be there. And with SmartSuite Millennium Edition you can be there! This part covers the special Web-enabled features of the core SmartSuite programs — Word Pro, 1-2-3, and Freelance — and it introduces FastSite, a new SmartSuite program dedicated to easily building and maintaining Web sites.

Chapter 22

Boot Camp for Web Spinners

· ·

In This Chapter

▶ Using Word Pro to create Web pages

▶ Working with 1-2-3 worksheets on the Web

▶ Using Freelance to create presentations on the Web

▶ Printing Web documents

· ·

*T*he Internet and the World Wide Web are the "really big thing" these days, and everyone wants to get into the act by joining the rush to publish documents on the Web. And with good reason, too. Posting documents on an Internet Web server is a great way to make your message available to anyone, anywhere in the world.

The key to the Web is the HTML (HyperText Markup Language) file format — a system of embedding formatting codes and links to graphics and other documents into simple text files. When viewed with a Web browser, HTML files appear as nicely formatted documents with graphics and hyperlinks. Web servers are specially equipped computers that store Web documents (HTML files) and make them available to users' Web browsers. To publish a document on the Web, you first save or convert the document to the HTML format, and then you *post* the document (copy the file or files) on a Web server.

The Web grew to prominence on the Internet, but now that many local area networks support the same standards as the Internet, Web servers have become a popular and convenient way to share documents with coworkers as well. Nowadays, "on the Web" is as likely to mean on your local network as it is to mean on the World Wide Web.

With the increased use of Web documents in networks of all sizes, many people have an increased need for easy, convenient ways to create Web documents and to transform regular documents, worksheets, presentations, and reports into Web documents. SmartSuite is ready, willing, and able to meet that need. (Eager little rascal, isn't it?) Word Pro, 1-2-3, and Freelance all have some special Web document creation capabilities, and we cover those in this chapter. And all the SmartSuite programs can at least create Web documents by using a utility that enables you to "print" to the Web, which we also cover in this chapter. FastSite is a new member of the SmartSuite family that enables you to easily create and maintain Web sites. We cover FastSite in Chapter 23.

 In order to post files to a Web server, you must know how to access that server. You need to know things like the address to use for file transfers, the directory where your Web files should be stored, a user name and password to gain access to the server, and perhaps other details as well. You should check with your neighborhood network guru or the technical support staff of your Internet service provider for the information.

Creating Web Pages with Word Pro

Of all the SmartSuite programs, Word Pro is the one with the most extensive Web page creation and editing capabilities. In fact, Word Pro makes a pretty decent Web page design tool for basic pages. That's not too surprising because the most common elements on most Web pages are text and graphics — two things that Word Pro handles very well. Just add the ability to handle hyperlinks and to save documents in the HTML format that is used on the Web, and Word Pro becomes a real Web page authoring tool. Of course, the real advantage of using Word Pro to create Web pages is that you already know how to use Word Pro — you don't need to find out how to work with another new program. (Check out Chapters 4, 5, 6, and 7 for more on using Word Pro.)

Converting your existing documents to Web pages

Suppose that you have some existing Word Pro documents, duly saved on your hard disk in Word Pro's own file format, that you want to post on a Web server. Those documents can be anything from product specification sheets, to project schedules, to that short story that you're so proud of. In order to post those documents on the Web, you need to resave them in files using the HTML file format, which involves a little more than just saving the files. (For example, any pictures or other graphics in your document must be saved in separate files from the text.) Word Pro takes care of these details and makes the process easy! Here's how you do it:

1. **Open the document you want to convert to a Web page, and perform any editing that may need to be done before the conversion.**

2. **Choose File➪Internet➪HTML Export Assistant to open the HTML Export Assistant dialog box, shown in Figure 22-1.**

   The HTML Export Assistant dialog box appears with the Content tab selected.

Figure 22-1:
The Content tab of the HTML Export Assistant dialog box.

3. **Using the options on the Content tab of the dialog box, select the portion of the document that you want to convert to a Web page and select the document elements (such as header and footer) that you want to include.**

4. **Click Next to display the options on the Layout tab, as shown in Figure 22-2.**

Figure 22-2:
The Layout tab of the HTML Export Assistant dialog box.

5. **If you want Word Pro to automatically add Web navigation features to the Web document you're creating, specify those on the Layout tab.**

The Table Of Contents check box is normally grayed out unless you're converting a long document that is divided into sections and, on the Contents tab, you instructed Word Pro to save each division as a separate file. If you check the Table Of Contents check box, Word Pro creates a frame on the left side of the Web pages that displays a table of contents with links to each division of the document. If you elect to use the table of contents, you can also add navigation arrows to your Web pages to enable viewers to jump to the previous or next division of the document.

If you want to add a hyperlink (such as a link to your corporate home page) on the bottom of each Web page, check the Include Link To URL check box. Then enter the address of the link in the URL Address box and enter the text that should appear on the page in the URL Description box.

URL stands for *Uniform Resource Locator,* which is a fancy name for *Internet address.*

6. **Click Next to display the options on the Preview & Save tab, as shown in Figure 22-3.**

Figure 22-3: The Preview & Save tab of the HTML Export Assistant dialog box.

> **HTML Export Assistant**
>
> Content \ Layout \ Preview & Save \
>
> Choose options for saving your document. Preview and save your web page, or click Done just to save the settings.
>
> Saving options
>
> Location of files when saving:
>
> Single directory
>
> □ Include linked files
>
> Save graphics as:
> ○ JPEG (.jpg)
> ○ PNG (.png)
>
> Preview in Browser
>
> Save Locally...
>
> Save to Notes...
>
> Save to Internet...
>
> Cancel   Help   << Back   Next >>   Done

7. **Click Preview In Browser.**

Word Pro saves a temporary version of the Web page (or pages), opens your Web browser, and loads the Web page into it. This gives you a preview of what your Web page will look like when it is posted on a Web server and accessed with a Web browser. You can see the effect of the inevitable formatting changes that occur when a regular document is converted to a Web page.

8. **Close the browser or click the Word Pro button in the Windows taskbar to return to Word Pro and the HTML Export Assistant dialog box.**

If your document looked good in the browser, you're ready to proceed to Step 9. Otherwise, you can click Back to go back and change options and preview the document again until it looks the way you want it to.

9. **Specify the Saving Options and then click Save Locally, Save To Notes, or Save To Internet.**

   Depending on the Saving Options you select and the Save button you click, Word Pro displays one or more Browse or Save dialog boxes for you to specify the location and filenames of the Web page files that the program creates from your document.

10. **Click Done to close the HTML Export Assistant dialog box.**

Converting a Word Pro document to a Web page does not destroy or alter the original document. It merely creates a copy of the document saved in the appropriate file format for display on the Web.

Building Web pages from scratch in Word Pro

Creating a Web page in Word Pro is very much like creating any other Word Pro document. You enter and format text, you import and move pictures, and you can even work with tables in your document. All these tasks work the same whether the document you're creating is destined to be printed on paper or published on a Web server.

The distinctive features of a Web page are the hyperlinks that, when you view the page in a Web browser, enable you to jump from one Web page to another by just clicking some underlined text or a linked graphic. So, to be able to work effectively with Web pages, you need facilities for creating and editing hyperlinks. Well, you can rest assured that Word Pro has the hyperlink tools you need.

Working with Web tools

To make working with Web pages easier, Word Pro includes a special toolbar with buttons for some of the tasks you need to do frequently when editing Web page files. To display the Web Tools bar (shown in Figure 22-4), choose File➪Internet➪Show Web Tools.

Figure 22-4:
The Web Tools bar keeps Web page editing tools handy.

Here's what the buttons in the Web Tools bar do:

- ✔ **Create Link.** Clicking the Create Link button opens the Create Hyperlink dialog box, where you can define a hyperlink. You find out more about hyperlinks in the next two sections of this chapter.

- ✔ **Preview in Browser.** Click this button to open your Web browser and see how the page that you're editing will look when viewed in the browser.

- ✔ **Export Assistant.** Click this button to open the HTML Export Assistant dialog box — the same one you discovered how to use in the "Converting your documents to Web pages" section, earlier in this chapter.

- ✔ **Done.** Clicking the Done button closes the Web Tools bar.

- ✔ **The Previous, Next, Reload, and Stop navigation buttons.** These buttons (located just below the Web Tools bar name) work just like their counterparts in a Web browser. However, the navigation buttons are grayed out unless you are working on a Web page that you load from a server.

- ✔ **Address.** This button is another feature borrowed from a Web browser. You type the URL for a Web page in the Address box, and Word Pro attempts to establish a link to the Internet (or your intranet or local hard disk) and display the page you specify.

Adding hyperlinks

Hyperlinks are the very essence of the Web. So, if you plan to create Web pages in Word Pro, you need to know how to create hyperlinks in your Web documents. To work with hyperlinks effectively, you need to have a basic understanding of what they are and how they work. Unfortunately, we don't have space available in this book to give you much background information on the Web. However, if you have done much Web surfing (or any Web page creation in another program), you probably already know hyperlinks well enough to work with them. (You can also find a thorough explanation of hyperlinks and other Web topics in *World Wide Web Searching For Dummies,* 2nd Edition, by Brad Hill, published by IDG Books Worldwide, Inc.) If you know what a hyperlink is supposed to do, creating it in Word Pro is a simple matter of following these steps:

1. **Position the insertion point (click with the I-beam pointer) at the location in your document where you want to insert the hyperlink.**

2. **Click the Create Link button in the Web Tools bar or choose Create⇨Hyperlink to open the Create Hyperlink dialog box, shown in Figure 22-5.**

Figure 22-5:
The Create
Hyperlink
dialog box.

3. **In the Action drop-down list box, select the action that you want to happen when the viewer clicks the hyperlink.**

   The list of available actions is fairly extensive, covering almost anything that you want a hyperlink to do. Typically, you want to choose Go to Web document (http://) or Go to another document in this Web site, but you can also create hyperlinks that do things like start file transfers or create e-mail messages.

4. **Click in the Link To box and type the URL of the Web page that you want to link to.**

   Depending on your choice in the Action drop-down list, you may need to enter a URL for a different kind of Internet resource instead of a Web page.

   As an alternative to typing the URL in the Link To box, you can click the Browse button to open your Web browser and surf your way to the page you want to link to. Then you can copy the URL from the browser's address box (press Ctrl+C), return to Word Pro and the Create Hyperlink dialog box, and paste the URL (press Ctrl+V) into the Link To box.

5. **In the Linked Text box, type the text that should appear on the Web page as the hyperlink.**

   The viewer will see the Linked Text on the Web page and click it to follow the hyperlink. In most browsers, the linked text of hyperlinks appears in a color (usually blue) and with an underline to distinguish it from other text.

6. **Click OK to close the dialog box and insert the newly defined hyperlink into your Web page.**

If you highlight some text on your Web page before opening the Create Hyperlink dialog box, Word Pro automatically treats that text as the Linked Text for the hyperlink you define.

Editing an existing hyperlink is very similar to creating one from scratch. You can click the linked text for a hyperlink and then click the Edit Link button in the Web Tools bar (the Create Link button changes to the Edit Link button when you click an existing hyperlink). Or you can right-click the linked text and choose Edit Hyperlink from the pop-up menu. Either action opens the Edit Hyperlink dialog box, which is identical to the Create Hyperlink dialog box except for the title and the fact that the Linked Text box is not editable. Change the Action and Link To settings as needed and then click OK to close the dialog box and update the hyperlink. If you need to edit the Link text of an existing hyperlink, you can simply select and edit the text directly in the Word Pro document.

Adding a hyperlink to a graphic

Not all hyperlinks are linked to text on the Web page. Some hyperlinks are linked to graphics. If you want to create a hyperlink to a graphic on your Web page, follow these steps:

1. **Insert the desired picture into your document. Size, position, and crop the picture the way you want it.**

2. **Select the picture by clicking it.**

3. **With the picture selected, click the Create Link button in the Web Tools bar or choose Create⇨Hyperlink.**

   This action opens the Create Hyperlink dialog box, shown in Figure 22-6. Notice that the dialog box is almost exactly the same as the one shown in Figure 22-5. The only difference is that the Linked Text box has been replaced by the Graphic Description box. Although neither the picture itself nor its filename appears in the Create Hyperlink dialog box, the hyperlink will be linked to the selected picture.

Figure 22-6:
Creating a
hyperlink to
a graphic.

4. **Select the appropriate action for the hyperlink in the Action drop-down list.**

5. **Enter the URL for the target of the hyperlink in the Link To box.**

6. **In the Graphic Description box, type a brief description of the link.**

   This is the text that the Web browser displays as a placeholder while waiting for the graphic to download over the Internet.

7. **Click OK to close the Create Hyperlink dialog box and record the hyperlink definition in your document.**

Editing existing Web pages

You can do more than convert Word Pro documents to Web pages and create Web pages from scratch in Word Pro. You can also open existing Web pages in Word Pro and edit them. In fact, editing existing Web pages is easy.

If the Web page file exists on your hard drive, just use your favorite technique for opening a document (choose File⇒Open or click the Open File SmartIcon). When the Open dialog box appears, select HTML or All Files in the Files Of Type list box so that you can see Web page files as well as Word Pro documents listed in the dialog box. Then select the file you want to edit, and click Open.

If the Web page that you want to edit is on a Web server someplace, the easiest way to get to it is by using the Address box in the Web Tools bar. First, make sure that the Web Tools bar is displayed in Word Pro (as covered in the "Working with Web tools" section, earlier in the chapter). Click the Address box in the Web Tools bar, type the URL of the Web page you want to edit, and then press Enter. Word Pro reaches out over the Internet (or your corporate intranet) to locate the file and load it into the Word Pro window so that you can edit it.

After Word Pro opens the Web page, you can edit and save it just like a Web page or document that started out in Word Pro to begin with. See, we told you it's easy.

Word Pro can open and edit most basic Web pages, including pages with graphics and tables, but Word Pro can't deal with pages that include frames. (We're talking about Web page frames here, not the Word Pro frames that hold pictures and text in a Word Pro document.) Oddly, that means that you can't open and edit some Web pages that you create with Word Pro because choosing the Table Of Contents option in the HTML Export Assistant causes Word Pro to create Web pages with frames for the table of contents.

Working with Web Pages in 1-2-3

Working with Web-based data in 1-2-3 is a two-way street. 1-2-3 has the capability to reach out to the Web for data and import it into your worksheet. Like its sibling, Word Pro, 1-2-3 also has the capability to save worksheet data in a format that can be viewed with a Web browser.

Working with Web tables

Finding statistical data and other numeric information published in tables on Web pages is fairly common. If you wanted to use some of that information in a 1-2-3 worksheet, you could visit the Web site and view the relevant Web page, jot down the information on a scratch pad or print a copy of the page, and then type the data into cells in your 1-2-3 worksheet. At least, you could do that if you insist on doing things the hard way. It's tedious, time-consuming, and error-prone.

Fortunately, SmartSuite has a much better way to get information from the Web *into* 1-2-3. Here's how you do that:

1. **Open the worksheet into which you want to import data, and locate an area of the worksheet where that data will fit.**

   You don't need to select the range of cells where the Web table will go. You just need to identify a suitable area and make a note of it.

2. **Choose File➪Internet➪Get Data from Web to open the Get Data from Web dialog box, shown in Figure 22-7.**

3. **In the Web Address (URL) box, type the Internet address of the Web page that contains the table you want to import into 1-2-3.**

   If you want to save yourself some typing, you can click the Browse button to open your Web browser and use it to open the Web page containing the data you want to import. Then you can copy the Web page address from the Address box in your Web browser, close the browser window, and paste the address into the Web Address (URL) box in the Get Data from Web dialog box.

4. **Click in the Select The Sheet Location For The Web Table box and enter the range of cells where you want the Web table to be inserted into your 1-2-3 worksheet.**

   You can type in a range name or the cell addresses for a range in the text box. Or you can click the range selector button at the right end of the text box; the range selector button enables you to temporarily switch from the dialog box back to your worksheet where you can define a range by dragging the mouse pointer to select a group of cells in your worksheet. As soon as you complete the selection, 1-2-3 reopens the Get Data from Web dialog box.

Figure 22-7:
The Get
Data from
Web dialog
box.

5. **Click the Adjust Column Widths To Fit Web Data option.**

Normally, you want to make sure that you enable this option to instruct 1-2-3 to automatically adjust its column widths to accommodate the data in the Web table you import.

6. **Click OK to close the dialog box and import the Web table.**

1-2-3 establishes a connection to the Internet, locates the Web page you specified, extracts data from the table that it finds on the Web page, and inserts that data into your worksheet.

After you import the Web table into your 1-2-3 worksheet, you can use that data in formulas and calculations throughout the workbook by simply referring to the cells that contain the data you want to use.

After you finish importing the Web table, 1-2-3 doesn't forget where that table came from. If you want to go back to get updated information from the Web page, you won't have to go back through the whole process of defining the Web table again. Instead, you can simply choose File⇪Internet⇪Refresh Web Data to instruct 1-2-3 to re-download the latest data from the Web site. Of course, 1-2-3 then automatically updates all your calculations with the new data from the Web.

Putting your numbers on the Web

The previous section shows you how to get data from a Web table into a 1-2-3 worksheet. However, the data exchange between 1-2-3 and the Web can be a two-way street. You can also convert 1-2-3 worksheets into Web documents that are viewable with any Web browser. To convert 1-2-3 worksheets to Web pages, follow these steps:

1. **Open the 1-2-3 workbook file that you want to convert to a Web page (or pages).**

2. **Choose File⇪Internet⇪Convert to Web Pages to open the Convert to Web Pages dialog box, shown in Figure 22-8.**

Figure 22-8:
The
Convert to
Web Pages
dialog box.

3. **In the File Name For Web Page box, type a filename for the Web page file you are creating.**

4. **In the What To Convert area, select the portion of the current 1-2-3 workbook that you want to convert to a Web page.**

You can choose to convert the entire multipage workbook, the current worksheet page, or a selected range of cells. If you choose Selected Range, you need to define the range by typing the range address in the text box or by clicking the button at the right end of the text box and highlighting the range of cells in your worksheet by dragging the mouse pointer diagonally across a block of cells while pressing the left mouse button.

5. **Select the format for the Web table by choosing HTML Table or jDoc (Print Snapshot) in the Format area near the bottom of the dialog box.**

Actually, you have a choice of formats only if you chose Selected Range in the previous step. For Web table conversions from the entire work-book or from the current sheet, 1-2-3 always uses the jDoc format.

6. **Click Next to display the next page of Web table conversion options.**

7. **Adjust the layout options for your Web table as desired.**

If you chose the HTML Table format option in Step 5, you have the opportunity to define several layout options, as shown in Figure 22-9. You can define an optional header, description, author name, and e-mail address to appear on the Web page. You can choose whether to display table borders, and you can elect whether to add a link to the page to allow viewers to download a copy of the 1-2-3 file that is the basis for the Web table.

Figure 22-9:
The HTML
table
formatting
options.

If, on the other hand, you (or 1-2-3) chose the jDoc format in Step 5, you have only a single formatting option: whether or not to include on the Web page a link to allow viewers to download the 1-2-3 file.

8. **Click Next to display the final page of options for creating Web tables.**

9. **Click the Preview In Browser button to open your Web browser and display a temporary copy of the Web page.**

   This step is optional but highly recommended. It allows you to preview the Web page and see any unexpected formatting changes before committing to save the file.

10. **Close the Web browser and return to the Convert to Web Pages dialog box in 1-2-3.**

    If everything looked good in the browser, proceed to the next step. Otherwise, click the Back button to back up and change some settings until you achieve the effect you want.

11. **In the Save area, choose a Location (either a Local Or Network Drive or an Internet Server) and type in a path and folder name or an Internet address in the Directory box.**

12. **Click Save to start the conversion process.**

    1-2-3 converts your worksheet to a Web page file according to your specifications. The program displays a message when the conversion is complete. Just click OK to dispose of the message box.

Now you know how to get data from Web tables and how to create Web tables from your 1-2-3 worksheets, too.

Presenting the Web from Freelance

Freelance is the other SmartSuite program (besides Word Pro and 1-2-3) that has special built-in Web page creation capabilities. The Freelance Web page converter enables you to transform an entire Freelance presentation into a series of Web pages that can be viewed with a Web browser. You even have the option of creating a Web-viewable version of a Freelance screen show, complete with slide transitions, bullet builds, and animations. The following steps describe how you can create presentation magic on the Web.

1. **Open the Freelance presentation that you want to convert to Web pages.**

2. **Choose File➪Internet➪Convert to Web Pages.**

   The first time you choose the Convert to Web Pages command, Freelance displays a dialog box that gives you an overview of the conversion process. If you don't want to see the Overview dialog box in the future, check the Do Not Show Me This Message Again option before clicking OK to close the Overview dialog box and display the Convert to Web Pages – Step 1 dialog box, shown in Figure 22-10.

Figure 22-10:
Step 1 of
the Convert
to Web
Pages
process in
Freelance.

3. **Select a format for your presentation from the Web Style list.**

   You have four choices in the Web Style list. For best results, you need to understand the difference between the formats:

   • **Single Image.** This option saves each slide in your presentation as an individual graphic image and displays it on a separate Web page. Viewers will be able to browse through the Web pages to see your slide images one at a time and even access the Web pages for various slides in random order. (Don't let the name mislead you into thinking that only one slide will be converted. This process converts all the slides in your entire presentation file.)

- **Tiled Background.** Like the Single Image option, this option causes Freelance to create a series of individual Web pages — one for each slide in your presentation. The difference is that Freelance attempts to break each slide image into component parts (such as a background color and text blocks) instead of saving each slide as a graphic image. If your slides are mostly text on a solid-color or tiled background, the result is smaller files that load and display faster. However, if your presentation includes photographic or graduated-color backgrounds, the Single Image format usually works better.

- **Screen Show With Plug-In.** Choosing this format saves your presentation as a screen show — one large file that contains all the slides in your presentation and includes transition effects and such. You gain control over the order of presentation of your slides and the transition effects are nice, but you pay a price for the slick presentation. The screen show file is large and takes a while to download. (The screen show file is usually about the same size as all the individual slide files combined, but the download time is more noticeable because you must wait for the entire file to download before viewing the presentation, instead of being able to view each page as it is downloaded.) In addition, the people who view your presentation on the Web first need to download and install a plug-in for their browser. The introductory page for the presentation makes the plug-in easy to get, and you have to download and install it only once, but it's an extra step that takes some time.

- **Screen Show With ActiveX.** This option is essentially the same as the Screen Show With Plug-In option. You get a screen show presentation complete with transition effects, bullet builds, and animations. The difference is that you don't need to download and install a browser plug-in module in order to view the presentation, because the screen show display module is an ActiveX control — which means you must view it by using a browser that supports ActiveX. Microsoft Internet Explorer supports ActiveX, but Netscape Navigator requires a third-party plug-in to display ActiveX controls.

4. **Enter the base filename for your presentation Web pages in the File Name box.**

   Freelance uses that name for a screen show, but for presentations that it converts to individual pages, Freelance adds a number to the end of the filename that you enter and increments that number for each successive page in the presentation.

5. **Click Next to display the Convert to Web Pages – Step 2 dialog box, shown in Figure 22-11.**

Figure 22-11:
Step 2 of
the Web
conversion
process in
Freelance.

6. Choose the layout options for the Web pages that serve as the background for each slide in your presentation.

The thumbnail image on the left side of the dialog box gives you a preview of the Web page layout. As you click the check boxes to enable or disable the various layout options, the thumbnail image changes to reflect your current choices. If you chose one of the screen show formats, the layout options are grayed out because the layout for the screen show Web page is predetermined.

7. In the Images area, choose the Format and Resolution settings appropriate for your presentation.

Your format choices are either GIF or JPEG — both are standard file formats for graphics on the Web. The GIF format does a slightly better job of handling charts, graphs, and blocks of solid color, and the JPEG format is better for handling photographic images and smooth shaded backgrounds. Choose the appropriate one for your presentation based on the kind of graphics and backgrounds in your slides. (The Format option is disabled when you are creating a Screen Show With Plug-In or a Screen Show With ActiveX.)

The Resolution setting determines how much information is recorded in the slide images, which, in turn, determines the size of the image files and the length of time that they take to download. The choices that are available depend on the capabilities of your display driver. Choosing 800 x 600 resolution is usually a good compromise between recording adequate detail and controlling file size.

8. Click Next to display the Convert to Web Pages – Step 3 dialog box, shown in Figure 22-12.

Depending on the conversion format you chose, Freelance may display a status message as it creates a series of temporary files before displaying the dialog box.

Figure 22-12:
Step 3 of
the Web
conversion
process in
Freelance.

9. **Click Preview In Browser to open your Web browser and load the first page of your Web presentation. Test the presentation by viewing the pages.**

   If you are creating a screen show, you need to be connected to the Internet in order to successfully load and view the Web presentation.

10. **Click Save Locally or Save To Internet.**

    Clicking Save Locally opens a Browse for Folder dialog box. Select the folder where you want to save the Web presentation files, and click OK. Clicking Save To Internet opens a Browse for Directory dialog box where you can specify an FTP server and directory location for saving the Web presentation. Select (or set up) the FTP server and click Connect. Freelance displays a message when the files are saved. Click OK to clear the message box.

11. **Click Done to close the Convert to Web Pages dialog box.**

Printing to the Web

All the SmartSuite programs share a rudimentary Web page creation capability in the form of a printing utility that allows you to "print" to a Web page document instead of to a real printer. As a result, any document, worksheet, form, memo, database report, presentation handout, calendar printout, or other printed output from any of the SmartSuite programs can become a Web page document.

The printing utility that makes this possible — Net-It Now! Starter Edition — is installed automatically as part of the standard SmartSuite installation so that it's ready and waiting when you need it. Instead of trying to translate the formatting of your document into the HTML codes that Web browsers understand, Net-It Now! prints a "picture" of each page of your document and then creates Web pages to contain each of those pictures. The result, called the jDoc format, gives you a faithful reproduction of your original document — something that often isn't possible when converting documents to normal Web pages. jDocs can be viewed with any Web browser that supports Java (and most browsers support Java).

Using Net-It Now! is almost as easy as using a regular printer. Just follow these steps to print a Web document to a jDoc:

1. **Open the appropriate SmartSuite program and prepare to print the document, worksheet, database report, or other item just as you would if you wanted to print the item on paper.**

2. **Choose File⇨Print or click the Print SmartIcon to open the Print dialog box.**

3. **In the Print To list box, select Net-It Now! SE.**

4. **Adjust the other print settings as desired and then click Print.**

   After a short delay, the Net-It Now! Starter Edition dialog box appears, as shown in Figure 22-13.

Figure 22-13:
The Net-It
Now!
Starter
Edition
dialog box.

Net-It Now! Starter Edition	✕
Select a folder in which to build your Web document:	
C:\My Documents\jdoc10	Browse
Note: Each Web document should have its own folder.	
Options:	
Web page navigation style: Default	Select...
☑ View in Web browser after the build.	
Build · Cancel · Upgrade... · Help	
Status: Received Freelance Graphics - Untitled1 · Version 1.62.523 · *jdoc*	

5. **Enter an appropriate folder name in the Select A Folder In Which To Build Your Web Document box.**

   Be sure to put each Web document you create with Net-It Now! in a separate folder because each document may actually be composed of numerous separate files.

6. **Click Select to open the Navigation Style dialog box, shown in Figure 22-14.**

Figure 22-14:
Buttons,
buttons,
what kind of
buttons?

7. **Select a style for the navigation buttons that appear on the background page that contains your document and click OK to return to the Net-It Now! Starter Edition dialog box.**

   If the item you're printing consists of multiple pages, you should include navigation buttons to allow the viewer to move from page to page through the finished Web document. However, if you're printing a single-page item, you probably want to choose (none) to dispense with the navigation buttons.

8. **Check or clear the View In Web Browser After The Build option, according to your preference.**

   You can disable this option to save time, but viewing the finished jDoc in your Web browser is the best way to check the results.

9. **Click Build to create the jDoc Web page documents.**

   Net-It Now! displays status messages as it creates the images, Web pages, and other files that make up the jDoc document. After the program creates the necessary files, it launches your Web browser and displays the Web document there.

Net-It Now! Starter Edition is designed to work exclusively with the SmartSuite programs. However, the same technology could allow you to print jDoc Web documents from other programs as well. The catch is that you must buy an upgrade to the Net-It Now! program to enable it to work with non-SmartSuite programs. Choose Start➪Programs➪Net-It Now! Starter Edition➪Upgrade Net-It Now! Starter Edition to purchase the upgrade online.

Chapter 23

Publishing a Web Site with FastSite

● ●

In This Chapter

▶ Getting to know FastSite

▶ Creating a Web site with FastSite

▶ Editing and refining a site

▶ Posting your Web site on a server

● ●

*I*n the past, you could fit most Web sites into two general categories. First, you had the big, elaborate multipage Web sites that were designed and created by a staff of computer professionals and maintained by a full-time Webmaster. Then you had the small "home page" sites that individual Web users created and maintained on their own. The small Web sites often consisted of a single page and rarely exceeded a half-dozen pages or so.

Today, the face of the Web is changing. The proliferation of intranets is bringing Web technology to corporate local area networks, and Internet service providers are making Internet Web sites available to anyone who needs one. As a result, Web sites of all sizes and descriptions are cropping up everywhere. The Web has become a publishing medium that enables anyone with basic computer skills (hey, that includes you!) to share information with others. You can share your literary efforts with the world on an Internet Web site, or you can share project documents with other members of your workgroup on a corporate intranet. Often, the information that you need to publish on the Web already exists as word processor documents and other files. To make Web publishing work, you need a convenient way to convert existing documents to a format that you can use on the Web, and you need a way to manage and update the pages on a Web site without requiring the services of a professional Webmaster. That's where FastSite comes in.

Introducing FastSite

FastSite is the newest member of the SmartSuite family, designed to make the job of creating and maintaining multipage Web sites faster and easier than it has been before. FastSite makes it simple for you to create a Web site by assembling a collection of existing document files. The program uses SmartMaster templates to make creating a home page and section pages a snap, and it automatically adds navigation buttons to your Web pages so that visitors to your Web site can move around easily. FastSite automates the processes of converting existing documents to Web pages and of posting those Web pages on a server. When the original documents change, you can update the Web site with a few mouse clicks in FastSite.

FastSite, and the Web sites you create with it, may not have lots of fancy bells and whistles, but the program is a great tool for efficiently publishing existing documents on a Web server. If you're charged with the responsibility of maintaining a library of documents on a workgroup Web server, FastSite is made for you.

Starting FastSite

Like the rest of the SmartSuite programs, you can start FastSite in any one of several ways. Pick the technique you like best from the following list:

Lotus FastSite

✔ Click the Start button in the Windows taskbar and choose Programs⇨Lotus SmartSuite⇨Lotus FastSite.

✔ Click the SmartSuite drawer in the SmartCenter bar, click the Lotus Applications folder, and then double-click the Lotus FastSite icon.

✔ If SuiteStart is running, you can simply click the FastSite icon in the system tray.

When you start the program, the FastSite window appears; but unlike with most of the other SmartSuite programs, no welcome dialog box prompts you to open a file to work on. That's because FastSite doesn't work on individual files; it deals with an overview of all your Web sites, and it loads that Web site data automatically when you start the program.

Finding your way around the FastSite window

The FastSite window, shown in Figure 23-1, may look a little strange at first glance — particularly when compared to the windows of the other SmartSuite programs. The FastSite window has a standard title bar and menu bar at the top, but below the menu bar you find an icon bar with a fixed set of buttons instead of the SmartIcon palettes that are typical of other SmartSuite programs. The status bar at the bottom of the FastSite window gives you information about the selected item but doesn't include any clickable buttons that you can use for things like formatting text. (The fact that FastSite is intended for manipulating whole files instead of the text and numbers within those files probably has something to do with the lack of formatting controls on the status bar.)

The main work area of the FastSite window is divided into two panes. (Fortunately, these panes don't cause pains.) The Site pane on the left contains the Site Hierarchy — an outline-style list of Web sites and all the section pages, Web documents, and hyperlinks that those sites contain. (Initially, the Site Hierarchy is empty, but it will grow to look more like the example in Figure 23-1 as you create Web sites and add files to those Web sites.) The Tabbed pane consumes the remainder of the FastSite window. You probably guessed that it's named for the two tabs at the top of that

Figure 23-1:
FastSite looks a little different from most SmartSuite programs.

pane. You use the tabs just like you do the tabs in tabbed dialog boxes. Click the Choose Task tab to display a list of tasks like those shown in Figure 23-1. Click the Preview Web Pages tab to convert the tabbed pane into a Web browser window where you can view the Web page document that is selected in the site hierarchy.

Building a Web Site

Building a Web site in FastSite is a fairly straightforward process. You begin by giving your Web site a name and picking a SmartMaster look. FastSite then creates a home page for your Web site that acts as a table of contents for the site. Then you begin adding files to the site. Each new file becomes a separate Web page that includes a Web-viewable version of the original SmartSuite document plus a set of navigation buttons that allow viewers to move through the Web pages and back up to the home page. FastSite also automatically adds a link for that page to the table of contents on the home page. For more complicated sites, you can add *sections* — table of contents pages that contain links to a group of pages in that section. The section pages are, in turn, linked to the main table of contents page for the site.

Creating a site

The first stage of building a Web site in FastSite is called creating a site. Actually, what you're creating is the top-level home page or table of contents for the site. Here's how you do it:

1. **Click the Choose Task tab in the tabbed pane (if it isn't already selected) and then click the underlined <u>Create a site</u> hyperlink. Or you can click the New Site button in the icon bar; choose <u>F</u>ile➪ <u>N</u>ew Site; choose <u>C</u>reate➪<u>S</u>ite; or press Ctrl+N.**

   FastSite opens the Create Site – Basics dialog box, shown in Figure 23-2.

2. **Type in a name and a description for your Web site in the text boxes provided.**

   The Name appears as a title on the top-level home page, and it also appears in the Site Hierarchy and serves as the name of the staging folder where the Web site files are stored. The Description appears as a block of text just below the title on the home page.

Figure 23-2:
Begin
creating a
Web site
in this
dialog box.

3. **(Optional) Click the Browse button to open the Browse for Folder dialog box. Then select a folder and click OK to designate a different staging directory.**

   FastSite automatically creates a folder with the same name as the name of your Web site and uses it to store your Web page document files. The program calls this folder the *staging directory.* By default, the site folder is created in the c:\lotus\work\fastsite folder, but you can designate a different parent folder for the site folder.

4. **Click either the HTML Pages radio button or the jDoc radio button to select the preferred format for the Web page documents that FastSite will create from the files you add to the site.**

   Selecting HTML Pages instructs FastSite to convert files to the editable HTML format whenever possible. Selecting jDoc, on the other hand, creates pictures of your documents, as explained in Chapter 22 in the section on printing to the Web with the Net-It Now! utility. Even if you select HTML Pages, FastSite converts certain files (some 1-2-3 files and all Approach files) to the jDoc format.

5. **Click Next to display the options shown in Figure 23-3.**

6. **Select a Web SmartMaster look from the list box in the upper-left portion of the dialog box.**

   When you select a look, FastSite displays a sample of the Web SmartMaster in the middle of the dialog box.

7. **Click Done to close the dialog box and create the site.**

   FastSite adds the site to your Site Hierarchy and creates the home page for your site.

So far, so good. You've got the beginnings of a Web site defined, but the site is pretty useless at this point. So far, your Web site consists of a home page without links to any other pages.

Adding files to a site

After you create the initial home page for a site in FastSite, you can begin building the site by adding pages to it. You can add Word Pro documents, 1-2-3 worksheets, Approach database reports, Freelance presentations, and just about any other kind of file that you create with a SmartSuite program. (You can also add Microsoft Word document files to a FastSite Web site without first converting them to another format.) Each file becomes a separate page in the Web site. Later, FastSite converts the files to Web page documents before posting them on the Web server.

To add a file to a FastSite Web site, follow these steps:

1. **If you have more than one Web site defined in FastSite, select the site you want to add files to by clicking the site's home page in the Site Hierarchy.**

2. **Click the Choose Task tab to display the task list pane and then click <u>Add more files to a site or section</u>; or click the Add File button in the icon bar; or choose <u>F</u>ile➪<u>A</u>dd File; or choose <u>C</u>reate➪Add <u>F</u>ile; or press Ctrl+A.**

   Any of these actions opens the Add Files dialog box (shown in Figure 23-4), which looks and works like a typical Browse or Open dialog box.

3. **Select the file you want to add to the Web site.**

   Normally, you want to select the Shortcuts To Selected File radio button in the Add Files As area in the lower-left corner of the Add Files dialog box. This option preserves any dependencies between the selected file and other files in its home directory (such as an Approach file's dependence on separate files for storing database forms and data). You can select the Copies Of Selected Files radio button to copy the selected files to the FastSite staging directory.

   You can select multiple files in the Add Files dialog box by pressing and holding the Ctrl key as you click files to select them. FastSite adds all the selected files to your Web site at once.

4. **Click Add to close the dialog box and add the selected files to your Web site.**

   FastSite adds the files to your Web site. They appear in the Site Hierarchy with yellow dots beside them to indicate that those files have not yet been converted to Web documents. In addition to adding the files to the Site Hierarchy display, FastSite automatically adds links to those files in the site's table of contents on the home page.

Organize your site with sections

A large multipage Web site with lots of pages would become almost unmanageable if all the pages in the site linked directly to the top-level home page. So FastSite lets you organize your site into *sections*. Each section has a section page that serves the same purpose as the home page does for the site — it's a table of contents with links to each of the pages in the section. The section page appears as a link on the home page. This lets you keep the number of links on the home page at a manageable level, even though the Web site includes dozens of files.

When Web visitors view your site, they can click a link on the home page to go to a section page and then click a link on the section page to go to a document. Actually, a link on a section page might lead to another section page because you can nest sections within sections just as you can create folders within folders within folders to organize files on your hard drive.

Here are the steps for adding a section to a FastSite Web site:

1. **In the Site Hierarchy, select the Web site home page (or existing section page) under which you want to create a new section.**

 2. **Click the Choose Task tab to display the task list pane. Then click** <u>**Create a section**</u>**. Or you can click the Create Section button in the icon bar or choose** <u>**C**</u>**reate**⇨**S**<u>**e**</u>**ction.**

   FastSite immediately creates the section and adds it to the Site Hierarchy. By default, the section has the generic name New Section, a yellow triangle appears beside the name, and the name is highlighted.

3. **Type a new name for the section and press Enter.**

   The new name that you type in replaces the generic *New Section* text in the Site Hierarchy. The name you enter into the Site Hierarchy also appears later as the title of the section page itself. Initially, FastSite creates section pages with the same Web SmartMaster look as the Web site (or, if the new section is nested within an existing section, the same look as the parent section). You can change the Web SmartMaster look for the section page later if you want. (See the section "Changing the Web SmartMaster look," later in this chapter, for more details.)

Adding files to a section of your Web site is easy. The procedure is the same as adding files to the site's home page; you just select the section (rather than the home page) in the Site Hierarchy before you open the Add Files dialog box.

Adding hyperlinks

FastSite does more than provide links on your Web site's home page and section pages that go to other section pages and to Web page documents that originated as SmartSuite files. FastSite also enables you to create hyperlinks that jump to other locations in your Web site or to an Internet location such as a Web page or other file on a different Web server. Hyperlinks enable you to break out of the rigid hierarchical structure of a FastSite Web site and to add links to all sorts of Internet resources.

Follow these steps when you want to add a hyperlink to your Web site:

1. **Select the Web site home page or the section page to which you want to add the hyperlink by clicking it in the Site Hierarchy.**

2. **Click the Choose Task tab to display the task list pane. Then click <u>Create a hyperlink</u>. Or you can click the Create Hyperlink button in the icon bar or choose <u>C</u>reate➪<u>H</u>yperlink.**

   FastSite opens the Create Hyperlink dialog box, shown in Figure 23-5.

Figure 23-5: The Create Hyperlink dialog box.

3. **Select a hyperlink action from the <u>A</u>ction drop-down list.**

   Selecting `Go to a FastSite section or file` creates a hyperlink to another location within the current Web site. On the other hand, selecting `Go to an Internet location` creates a hyperlink that can link to any available Internet resource address. Usually, a hyperlink to an Internet location loads a Web page from another Web server, but it can also start a file download or open an e-mail message composition window.

4. **Select or fill in the destination for the hyperlink in the <u>L</u>ink To box.**

   If you chose `Go to a FastSite section or file` in Step 3, the Link To box displays a list of available section pages and files in a format similar to the Site Hierarchy. To choose a destination for the hyperlink, just click the item that you want to link to in the Link To list box.

   If you chose `Go to an Internet location` in Step 3, the Link To box changes to a text box where you can type the URL (*URL* stands for *Uniform Resource Locator,* but it's just a fancy way of saying Internet address) of the Web page or other Internet resource that you want to link to. As an alternative to typing the URL, you can click the Browse button to open a mini-browser window and use it to view the desired location. Then click OK to close the browser window. FastSite enters the URL into the Link To box for you.

5. **Type a descriptive name for the hyperlink in the Description box at the bottom of the Create Hyperlink dialog box.**

The hyperlink goes by this name in the Site Hierarchy, and the name is also the link text that appears on the home page or section page.

6. **Click OK to close the Create Hyperlink dialog box.**

Adding a hyperlink to a Web site is, in some ways, similar to adding a file. The finished hyperlink shows up on the site's home page or on a section page as a link, just like the links to Web document files. The hyperlink also shows up in the Site Hierarchy on a separate line like a document file. However, you can easily distinguish hyperlinks from section pages and document files in the Site Hierarchy. Hyperlinks are marked with an icon that looks like a link of chain.

 Creating a hyperlink adds the link to the Site Hierarchy but it doesn't automatically re-create the section page that will contain the hyperlink. That doesn't happen until you convert or update your site — converting documents to Web pages — in preparation for posting the site on a Web server.

Editing a Web Site

After you create the basic Web site in FastSite, you probably need to revise, refine, and tweak it a bit. (Well, I don't suppose that you need to edit your Web site if you got everything perfect to begin with. But naahh! The first thing you learn when you start creating Web sites is that they're never perfect and they're never finished. Fortunately, with FastSite, making changes is a snap.)

What's in a name?

When you add a Web site, section page, or hyperlink to the Site Hierarchy, you have the option of defining a name for the item. However, when you add a file to a Web site, FastSite does the naming for you — using the document's filename. These names aren't bad for filenames in the Site Hierarchy, but the same name also shows up on the home page or section page as the link to the document. You probably want to rename the Web page documents in your Web site so that visitors to your site can easily identify the links to the documents they are interested in.

Renaming a Web page document in the FastSite Site Hierarchy employs a technique that you probably already know from renaming files in Windows Explorer. Simply click the item you want to change in the Site Hierarchy to select it, wait a second, and then click the text portion of the item again.

(You can also right-click an item and choose Rename from the pop-up menu.) FastSite highlights the text in a box to show that it is ready for editing. Type in the new name for the document and press Enter. The document name is changed in the Site Hierarchy and in the link on the home page or section page.

Renaming items in the Site Hierarchy works for home pages, section pages, and hyperlinks, as well as Web document files.

Editing a home page or section page

Suppose that you want to edit more than just the name on a site's home page or on a section page. (The other text you may want to edit is the Description text that appears below the title.) Select the home page or section page you want to edit and then choose Edit⇨Properties to open the Site Properties or Section Properties dialog boxes. (You can also open the dialog boxes by right-clicking the home page or section page and choosing Properties.) Both of these dialog boxes include Name and Description boxes. Edit the text in those fields as appropriate and then click OK to record the change.

Changing the Web SmartMaster look

If you want to change the appearance of your site's home page or a section page, you can do so by changing the Web SmartMaster that FastSite uses as a template for the page. By default, the section pages use the same SmartMaster as their parent section page or home page. But you don't have to stay with the same SmartMaster; you can use a different Web SmartMaster for each section if that pleases your fancy. To change a Web SmartMaster look, follow these steps:

1. **In the Site Hierarchy, select the section page that you want to change, or select any item under the home page that you want to change.**

2. **Choose File⇨Choose Another Web SmartMaster Look⇨For Current Section to change the section page, or choose File⇨Choose Another Web SmartMaster Look⇨For Site to change the home page.**

   FastSite opens the Choose Web SmartMaster Look For Site dialog box, shown in Figure 23-6, or the nearly identical Choose Web SmartMaster Look For Section dialog box.

3. **Select a SmartMaster in the Select A Web SmartMaster list box.**

   FastSite displays a generic sample of the selected Web SmartMaster in the preview box that occupies the lower two-thirds of the dialog box. Keep selecting different Web SmartMasters and viewing the samples until you find a look that you like.

Figure 23-6:
Pick your
Web
SmartMaster
template
here.

4. Click OK to close the dialog box and apply the new SmartMaster look.

FastSite applies the new SmartMaster look to the page you specified. If you apply a new look to a Web site's home page and you haven't previously applied different looks to the section pages in that site, the section pages automatically change to have the same SmartMaster look as the home page.

Moving and removing files

Another characteristic of your FastSite Web site that you may want to change is the order in which the Web pages, section pages, and so forth appear. After all, if you're posting the chapters of your new historical novel on the Web site, you want to make sure that Chapter 1 comes first and the suspenseful conclusion in Chapter 25 appears at the bottom of the list. In FastSite, everything is controlled from the Site Hierarchy, so if you want to change the order of the links that FastSite creates on a home page or section page, you need to rearrange the order of the items in the Site Hierarchy. You can rearrange the order with a simple drag-and-drop operation.

To change the order of the items in the FastSite Site Hierarchy, just click the item that you want to move to select it; then click and hold down the left mouse button as you drag the mouse up or down the Site Hierarchy. When the horizontal bar that appears near the tip of the mouse pointer is in the desired location, release the left mouse button to drop the selected item there. Use this technique to rearrange the order of the items within a section. If you want to move an item to a different section, you use basically the same technique, except that you drop the item on the section page (or home page) for the section to which you want to move the item.

Removing an item from your Web site is also easy. Simply select the item in the Site Hierarchy, and either choose Edit⇨Clear or press Delete; or you can right-click the item in the Site Hierarchy and choose Delete. FastSite presents the Remove Confirmation dialog box. Click Remove to remove the selected item from your Web site and keep the associated files stored on your hard drive. Click Delete if you want to not only remove the selected item from your Web site but also delete all its files. Click Cancel if you made a mistake and don't want to delete the item after all.

Editing source files

If you discover that you need to make a change to the content of one of your Web page documents after adding it to your Web site, you don't need to remove the file from the Web site and then re-add it to the Web site after editing. You can make the change to the source document, and the page remains in your FastSite Web site. Simply select the page in the Site Hierarchy and choose Edit⇨Open Document, or right-click the page in Site Hierarchy and choose Edit Document. FastSite opens the SmartSuite program used to create the original document and loads the document into the program window for editing. After you edit the document in the SmartSuite program, save your work and close the program window. FastSite keeps track of the status of the edited document and reminds you to update the document in your Web site before publishing your Web site on the server by changing the color of the document's icon in the Site Hierarchy to yellow. If you attempt to post your Web site to the server, FastSite alerts you to any outdated documents and prompts you to update them before copying the files to the server.

Publishing a Web Site

Creating a Web site and adding files to it in FastSite are really only the beginning. The whole point is to create a Web site on a Web server where your documents will be available to members of your workgroup or to visitors from the Internet. After you define the Web site in FastSite, the program can do most of the tedious work involved in getting your site posted on a Web server. FastSite converts your document files from their original format to a Web-viewable form and even lets you check the results in a Web browser window right in FastSite. After all the files are converted, FastSite automates much of the process of copying those files to the Web server.

Converting files to Web pages

FastSite really earns its keep when it starts converting your SmartSuite document files to a Web-readable format. You don't have to have FastSite to do that converting because each SmartSuite program has the capability to export files in a Web-compatible format (as covered in Chapter 22). But if you have more than a few documents, opening the individual SmartSuite programs and converting files one by one is a really unpleasant chore. FastSite keeps track of which documents in your Web site have been converted and which ones need to be updated. Then, with a single command, you can instruct FastSite to convert a single document or all the documents in your Web site. FastSite does the deed automatically, even if the documents come from several different SmartSuite programs.

To start the file conversion process, follow these steps:

1. **In the Site Hierarchy, select the Web site that you want to convert and then choose File⇨Convert to Web Pages or click the Convert To Web Pages icon in the icon bar. Or you can right-click the home page or any section page in the Site Hierarchy that is part of the desired Web site and choose Convert to Web Pages.**

   FastSite opens the Convert to Web Pages dialog box, shown in Figure 23-7.

2. **Select the page or pages that you want to convert from the list box in the Convert to Web Pages dialog box.**

   The page list in the Convert to Web Pages dialog box is very similar to the Site Hierarchy. You can select an item for conversion by clicking it. You can select several items by holding down the Ctrl key as you click. To select all the documents in the Web site, click the All button. Click the Out Of Date button to have FastSite automatically select all the documents that are not yet converted or that have been changed since being converted.

Figure 23-7:
The Convert
to Web
Pages
dialog box.

3. Click Convert to close the Convert to Web Pages dialog box and begin the conversion process.

FastSite displays a message box to keep you apprised of its progress as it converts documents to Web pages. Depending on the number and complexity of the documents, the process could take a while. As FastSite completes the conversion of each document, it updates the Site Hierarchy by switching the document icons from yellow (needs conversion) to blue (Web page conversion complete and up to date).

If you want to convert an individual document to a Web page, you can right-click the document in the Site Hierarchy and choose Convert to Web Pages from the pop-up menu. FastSite then skips the Convert to Web Pages dialog box and immediately begins converting the selected document.

Previewing your site

After you convert your document files to Web pages, you may want to see what your Web site looks like before you post it on the Web server. You don't have to open a separate Web browser to preview your Web site. You can do it right in the FastSite window. Just click the Preview Web Pages tab in the tabbed pane of the FastSite window. FastSite displays the Web page that is currently highlighted in the Site Hierarchy. (See Figure 23-8.) To preview another page, simply click it in the Site Hierarchy.

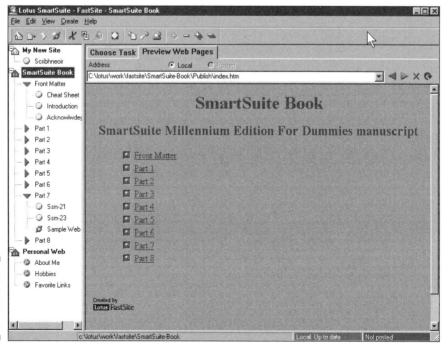

Figure 23-8: Previewing Web pages in FastSite.

Posting your site on a Web server

After you've built your Web site, converted documents to Web pages, and checked everything out, you're finally ready to post your Web site on a Web server. FastSite takes care of most of the details for you; you just need to get things started. To get started, follow these steps:

1. **Select the Web site that you want to publish by clicking its home page in the Site Hierarchy. Choose File⇨Post Web Pages to Server or just click the Post Web Pages to Server icon in the icon bar.**

   FastSite opens the Post to Server dialog box.

2. **Select the type of Web server that you're posting to and enter your Web site's full address on the server in the Path box.**

   To save yourself some typing in the Path box, you can click the Browse button. FastSite displays a Browse dialog box with options appropriate for the kind of server you selected. For example, if you chose Internet server, the Browse for Directory dialog box appears where you can select (or set up) the FTP server that you use to access your Web site. After specifying a server the first time, you can select it from the drop-down list in the Path box when you post files to the server in the future. (You may want to get your local network guru to help you set up access to the FTP server for your Web site.)

3. **Click OK to close the Post to Server dialog box and begin copying files to the server.**

   FastSite displays a Posting to Server message box to keep you informed of its progress as it copies converted Web pages from its staging directory to the Web server. By the way, be sure to check out the animation in the message box — the paper airplanes are just too cute.

That's it! When FastSite finishes copying files to the server, your Web site is available for all to see. But after you create a Web site, you need to maintain it. FastSite does a great job in maintenance mode. You can easily add, update, and rearrange files in FastSite. The program keeps track of what has changed and automatically copies the appropriate files the next time you post Web pages to the server.

Part VIII
The Part of Tens

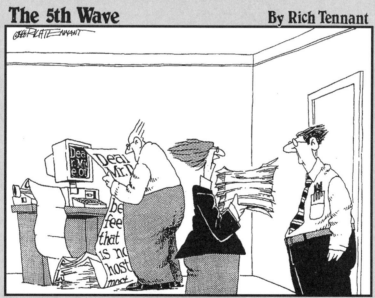

"YES, WE STILL HAVE A FEW BUGS IN THE WORD PROCESSING SOFTWARE. BY THE WAY, HERE'S A MEMO FROM MARKETING."

In this part . . .

This part covers several tips and tricks to help you get your work done more efficiently. You find shortcuts for all the SmartSuite Millennium Edition programs, as well as some shortcuts that apply everywhere, no matter which program you're using. This part is a veritable treasure trove of neat stuff.

Chapter 24

Ten Best Tips and Shortcuts that Work Anywhere in SmartSuite

In This Chapter

▶ Creating a user dictionary

▶ Using the SuiteStart icons

▶ Opening files quickly

▶ Using shortcuts for bold, italic, or underlined formatting

▶ Right-clicking to use context menus

▶ Saving regularly

▶ Keeping the InfoBox instantly available

▶ Speeding up your work with the status bar buttons

▶ Using Shift+Click

▶ Cutting and pasting with keyboard shortcuts

*L*est you forget that all the SmartSuite Millennium Edition applications have a lot in common, here are ten tips and shortcuts that you can use to save time and sanity almost anywhere in the SmartSuite universe.

Create Your Own User Dictionary

You probably use a lot of words that don't exist in any dictionary: people's names, esoteric terms that no one outside your field has heard of — stuff such as that. For the spell-checker to have to stop every time it sees the name *Mordensky,* for example, is a waste of time, especially if that's part of your company name and you use it repeatedly in just about every document.

After the spell-checker stops on a word that's not in the SmartSuite dictionary but is a word that you use all the time, just click the Add To User Dictionary button. From then on, whenever you run a spell-check, SmartSuite recognizes the word and doesn't bug you about it. (Hallelujah!)

The only application in which this doesn't work is Organizer, because that program doesn't have a spell-checker. As a side note to this tip, if you're putting a bunch of text into an Organizer file (probably a Notepad page), you may just want to create the document in Word Pro first so that you can spell-check the text and then retrieve the Word Pro document into your Organizer file.

Use the SuiteStart Icons to Switch Applications

Take advantage of the integration features of SmartSuite by keeping the SuiteStart icons in the system tray of the Windows taskbar. Then, whenever you want to switch to a different SmartSuite application, all you need to do is click a SuiteStart icon.

If you don't have those little SuiteStart icons in your system tray (next to the clock display), here's how you can make them appear:

1. Click the Start button in the taskbar to open the Windows Start menu.

You can also press Ctrl+Esc or the Windows key (the key between Ctrl and Alt with the Windows logo on it) to open the Start menu.

2. Choose Programs⇨Lotus SmartSuite⇨Lotus Accessories from the Windows Start menu to open the series of cascading menus.

3. Choose SuiteStart from the menu.

Your Lotus SmartSuite program menu may be called something else. If it's not called Lotus SmartSuite and you don't know what else it may be, check with whoever set up your system.

Open Files in a Flash

All the SmartSuite programs keep track of the files you've worked on most recently. (The actual number of files depends on the program.) This means that you can often avoid the hassle of going through the Open dialog box, changing drives and directories, and scrolling around to find the file you want. When you're working in a SmartSuite program, just open the File menu and take a look at the very bottom of the menu. The last few files you used are listed right there with numbers next to them. To open one of the files, just click its filename in the menu or use your keyboard to press the number listed on the menu for that file.

Windows also keeps track of the last few files you've worked on and enables you to choose them from the Start menu. Just click the Start button, point to Documents on the Start menu, and choose the file you want to work on from that menu.

Make a Bold (Or Italic or Underlined) Statement

Word Pro, Approach, Freelance, and 1-2-3 all use the same keystroke shortcuts for text attributes, as shown in the following list:

- Ctrl+B for boldface
- Ctrl+U for underlining
- Ctrl+I for italics

Use these keys to apply attributes quickly throughout SmartSuite.

Right-Click for Super Shortcuts

The right mouse button is a very useful (and often under-used) button. Right-clicking almost anything in any of the SmartSuite programs opens a menu of options that apply to the object you clicked. For example, right-clicking a cell in a 1-2-3 worksheet opens a menu that includes commands to open the Range Properties InfoBox; the Cut, Copy, and Paste commands; Insert and Delete commands, and more — all the most-used commands that apply to the cell you clicked. The context menu you get when you right-click an object is usually the fastest way to access common commands to work with the object you clicked.

A File Saved Is a File You Don't Need to Do Over

Save, save, and save again! Save after you do a spell-check, save before you use a feature you haven't worked with before; save before you make complex changes that may not turn out the way you expect; save when the skies are cloudy. . . .

But seriously, folks, saving frequently is one of the best ways to set your mind at ease so that you can confidently play with new features and expand your SmartSuite repertoire. If you save whatever you're working on before you try something you're not sure of, you don't need to worry about messing up your document. If everything turns to Silly Putty on you, just close the document without saving it. Then reopen the document and — hey, it's just like it was before it fell apart.

The Instant-On InfoBox

The InfoBox is a versatile and powerful formatting tool. You probably use it so much that you'd like to just leave it open all the time. The only trouble is that the InfoBox occupies too much space on-screen when it's open. Well, not if you use this trick. Double-click the InfoBox's title bar and watch what happens. The InfoBox shrinks to display only the title bar and the row of tabs. The InfoBox is still open and available at the click of a mouse, but it now occupies only a fraction of the normal space. You can drag it off into a corner of your document where it won't interfere with anything. To restore the InfoBox to regular size so that you can access its many formatting options, just add water, er, I mean click one of the tabs.

Use the Status Bar Buttons

Not only is the status bar a great place to get information about your program or document, but you can also find a lot of action going on there. In Word Pro, for example, if you click the status bar button that displays the current style name, you get a list of all the styles in the document. You can change the style just by clicking a different style name in this list. This process is much easier than going through a bunch of menus and dialog boxes for the same results.

As you work with the different SmartSuite applications, check out the different status bar buttons and see what they do. They're not just pretty faces.

Use the Shift+Click Trick

SmartSuite offers all sorts of different ways to select text, but the Shift+Click trick is one of the handiest and most precise. Just put your insertion point at the beginning of the text you want to select, move the mouse pointer to the end of the selection, and press and hold the Shift key as you click the left mouse button.

The only caveat here is that you need to be careful not to move the insertion point from the starting point until you're ready to Shift+Click. Use the mouse or the scroll bars to move the mouse pointer; using the arrow keys on the keyboard moves the insertion point, which you don't want for this trick.

Cut and Paste without Clicking

The Cut, Copy, and Paste commands on the Edit menu aren't hard to use, but using keyboard shortcuts for those commands is usually much faster. The shortcuts in the following list work in all the SmartSuite programs (and nearly all other Windows programs as well):

- Ctrl+C for Copy
- Ctrl+X for Cut
- Ctrl+V for Paste

C for Copy is easy to remember, and *X* for Cut makes some sense, even if it isn't an obvious mnemonic. The *V* for Paste must come from some strange foreign language or twisted logic, but you soon get so used to using this key that its weirdness doesn't make any difference. All three keyboard shortcuts become second nature.

Chapter 25

Ten Best Tips and Shortcuts for Individual SmartSuite Programs

. . . .

In This Chapter

▶ Using the Reset to Style feature of Word Pro

▶ Clicking to select in Word Pro

▶ Adjusting your 1-2-3 column widths automatically

▶ Using F5 to move quickly in 1-2-3

▶ Modifying an Approach database template

▶ Moving groups of Freelance Graphics objects

▶ Shuffling the order of your Freelance Graphics pages

▶ Duplicating repeating Organizer address fields

▶ Clicking Organizer's Backtrack SmartIcon

▶ Dragging and dropping in the FastSite Site Hierarchy

. . . .

*O*kay, Chapter 24 gives you the ten best tips and shortcuts that you can use anywhere in SmartSuite Millennium Edition. This Part of Tens chapter gives you the ten best tips and shortcuts for the individual SmartSuite applications: Word Pro, 1-2-3, Approach, Freelance Graphics, Organizer, and FastSite (in that order). We include only one or two tips per program. But they're *good* tips! Try 'em and see if you don't agree.

Get Out of Word Pro Jams by Using Reset to Style

Word Pro has this really cool feature called Reset to Style, which enables you to make a total mess out of things with wild formatting changes and then say, "Yuck! I don't like any of that. Put the document back the way it

was." You don't even need to stamp your feet and pout. If you make formatting changes and then decide that you don't like them, just select the text
and choose Text⇨Named Styles⇨Reset to Style from the menu bar (or just
click the Reset to Style SmartIcon). Your text reverts to the formatting
defined in the named style applied to that paragraph. If you just want to
remove the last formatting change but want to keep previous changes, use
the Undo command instead of Reset to Style.

Click to Select in Word Pro

Dragging can be a real drag. Here's a Word Pro tip that can cut down on your
dragging: With your insertion point anywhere in a sentence, press and hold
the Ctrl key while you click the left mouse button to select the entire
sentence. If you want to select a whole word, don't waste time dragging the
mouse pointer through the word. Just put your insertion point anywhere in
the word and double-click. Voilà!

Have 1-2-3 Adjust Your Column Widths for You

Don't waste time trying to figure out how wide to make a 1-2-3 column. Just
move the mouse pointer over the border on the right side of the column
label button at the top of the column so that the pointer turns into a two-
headed arrow. Then double-click. The column instantly adjusts to accommodate the longest entry currently occupying any cell in the column.

Get There Fast in 1-2-3 by Using F5

If you can see the 1-2-3 cell you want to move to on-screen, the fastest way
to get there in 1-2-3 is just to click that cell. If, however, you need to make a
larger leap, press F5 — the Go To key — to display the Go To dialog box.
Then just type the address of the cell (or chart or drawn object) in the
dialog box that you want to get to or click the range name in the list of
names; then click the OK button. Hey! You're there already. (Boy, are *you* a
fast learner!)

Modify an Approach Database Template

Approach provides more than 50 different SmartMaster applications and templates — predesigned databases in which to store information ranging from mailing lists and employees to art collections and musical groups. Using an existing database template and deleting the fields you don't need is almost always easier than creating a database from scratch. Each time you load Approach, a Welcome to Approach dialog box appears, asking whether you want to open an existing database or create a new one. If you choose to create a new database, Approach displays the available SmartMasters in a list box. Just choose one and alter away.

Move Freelance Graphics Objects as a Group

To maintain the relationship in Freelance Graphics between several drawn graphic objects on a page so that you can manipulate them as one object, group them. To create a group, select the objects you want to group and then choose Drawing⇨Group. If you later need to manipulate the objects separately, select the group and choose Group⇨Ungroup. You can select all the objects on a page by pressing F4. This action doesn't officially group the objects but does enable you to work with the objects as a group on a temporary basis (until you deselect them).

Shuffle the Freelance Graphics Deck

The order of your pages in a Freelance Graphics presentation can make all the difference. The easiest way to get your pages in the order you want them is to switch to Page Sorter view by clicking the Page Sorter view tab and then dragging the pages to the desired positions.

Don't Type Repeating Organizer Address Fields — Duplicate!

Rest those tired fingers. Why retype duplicate entries if Organizer can do it for you? If you have several contacts from the same company, have Organizer do the dirty work. First, open the Create Address dialog box by clicking the Address tab and then clicking the Entry icon. Type the person's name, job title, and company in the Create Address dialog box. After you press the Tab key to go to the address field, the Similar Address Found dialog box appears. Select the company from the drop-down list box, and Organizer fills in the duplicate information. If you need more info on this feature, see Chapter 20.

Make a Long Leap with the Click of a Mouse

In Organizer, if you have sections such as Notepad set up with an Organizer index page, you can flip to any page in that section quickly. Double-click the page number in the index, and Organizer opens the Notepad to that page. Flip back to the index page by clicking the Backtrack SmartIcon (the one that appears to have footprints on it).

Drag and Drop in the FastSite Site Hierarchy

The Site Hierarchy in the FastSite Site Pane (the frame on the left side of the FastSite window) is a terrific tool that enables you to do all sorts of Web site management tasks by simply dragging with your mouse pointer. You can move a document from one part of your site to another by just pointing to the item you want to move, pressing and holding the left mouse button as you drag the pointer to the new location for the item, and then releasing the mouse button to drop the item in its new location. The really slick trick is that you can drag documents from other windows (such as a Windows Explorer window displaying a folder of files) and drop them on a site icon in the FastSite Site Hierarchy to add them to the site. No menu commands and dialog boxes — just drag, drop, and you're done. You can even select several files and drag and drop them onto your site all at once.

Index

(continued)

(continued)

GET THE MOST FROM YOUR PC!

Every issue of PC World is packed with the latest information to help you make the most of your PC.

- Top 100 PC and Product Ratings
- Hot PC News
- How Tos, Tips, & Tricks
- Buyers' Guides
- Consumer Watch
- Hardware and Software Previews
- Internet & Multimedia Special Reports
- Upgrade Guides
- Monthly @Home Section

Make the Most of Windows® 98 with Your FREE ...For Dummies® Mouse Pad!

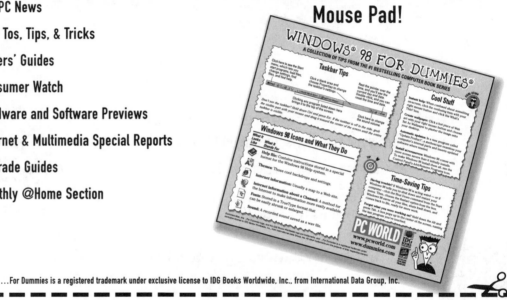

SEND TODAY
for your sample issue and FREE Windows® 98 Tips For Dummies® Mouse Pad!

How to order your sample issue and FREE mouse pad:

✉ Cut and mail the coupon today!
Mail to: PC World, PO Box 55029, Boulder, CO 80322-5029

☎ Call us at 1-800-825-7595 x434
Fax us at 1-415-882-0936

☞ Order online at www.pcworld.com/resources/subscribe/BWE.html

PC WORLD

IDG BOOKS WORLDWIDE
BOOK REGISTRATION

Register This Book and Win!

We want to hear from you!

Visit **http://my2cents.dummies.com** to register this book and tell us how you liked it!

- ✔ Get entered in our monthly prize giveaway.

- ✔ Give us feedback about this book — tell us what you like best, what you like least, or maybe what you'd like to ask the author and us to change!

- ✔ Let us know any other *...For Dummies*® topics that interest you.

Your feedback helps us determine what books to publish, tells us what coverage to add as we revise our books, and lets us know whether we're meeting your needs as a *...For Dummies* reader. You're our most valuable resource, and what you have to say is important to us!

Not on the Web yet? It's easy to get started with *Dummies 101*®*: The Internet For Windows*® *95* or *The Internet For Dummies*®*,* 5th Edition, at local retailers everywhere.

Or let us know what you think by sending us a letter at the following address:

...For Dummies Book Registration
Dummies Press
7260 Shadeland Station, Suite 100
Indianapolis, IN 46256-3945
Fax 317-596-5498

**BUSINESS AND
GENERAL
REFERENCE
BOOK SERIES
FROM IDG**

**COMPUTER
BOOK SERIES
FROM IDG**